Gifts from the Dark

Critical Perspectives on Race, Crime, and Justice

Series Editor

Tony Gaskew, University of Pittsburgh, Bradford

This book series seeks interdisciplinary scholars whose work critically addresses the racialization of criminal justice systems. Grounded within the connective space of history, the nuances of race continue to define the standard of how justice is applied throughout policing, courts, and correctional systems. As such, this series is open to examine monographs and edited volumes that critically analyze race from multiple narratives—sociopolitical, cultural, feminist, psychosocial, ecological, critical theory, philosophical—along criminal justice lines. The Critical Perspectives on Race, Crime, and Justice book series speaks to the significant scholarship being produced in an era where race continues to intersect with crime and justice.

Titles in the series

Gifts from the Dark: Learning from the Incarceration Experience by Joni Schwartz and John R. Chaney

Stop Trying to Fix Policing: Lessons Learned from the Front Lines of Black Liberation by Tony Gaskew

Race, Education, and Reintegrating Formerly Incarcerated Citizens: Counterstories and Counterspaces edited by John R. Chaney and Joni Schwartz

Law Enforcement in the Age of Black Lives Matter: Policing Black and Brown Bodies, edited by Sandra E. Weissinger and Dwayne A. Mack

Gifts from the Dark

Learning from the Incarceration Experience

Joni Schwartz and John R. Chaney

LEXINGTON BOOKS
Lanham • Boulder • New York • London

Published by Lexington Books
An imprint of The Rowman & Littlefield Publishing Group, Inc.
4501 Forbes Boulevard, Suite 200, Lanham, Maryland 20706
www.rowman.com

6 Tinworth Street, London SE11 5AL, United Kingdom

British Library Cataloguing in Publication Information Available

Library of Congress Cataloging-in-Publication Data
Names: Schwartz, Joni, author. | Chaney, John R., 1951– author.
Title: Gifts from the dark : learning from the incarceration experience /
    Joni Schwartz and John R. Chaney.
Description: Lanham : Lexington Books, 2021. | Series: Critical
    perspectives on race, crime, and justice | Includes bibliographical
    references and index. | Summary: "Without minimizing the systemic
    injustices and disparities of mass incarceration, Gifts from the Dark
    challenges the mindset of incarceration as a solely one dimensional,
    deficit event. Instead, this book argues that the prison experience can
    potentially be one of transformational learning"— Provided by
    publisher.
Identifiers: LCCN 2021005508 (print) | LCCN 2021005509 (ebook) | ISBN
    9781498591706 (cloth) | ISBN 9781498591713 (ebook)
    ISBN 9781498591720 (pbk)
Subjects: LCSH: Prisoners—Education—United States. |
    Criminals—Rehabilitation—United States. | Education and crime—United
    States. | Ex-convicts—United States. | Imprisonment—United States.
Classification: LCC HV8881.3.U5 C53 2021 (print) | LCC HV8881.3.U5
    (ebook) | DDC 365/.6660973—dc23
LC record available at https://lccn.loc.gov/2021005508
LC ebook record available at https://lccn.loc.gov/2021005509

Contents

PART III: LEARNING IN RELATION TO OTHERS

PART IV: LEARNING THAT TRANSFORMS THE WORLD

Acknowledgments

We first thank the individuals who inspired our thinking while offering guidance and support in bringing *Gifts from the Dark* to the world: our friends and writers who share the experience of incarceration. Their lives, friendship, solidarity, and influence appear throughout our book and include, but are not limited to the participants from New York State Queensboro Correctional Facility (QCF) and the Restoration Writing Groups—Marvin Wade, Dario Pena, Michael Colbert, P. Harris, Sonny Jackson, Carolina Soto, and Restoration facilitator John Proctor. We also wish to extend our appreciation to QCF Superintendent Dennis Breslin, Deputy Superintendent of Programs Michelle Yon, Director of Volunteer Services Obafemi Wright, and City University of New York (CUNY)-LaGuardia Community College President Kenneth Adams for their collaborative support.

Thanks to Tony Gaskew and Rowman & Littlefield for creating the series, Critical Perspectives on Race, Crime and Justice, of which this book is our second contribution. A special shoutout to Becca Beurer, our editor, who consistently provided professionalism, kindness, and support as we juggled with COVID-19 pandemic challenges in meeting our deadlines. To our copyeditors Cathy and Crystal Powell, thanks for being such a pleasure to work with. We also extend a special note of appreciation for receiving key input from the National Endowment for the Humanities (NEH) 2019 Summer Institute: Incarceration and the Humanities at CUNY-LaGuardia Community College. To NEH facilitators Shannon Proctor and Naomi Stubbs and our colleagues from Social Science and Humanities departments: thanks for your wise commentary and critiques, and for providing a forum for us to workshop the book's concept and revise its introduction.

The time and space to think and write is a great gift, so we appreciate CUNY-LaGuardia's awarding Joni a 2018–2019 fellowship/sabbatical. A special thanks to Gail Mellow and Michael Rodriguez for their support during that time.

Harlem poets/raconteurs Michael Boston and Ronald Smalls, as well as fellow friends and writers Birdie DeJesus and Sara Jorgensen: each of you are a cherished blessing in our lives. Finally, to Joyce and Joanne Chaney, your special brand of love and support mean much to us and will never be taken for granted. Thanks for all that you are and all that you do.

Introduction

Gifts are meant to be shared. And *Gifts from the Dark: Learning from the Incarceration Experience*, a book in the Lexington Books Critical Perspectives on Race, Crime, and Justice Series makes the case that despite its dark cruelty, the prison cell can be for some a counterspace of adult transformative learning for individuals inside and outside. This book includes counterstories of prison experiences challenging testimonial injustice that marginalizes the voices of people incarcerated. It is an effort to open the space of prison to avoid the erasure of the experience and to silence the shame associated with it. In doing so, *Gifts from the Dark* explores the place of prison as a site of learning that transforms. The gift or gifts are both singular and plural—the gift of the incarceration experience as transformation and the gifts of solitude and silence, organic intellectualism, the mind and body connection, emotional intelligence, community solidarity to mention but a few. In the words of Nelson Mandela, "the cell is an ideal place to learn to know yourself, to search realistically and regularly to the process of your own mind and feelings." This learning is both for society as a whole and for people who are or have been incarcerated.

The title and ensuing content of this book are an apparent paradox to the harsh reality, impact, and long-term individual and societal consequences of mass incarceration, imprisonment, and the carceral experience. The idea that a prison experience could be any kind of gift contradicts all we know. In fact, to even suggest that any good could evolve from incarceration is at worst inflammatory and dangerous, and at best contradictory and somewhat absurd. The authors emphatically concur with these premises and continue as staunch advocates for effective policy changes such as bail reform, decarceration, stopping harsh and long sentences, prosecutor discretion, policing reform, discriminatory sentencing, and drug sentencing reform. However, uncovering some of the unexpected jewels that have been found amid the madness is precisely the central theme of this book.

While the very real and pervasive evils, injustice, and inequality of prisons are a tragic and inhumane truth requiring and demanding massive reform, and perhaps complete abolition, the authors argue that something beneficial can still be gleaned from this phenomenon. This is a paradox. Because one part is true, the failures of the dark prison systems, does not mean that the other part cannot also be true; there is a gift to be gained from those who have had this experience. This is the argument that this book puts forward.

During the writing of this book, the authors read Heather Ann Thompson's Pulitzer Prize winner, *Blood in the Water,* the story of the Attica prison uprising of 1971. It is altogether a horrific, tragic, and beautiful book. It not only is a long overdue reporting of the facts of what happened that September of 1971 and a setting straight of history, but it also changes a paradigm of who persons in prison really are and who they are not—metaphorically as well as physically. It continues to challenge our perception of prisoners, prisons, and the power of the state to shape perception to protect political, economic, and personal reputations. It is a story about great evil but great good within an evil institution.

What Thompson has so masterfully done, we are humbly trying to do here—to shift the paradigm, to expose unexpected beauty and transformative learning excavated by persons imprisoned and the formerly incarcerated from the suffering and deprivation that is prison. What becomes clear in Thompson's book is the blurring of the lines between prisoners and correctional officers, police, prison administration, and that acts of reason, civility, charity and humanity were often exhibited by the prisoners, not the so-called free. Indeed, this is another argument the authors are making: there is a "blurring of the boundaries" as we are all prisoners of something, our own insecurities, addictions, relationships, ignorance, or fears. The inside and outside dichotomy of the prison experience is blurred (Thompson 2016).

"What happens inside the walls inevitably reflects the society outside" (Wicker 2005, xii), journalist and witness to the Attica uprising, Tom Wicker asserts. "So, this is who we are, the jailers, the jailed. This is the spirit of our age," (Wright 2007, ix) states the poet, C.D. Wright who visited and wrote from her experience in Louisiana state prisons. Our public institutions reflect the soul and spirit of any era. Prisons in America define who we are as a people.

But as it is with all of us, there is juxtaposition of the individual will with the context of the institution and society. Within and despite a dehumanizing system, there is individual choice. Individual choice or will for purposes of this book, does not refer to the commission of a crime, but instead to a choosing to transform once incarcerated. These are the individual experiences that the authors unpack and which stamp individuals in profound, often traumatic ways, but frequently transformative ways as well. Therefore, dismissing transformative aspects of the experience of incarceration for fear of idealization or romanticizing is not acceptable nor is it an option. When asked his opinion on Ban the Box (an American campaign to remove the check box that asks job and college applicants if they have a criminal record), National Association for the Advancement of Colored People (NAACP) award recipient and poet teacher, Dwayne Betts said:

> In some ways I am not in favor of Ban the Box as – the gaps we have when we were incarcerated should not be erased. I'm not saying incarceration in any way should be glorified, but it is a reality. But some of it can be an asset and we shouldn't erase it. Shame makes you silent. Opening up the space, to ignore this gap means we don't value at all that time in our lives. This time [incarceration] contributes to who we are (2019).

Opening this space then in the service of benefitting others through shared experiences so as not to be defined by humiliation, dehumanization, and brutality is often the desire of the incarcerated (Larson 2013). So, the voices of those most affected are included; it is their gift from the dark.

Throughout this book, the authors attempted to choose language that does not define individuals who are or have been incarcerated by that experience. Therefore, terms such as imprisoned or formerly incarcerated are used rather than prisoner, inmate, or felon. The idea that a person should not be defined and identified by the prison experience is crucial, and individuals should not be thought of abstractly but individually as people.

The authors are well positioned to speak to the theme of this book and came to it through their own experiences. John R. Chaney is currently a City University of New York professor and co-director of Criminal Justice at CUNY's LaGuardia Community College. He also served as the former executive director for the Brooklyn District Attorney's Office's nationally acclaimed prisoner reentry program ComALERT, responsible for providing community reintegration services for thousands of men and women. He too has lived the experience of incarceration, identifying his seven years of incarceration within city, state (including Attica), and federal facilities to be instrumental in creating what he considers to be his transformative gifts from the dark. Dr. Joni Schwartz has facilitated a volunteer writing class inside a New York State prison since 2017 and is founder and facilitator of a community writing group for newly released men and women. Her knowledge of physical incarceration comes through the hundreds of stories and narratives of the men and women she has met, befriended, and interacted with, several of whom have provided guidance and valuable critiques and insights in writing this book. In addition to critiquing the volume, more than a few individuals have demonstrated deep intellectual work and an organic approach to scholarship that has persuaded the authors that elements of the prison cell can serve as a paradigm for non-incarcerated people as a site of education. Schwartz and Chaney wrote this book because the overwhelming majority of writing identifies the all-too-familiar and true evils, humiliations, degradations, and injustices of the prison experience without offering a substantial and deep focus on the transformational phenomena, an occurrence that is just as real and familiar. *Gifts from the Dark* seeks to bend the paradigm.

Although this is not an edited volume, the authors often frame the incarceration experience by highlighting people and writers across generations. This selection is central to the argument of the ubiquitous qualities of the experience. Readers may wonder why writers like Antonio Gramsci or Viktor Frankl are included with others like Jack Henry Abbott. For purposes of this book, the catalyst or cause, as well the justice or injustice of the imprisonment, is not primarily relevant. The commonality of the prison experience is. Therefore, political prisoners, holocaust victims, those convicted for murder and drug offenses, and other types of incarcerated individuals are grouped together because of the shared experience of incarceration.

Gifts from the Dark is divided into four parts: Adult Transformative Learning and the Prison Experience (Chapters 1–4); Learning that Transforms the Self (Chapters 5–9); Learning in Relationship to Others; (Chapters 10–12); and Learning that Transforms the World (Chapters 13–14).

Chapter 1 frames this book in the tradition of classic prison writing by Nelson Mandela (*Conversations with Myself,* 2010), Viktor Frankl (*Man's Search for Meaning,* 1984), Antonio Gramsci (*Notebooks from Prison,* 1972), and Jack Henry Abbott (*In the Belly of the Beast,* 1981) as well as others. Unlike these texts, this book was not written in a prison cell. But congruent with these prison classics, the authors of this volume make the case that there are many kinds of prisons and the lessons from behind physical bars have relevance. Chapter 2 defines adult transformative learning and the disorienting dilemma of incarceration that can be a catalyst toward transformation. Critical Race Theory is introduced as both individual and collective transformative learning are developed. Chapter 3 explains transformative learning as a brave act in the face of the obstacles of *prisonization,* the inmate code, and substance abuse. Choosing transformative learning is hard. Assata Shakur, Susan Rosenberg, Angela Davis, and Ruth Wilson Gilmore are among the women included in Chapter 4 specifically centering on female prisons and race. In Chapter 5, silence and solitude are discussed in spite of the diabolical nature of solitary confinement is well known to be. This chapter provides context, history, and perspective to a discussion of solitary spaces for meditation, quiet, and intrapersonal communication. Chapters 6 through 9 cover the development and education of the organic intellectual, mental, physical and emotional intelligences while exploring prison art and college programs. Chapter 10celebrates the Black family and exposes the myth of family pathology by examining the contributions of families of incarcerated individuals. Chapters 11 and 12 address the digital divide as it relates to returning citizens and the proficiency of their non-verbal communication which is learned, honed and required for survival. The final two chapters look at giving back, community, loyalty, and reform as everyone's responsibility. *Gifts from the Dark* ends not with an American prison, but with African prisons in Gulu and Jinja, Uganda to round out the book's argument.

Finally, considering the somewhat polemical argument of this book, readers may approach it with initial uncomfortability. That seems a normal response. Granted, even a well-intentioned attempt to ascribe positive attributes to a prison cell, clearly a space of social and political punishment and torture, is a dangerous precipice to walk. This precipice, what the authors are calling paradox, is a counterspace that many prison literary social justice giants have walked including Mandela, Frankl, Gramsci, Baldwin, Himes, and Malcolm X. Some more explicitly than others; but all, in the company of hundreds if not thousands of other prison writers and artists, have with courage and tenacity inhabited and redeemed the cell.

REFERENCES

Abbott, J. H. (1981). *In the Belly of the Beast: Letters from Prison*. New York: Random.

Betts, D. (May 3, 2019). Conference at BMCC Re-entry/Entry Conference. Panel Presentation.

Frankl, V. E. (1984). *Man's search for meaning: An introduction to logotherapy*. New York: Simon & Schuster.

Gramsci, A., Hoare, Q., and Nowell-Smith, G. (1972). *Selections from the prison notebooks of Antonio Gramsci*. New York: International Publishers.

Larson, D. (2013). *Fourth city: Essays from the prison in America*. East Lansing, MI: Michigan University Press.

Mandela, N. (2010). *Conversations with myself*. New York: Farrar, Straus and Giroux.

Thompson, H. (2016). *Blood in the water*. New York: Pantheon Books.

Wicker, T. (2005). "Foreword," in D. Quentin Miller (ed.), *Prose and Cons: Essays on Prison Literature in the United States*. Jefferson, NC: McFarland & Company, Inc., p. 280.

Wright, C.D. (2007). *One big self: An investigation*. Port Townsend: Copper Canyon Press.

PART I

Adult Transformative Learning and the Prison Experience

Chapter 1

Prison Writing: A Literary Tradition

For as long as man has been imprisoned, the world has seen an abundance of prison authors. From them, emerged a genre of prison literature, often unacknowledged, in the academic canon (Blumenthal 2000). Whether the writing is for repentance, self-expression, reflection, prayer, creative outlet, protest, resistance or survival, the genre of prison literature is alive and well and is a vehicle of adult transformative learning for both the inmate and society. This book is an analysis of the prison experience, and the impact of that lived experience often expressed through that genre.

Cultural historian and scholar H. Bruce Franklin has chronicled the long history of prison writing in America. He recounted this writing genre from the plantation to the penitentiary, through the early American prisons, the civil rights movement and political prisoners, through to a prison renaissance to today's writers in prison (Franklin 1998). According to Franklin, the sheer quantity of writing by American convicts in the 19th and first half of the 20th centuries is huge and its historical significance profound (1998, 124). The progression from plantation to prison, particularly for men of color, resounds in songs of slavery, peonage, and chain gangs and represents the early writings within this genre. From a global perspective, Western Europe in the 19th century produced debtors' prisons and writing groups. The Middle Ages produced the likes of John Bunyan and his famous (1678) *The Pilgrim's Progress*. Prison is frequently a transformative experience and writing is its voice.

More contemporaneously, Joy James (2005) in the introduction to her book, *The New Abolitionists: (Neo) Slave Narratives and Contemporary Prison Writings*, equates prison writing with both slave narratives and abolitionists in America. She stated, "Through their narratives, imprisoned writers can function as progressive abolitionists and register as 'people's historians.' They become the storytellers of the political histories of the captives *and* their

3

captors. These narratives are generally the 'unauthorized' versions of politi-cal life, often focusing on dissent and policing and repression" (2005, xxxii).

The opening chapter frames this book in the tradition of classic prison texts by highlighting select writers. To be clear, this selection is neither represen-tative nor exclusive of the kinds of writing, convictions, personalities, geo-graphical locations, or political context of the many hundreds of individuals who could have been chosen. Instead, the selection points to the global nature and diversity of justice-involved experiences and the profound impact prison literary tradition has had upon our world.

The authors Antonio Gramsci (*Prison Notebooks*, 1971), Chester B. Himes, (*If He Hollers Let Him Go*, 1972), Viktor Frankl (*Man's Search for Meaning*, 2006), Nelson Mandela (*Conversations with Myself*, 2010), Jack Henry Abbott (*In the Belly of the Beast*, 1981), and Assata Shakur, (*Autobiography*, 1987) are in many ways the "people's historians" from prison. Unlike these texts and authors, this book was not written in a prison cell. However congru-ent with these prison classics, the authors make the case that there are many kinds of prisons and the lessons from behind physical bars have potential relevance to us all from both an historical and contemporary perspective.

A prison cell is sometimes an ideal space to write. There is quiet, time, isolation, focus, and more time. This focused time can provide space for both introspective self-reflection and the engagement of the sociologicalimagina-tion, where history connects with personal experience (Mills, 2000) which can be useful for writing. So, it is not surprising that a literary tradition of prison writing continues to emerge both in America and internationally. Prisons are spaces of revolution both internal to the individual and sometimes without in the political arena of social justice. The aforementioned authors Gramsci, Himes, Frankl, Mandela, Abbott, and Shakur have each produced a gift from the dark through their prison experience and subsequent writing. This is a disparate group of individuals from different countries, contexts, cul-tures, and circumstances of imprisonment. We make no distinction between common criminals, political prisoners, religious prisoners, or blue-collar or white-collar crime—he prison experience is still the prison experience. They have all contributed to the canon of prison writings, attested to the horrors of the experience, and raised their voices. Context for each contributor is dis-cussed along with how these prison writers have impacted our world. They are arranged in chronological order by incarceration dates.

PRISON LITERARY VOICES

Notebooks from Prison: Antonio Gramsci

Antonio Gramsci was arrested and imprisoned in the autumn of 1926 under Italy's Mussolini crackdown on bourgeois democracy. Any opposition to Mussolini's fascist regime in either print or through group organizing was cause for imprisonment. As a Marxist and communist politician, Gramsci was a member of Italy's parliament, a philosopher and writer. Because of his activism and scholarship, Gramsci was 35 years old when he was arrested as a political prisoner (Gramsci 1971). Prone to chronic illness most of his life, prison would ultimately kill him, although it did not stop him from thinking and writing profusely. Though he was too ill to complete his sentence, he was sentenced to 20 years in prison. During his 1928 trial, the judge was quoted as saying "We must stop this brain working for twenty years!" (Gramsci 1971, xviii.). This, however, was not accomplished. In fact, while in prison, Gramsci wrote 2,848 handwritten pages which became his volume *Prison Notebooks*. *Prison Notebooks* was later smuggled out of Italy by a family member. It would ultimately contain essays, historical analyses, critiques of fascism, notes from his readings, and general philosophical reflections on religion, economics and power. Gramsci suffered greatly with devastating despair, isolation, anxiety about his family, and physical ailments. But during the times he felt well enough, Gramsci wrote and read voraciously while in prison (Gramsci 1971). He died in a prison clinic from long-standing lack of medical attention but not before he taught briefly in an informal prison adult education school in Ustica Prison (Mayo 1999). He called his writing "the focus to my inner life" while others referred to his writing as "the continuation in Gramsci's prison cell of his life as a revolutionary" (Hoare and Smith 1971, xciv). For adult transformative education, Gramsci's prison writings inform basic questioning and challenging of the hegemonic implications of one's thoughts and actions (Brookfield 2000).

Would Gramsci have been as prolific had he not gone to prison? Would his thinking have been as rich and complex? We will never know. But the prison experience was utilized by Gramsci as a site to continue the revolution and a site of transformative learning for many who would embrace his thinking and read his prison essays. In fact, Gramsci influenced transformative adult educator, Paulo Freire, while Freire was exiled in Chile (Mayo 1999, 7). Both Gramsci and Freire emphasized the political nature of adult education and the role of institutions of civil society in social transformation, Gramsci in Italy and Freire in Brazil (Mayo 1999).

Fighter with a Pen: Chester B. Himes

Prisoner #59623 started publishing in mainstream magazines with his prison number—but later signed his work as Chester B. Himes (1909–1984). He was one of the most prolific and significant writers of the Black American literary tradition. Himes started his writing career while incarcerated in the Ohio State Penitentiary from 1928–1936; this was his transformative education both as an artist and a maturing man. Convicted for armed robbery and home invasion, he was originally sentenced to 20 years but due to prison overcrowding, the Ohio legislature in 1931 passed three laws reducing sentences and expediting paroles. Consequently, he only served eight of his 20 years (Jackson 2017).

A disorienting dilemma, a penitentiary cellblock fire on April 21, 1930, plummeted him into writing as a means of coping with the trauma of watching many of his fellow inmates die. One short story, *To What Red Hell*, and two novels based on the same manuscript, *Cast the First Stone* and *Yesterday Will Make You Cry*, launched his lifetime writing career. In the words of his biographer, Lawrence P. Jackson:

> Writing was one activity that helped him overcome lonely isolation and puzzles through the welter of emotions after the fire. Chester started putting pencil to paper on the ground floor of the E and H cell block in the crippled company. His efforts to deal with the personal tragedy of incarceration, loneliness, physical vulnerability, the conflict of homosexual desire, and the gruesome slush of human entrails in the yard during the long night of April 21st launched his writing career. He had the seed of a searing emotional experience to drive his ambition (2017, 88–89).

In his autobiography, *The Quality of Hurt,* Himes stated that prison was where he grew up to be a man after entering at the age of nineteen and being released at twenty-six. Prison taught him to be dependent only on himself and how to survive. More significantly, prison taught him how to write (1972). For Himes, prison was where he learned his craft. He would not become the famous Black literary giant who addressed issues of race until later in life. Through most of his career, Himes wrote fiction; particularly detective fiction. He wrote about Harlem and Black workers struggling to get ahead although he was born and grew up in the Midwest and Deep South of middle-class college-educated parents (Jackson 2017). But it was the racism Himes experienced when he relocated to Los Angeles in the 1940s as a screenwriter that enraged him and drove much of his later writing on race. He confessed in his emotional, open, and honest autobiography that after prison, he was confronted with racial prejudice:

Up to the age of thirty-one I had been hurt emotionally, spiritually, and physically as much as thirty-one years can bear: I had lived in the South, I had fallen down an elevator shaft, I had been kicked out of college, I had served seven and a half years in prison, I had survived the last five years of the Depression in Cleveland; and still I was entire, complete, functional; my mind was sharp, my reflexes were good, and I was not bitter. But under the mental corrosion of race prejudice in Los Angeles I had become bitter and saturated with hate (1972, 76).

This experience eventually drove him to self-exile in Europe in the 1950s. Himes was a controversial writer often compared to Richard Wright. Both wrote about strong Black male protagonists who raped and murdered whites. His writing was often full of rage, explicit sexual overtones, violence, and interracial relationships. During his lifetime, Himes's work did not receive much critical acclaim in the United States, but the French critics loved his writing, particularly his Harlem detective novels. These novels awarded him the 1958 Grand Prix de Littérature Policière award (Kentake 2015).

Though he was a contemporary of Ralph Ellison, James Baldwin, and Richard Wright, Himes did not receive the same acceptance and critical acclaim in America, perhaps because he wrote with less restraint. Himes is perhaps more relevant than ever before in the time of Black Lives Matter, an organized movement advocating for non-violent civil disobedience in protest of police brutality against African Americans, and the MeToo movement against sexual harassment and sexual abuse of women. Himes was arguably ahead of his time in the 1940s when he wrote uncompromisingly naturalistic fiction about race, the Black family, interracial marriage, and segregation (Jackson 2017) which rings true in current unrest movements today.

Making Meaning in Tragedy: ViKtor Frankl

Antonio Gramsci forged writing and thought that currently frames political, social, and philosophical scholarship. Chester Himes articulated a Black American collective voice against racism, white supremacy, and the practices of colonialization at a time when they were obscured. And Viktor Frankl's prison writing and thought informs the fields of psychology, counseling, and trauma studies with his perspectives on the psychology of survival.

Viktor Frankl was prisoner #119,104. He was a neurologist and psychiatrist who was imprisoned in several concentration camps, including Auschwitz, during the World War II Jewish Holocaust in Germany. He used his prison experience to write the classic of prison and survival literature, *Man's Search for Meaning* (2006). In its most basic theme, his writing suggests that life's quest is not power nor pleasure, but the quest for meaning. He implies that if anyone can make meaning, even in the most horrific and terrifying situations namely prison, they can survive any traumatic experience with health and wholeness. Through personal narrative, Frankl makes clear the undernourishment, torture, sickness, exposure to extreme elements, hard labor, and exhaustion experienced in the concentration camps:

> It is very difficult for an outsider to grasp how very little value was placed on human life in camp. The camp inmate was hardened, but possibly became more conscious of this complete disregard of human existence when a convoy of sick men was arranged. The emaciated bodies of the sick were thrown on two-wheeled carts which were drawn by prisoners for many miles, often through snowstorms, to the next camp. If one of the sick men had died before the cart left, he was thrown on anyway—the list had to be correct. The list was the only thing that mattered. A man counted only because he had a prison number. One literally became a number: dead or alive—that was unimportant; the life of a "number" was completely irrelevant. What stood behind that number and that life mattered even less: the fate, the history, the name of the man (Frankl 2006, 28).

He repeatedly heralded the value of suffering, the intensification of the inner life, saying yes to life and finding meaning and purpose that promotes human dignity. He maintained that purposeful work, love, and courage make life meaningful. He learned this amid prison terrorism.

Now, nearly 75 years later, this prison text has been reprinted more than 73 times, translated into 24 languages, sold over ten million copies, and is still being used in high schools, colleges, and prison classrooms (Noble 1997). Again, we ask the same question as that of Gramsci and Himes. Would Frankl have produced this book, influenced millions, and impacted the mental health profession in the way he did had he not gone to prison?

Both as a prisoner and as psychiatrist to the inmates, Frankl found that the ability to survive whole in prison, sound in body and mind, had to do with confronting the disorienting dilemma of the prison experience. This is adult transformative learning.

> What was really needed was a fundamental change in our attitude toward life. We had to learn ourselves and, furthermore, we had to teach the despairing men, that it did not really matter what we expected from life, but rather what life expected from us. We needed to stop asking about the meaning of life, and instead to think of ourselves as those who were being questioned by life—daily and hourly. Our answer must consist, not in talk and meditation, but in right action and in right conduct. Life ultimately means taking the responsibility to find the right answer to its problems and to fulfill the tasks which it constantly sets for everyone (Frankl 2006, 37).

Lessons from the Cell: Nelson Mandela

In the words of Nelson Mandela, in a letter written to his wife, "The cell is an ideal place to learn to know yourself, to search realistically and regularly the process of your own mind and feelings" (Mandela 2010, 211). Mandela wrote these words from Kroonstad Prison in 1975. Born in 1918 in Transkei, South Africa, Mandela fought throughout his adult life against the ruling South African National Party's policy of apartheid, a system of segregation or discrimination on grounds of race. Joining the African National Congress (henceforth, ANC) in 1944, he was arrested, detained, jailed, and sentenced to hard labor periodically from 1952–1963 for his resistance and political activity. His longest imprisonment began in 1964 when he was convicted and sentenced to life imprisonment for sabotage and treason. He was transported to Robben Island Prison where he spent most of the next 26 years until his release in February of 1990. His time spent in two other prisons, Pollesmoor and Victor Verster, were marked by hard labor, cramped uninhabitable cells, and the cruelty of Afrikaner guards (Mandela 1994). It was also marked by a trail of letters and writings articulating his seemingly unwavering optimism that South Africa would change and that the human spirit was resilient and forgiving.

Mandela and other Robben Island prisoners learned Shakespeare growing up in mission schools. As children they were required to memorize passages. Shakespeare inspired Mandela during his imprisonment, and Mandela repeated quotations from Shakespeare throughout his published and unpublished letters. Quotes like "the chains of the body are often wings to the spirit" which he used during his trial would be an encouragement to many in the fight against apartheid (Mandela 2010, 45). While he was imprisoned, his country, fueled in part by his sacrifice and example, increased their resistance and moved toward racial civil war in an attempt to end apartheid. To avoid civil war, authorities released Mandela in 1990.

Arguably, his time in prison more than prepared and positioned him to become South Africa's first Black president in 1994, achieving international recognition for rebuilding his country and dismantling apartheid. He built a broad coalition government and worked toward land reform, solutions to poverty, improvement of healthcare, and racial reconciliation, effectively healing a nation. One of his most notable achievements was the establishment of the Truth and Reconciliation Commission (TRC) to redress the crimes and atrocities of the years of apartheid and the anti-apartheid struggle. Nelson Mandela was many things: an anti-apartheid revolutionary, a political leader, and philanthropist who nurtured his patience, optimism, courage, and leadership in a minuscule prison cell and then offered these attributes to the world.

A Lifetime in the Beast: Jack Henry Abbott

Decades before mass incarceration and prison reform became political top-ics, prevalent issues of social protest, and mainstream issues of social justice, there was Jack Henry Abbott's 1981 book, *In the Belly of the Beast.* In the words of Norman Mailer in his introduction to this now famous and con-troversial analysis of penology and the American prison system, "There is a paradox at the core of penology, and from it derives the thousand ills and afflictions of the prison system. It is that not only the worst of the young are sent to prison, but the best — that is, the proudest, the bravest, the most dar-ing, the most enterprising, and the most undefeated of the poor. There starts the horror" (1981, xii).

In the Belly of the Beast was published as a result of written correspon-dence between Mailer and Abbott while Abbott was serving time in maximum security for forgery, manslaughter, and bank robbery. The letter-writing cor-respondence between Mailer and Abbott significantly informed the writing of Mailer's magnum opus about prison life that won him his second Pulitzer Prize in 1980, *The Executioner's Song* (Loving 2017). Abbott's book was released to a very favorable *New York Times Book Review* around the same time as his parole (Des Pres 1981). Six weeks after being paroled, Abbott was convicted of manslaughter in the death of a restaurant worker and returned to prison for life where he committed suicide in 2002 (Worth, 2002). Details of his return to prison and trial are developed in Abbott's second book, *My Return* (1987) with Naomi Zack, a scholar and philosopher (Loving 2017).

The bulk of Abbott's life was spent in various maximum security prisons. He died an author and writer. Through his writing, he revealed the horrors of the prison system and the violence within. He also questioned re-entry into mainstream society, especially for individuals returning after extended time in maximum security settings.

Critics of Abbott and Mailer do not believe Abbott should be a vehicle to discuss prison reform because of his violent criminal history. This does raise the question of why Abbott should be included in a group with the likes of Gramsci, Frankl, and Mandela. Our argument is that despite the nature of his crimes, it cannot be disputed that Abbott was an early critic of the prison system horrors, and his writing contributed to the canon of prison literature. Like Gary Gilmore, imprisoned for murder and dying by firing squad as well as the subject of Mailer's *The Executioner's Song* (1979); there seems little question that Abbott was an early spokesperson for the evils of the contem-porary prison industrial complex. In his voice, "When America can get angry because of the violence done to my life and the countless lives of men like me, then there will be an end to violence, but not before" (Abbott 1981, 108).

Civil Rights Advocate: Assata Shakur

At the time of this publication, Assata Shakur (Joanne Chesimard) remains the only woman and individual still alive among the six brief biographies in this chapter. Shakur was a member of the Black Liberation Army and a Black Rights fugitive who spent 6.5 years imprisoned for allegedly killing a New Jersey State trooper. She was given a life sentence but escaped from Clinton Federal Correctional Facility for Women in Union Township, New Jersey, and fled to Cuba where she is currently exiled (Shakur, 1987). The United States has tried to convince Cuba to return Shakur, but Cuba has consistently refused. Most recently former president Trump's former Secretary of State, Rex Tillerson, tried to extradite and re-imprison her. Cuba again refused (Revolt TV, 2017).

Shakur has always maintained her innocence in the death of the officer and the forensic evidence supported her account of the events, yet to this day she remains on the FBI's most wanted list. At the time of her arrest, she was labeled a terrorist and sentenced to life imprisonment. She has called her imprisonment a legal lynching as she has consistently fought for racial and social justice. In her autobiography, she outlines her work with the Black Panther Party and the Black Liberation Army. She also describes how the FBI's COINTELPRO, a Counterintelligence Program active from 1956–1979 and beyond conducted covert and illegal initiatives aimed at surveilling, infiltrating, discrediting, and disrupting American political organizations deemed subversive (Shakur 1987). Shakur was the first woman to be named on the FBI's Most Wanted Terrorist list as a domestic terrorist. In an open letter to Pope Paul II on a visit to Cuba, Shakur states she was neither a murderer nor a terrorist:

> I have advocated and I still advocate revolutionary changes in the structure and in the principles that govern the United States. I advocate self-determination for my people and for all oppressed inside the United States. I advocate an end to capitalist exploitation, the abolition of racist policies, the eradication of sexism, and the elimination of political repression. If that is a crime, then I am totally guilty (Shakur 2013).

In terms of her advocacy and speaking out on behalf of women in prison, Shakur said, "There are no criminals here at Riker's Island Correctional Institution for Women, (New York), only victims. Most of the women (over 95%) are Black and Puerto Rican. Many were abused children. Most have been abused by men and all have been abused by 'the system'" (Shakur 1978, 2).

Shakur remains a controversial figure. However, what we do know is that despite conflicting perspectives on her alleged crimes, Shakur represents a social activist and social justice icon in the tradition of prison writers and advocates.

GRAMSCI, HIMES, FRANKL, MANDELA, ABBOTT, AND SHAKUR

There is no question that Gramsci, Himes, Frankl, Mandela, Abbott, and Shakur were very different prisoners, writers, and people. Yet, despite the contextual differences of crimes, motives, social context, geography, race, and gender, they all utilized the space of prison in transformative ways. What is so remarkable, and we believe speaks to the dark gift of the prison experience, is that we could have highlighted any number of others including Robert Beck, Dietrich Bonhoeffer, Claude Brown, John Bunyan, Eldridge Cleaver, Angela Davis, Fyodor Dostoyevsky, Marcus Garvey, Jean Genet, Dashell Hammett, Piper Kerman, Martin Luther King, Jack London, Malcolm X, Nathan McCall, Thomas More, O'Henry, Alessandr Solzhenitsyn, or Oscar Wilde.

The brief descriptions of how these six extraordinary individuals transformed themselves and their corners of the world and still impact us through their legacy and writing and this is the learning that then becomes a gift to all of us. Gramsci's scholarship, hegemony, and adult education; Himes's outcries against racism through his art; Frankl's psychology, counseling, and trauma work; Mandela's civil disobedience, reconciliation, and political leadership; Abbott's witness to the horrors of prisons in America, and Shakur's civil rights and social justice activism all are gifts from prison that impact our world. Each one experienced a prison sentence, each one suffered emotionally and physically, each one experienced loss and dehumanization, and each one decided to make meaning. All decided to speak to their experiences.

Additionally, their lived experiences embrace an altered paradigm of who prisoners are, and are not, and a paradigm that embraces lifelong learning with all its complexities and paradoxes. The dark gift of the prison experience is born witness by all six. They inspired the content of this book and the questions it attempts to answer. These questions include: What is adult transformative learning and how are prisons sites of the phenomena? What is it about the incarceration experience that lends itself to potential human growth and not uncommonly makes this disorienting dilemma transformative?

REFERENCES

Abbott, J.H. (1981). *In the belly of the beast: Letters from prison.* New York: Random House.

Abbott, J.H. (1987). *My return.* New York: Prometheus Books.

Blumenthal, R., (2000, August 26). Confined in prisons, Literature breaks out. *The New York Times.* https://www.nytimes.com/2000/08/26/books/confined-in-prisons-literature-breaks-out.html)

Brookfield, S.D. (2000). "Transformative learning as ideology critique." In J. Mezirow and Associates (Eds.), *Learning as transformation. Critical perspectives on a theory in progress* (pp. 125–150). San Francisco, CA: Jossey-Bass.

Des Pres, T. (July 9, 1981). Child of the State [Book Review of *In the belly of the beast* by J. Abbott] https://www.nytimes.com/1981/07/19/books/a-child-of-the-state.html

Bunyan, J. (2003). *The Pilgrim's Progress,* W.R. Owens, ed. Oxford: University Press.

Frankl, V. E. (2006). *Man's search for meaning.* Boston: Beacon Press.

Franklin, H.B., (Ed.) (1998). *Prison writing in 20th-century America.* New York: Penguin Putnam, Inc.

Gramsci, A. (1971). *Selections from the prison notebooks.* Ed and translated by Hoare, Q. and Smith, G., New York: International Publishers.

Himes, C. (1972). *The Quality of Hurt.* New York: Thunder's Mouth Press.

Hoare, Q. and Smith, G. (1971). Selections from the prison notebooks of Antonio Gramsci. London: Lawrence & Wishart.

Jackson, L.P. (2017). *Chester B. Himes: A biography.* New York: W.W. Norton & Company Ltd.

James, J. (2005) (Ed.) *The new abolitionists: Neo slave narratives and contemporary writings.* Albany, NY: State University of New York Press.

Kentake, M. (July 29, 2015). Chester Himes. https://kentakepage.com/chester-himes/

Loving, J. (2017). *Jack and Norman.* New York: St. Martin's Press.

Mailer, N. (1979). *The executioner's song.* London: Hutchinson.

Mandela, N. (1994). *Long walk to freedom.* Little Brown & Co.

Mandela, N. (2010). *Nelson: Conversations with myself.* New York: Farrar, Straus and Giroux.

Mayo, P. (1999). *Gramsci, Freire & adult education: Possibilities for transformative action.* London: Zed Books.

Mills, C.W. (2000). *The sociological imagination.* New York: Oxford.

Noble, H.B. (1997, September 4). Dr. Viktor E. Frankl of Vienna, psychiatrist of the search for meaning, dies at 92. *The New York Times.* https://www.nytimes.com/1997/09/04/world/dr-viktor-e-frankl-of-vienna-psychiatrist-of-the-search-for-meaning-dies-at-92.html

Revolt TV. (June 18, 2017). Cuba will keep Assata Shakur, despite Trump's request to return her to U.S. https://revolt.tv/stories/2017/06/18/cuba-assata-shakur-trumps-request-return 0600303c69

Shakur, A. (1978). History is a Weapon. *The Black Scholar.* https://www.historyisaweapon.com/defcon1/shakurwip.html

Shakur, A. (1987). *Assata: An autobiography.* Chicago: Lawrence Hill Books.

Shakur, A. (2013). Transcript of Open Letter to Pope Paul II. https://www.
    democracynow.org/2013/5/2/ex_black_panther_assata_shakur_added_to_fbis_
    most_wanted_terrorist_list
Worth, R.F. (2002, February 11). Jailhouse author helped by Mailer is found dead.
    The New York Times. https://www.nytimes.com/2002/02/11/nyregion/jailhouse-
    author-helped-by-mailer-is-found-dead.html?rref=collection%2Fbyline%2Frober
    t-f. worth&action=click&contentCollection=undefined&region=stream&module=
    stream_unit&version=search&contentPlacement=1&pgtype=collection

Chapter 2

Incarceration: The Disorienting Dilemma toward Transformation

In a correctional facility classroom surrounded by imprisoned men who will return to civilian life within the next few months after serving years, often decades, in prison; we sit and listen to their lives as told through their writing and know we are receiving a gift. This is a counterspace. Through this three-hour-a-week writing group, we are engaged so that we don't remember we are in prison. The authors are a White woman and a Black man who are not significantly older than some of their students as several have spent twenty-five years imprisoned and others are hardly more than teenagers. Can we learn from the lived experiences of these mainly male, Black and Brown men? The answer is "yes." For many of the men, prison has been school and for some of them it has been a place of what Mezirow (1997) calls transformative learning. They are on a high learning curve, and we share in their process.

TRANSFORMATIVE LEARNING DEFINED

Adults learn differently than children. This fact is manifested in the approaches toward teaching adults. Teaching adults is referred to as andragogy as contrasted to pedagogy, the teaching and learning of children (Knowles 1975, 1984a & b). Not all scholars agree that there is a complete difference between pedagogy and andragogy (Holmes and Abington-Cooper 2000). However, there is a general consensus among educators that adults bring extensive prior life and school experiences to bear on their learning. Consequently, the teaching of adults (andragogy) is substantively different (Knowles 1984b) and often involves the changing or major altering of life perspective and orientation: transformative learning.

Age is the basic characteristic used to describe an adult learner (Holmes and Abington-Cooper 2000). Holmes and Abington-Cooper argue, in agreement with most adult educators, that defining adult and adulthood goes far beyond years to encompass psychological, emotional, biological, moral, and spiritual dimensions. Mature adults are (or are expected to be) responsible for their actions, behave in humane ways toward themselves and others, understand themselves, contribute to community and society, and think rationally while responding with appropriate emotional engagement within an increasingly complex global world (2000).

The term andragogy has Greek origins but was first introduced in the United States in the 1920s by Martha Anderson and Eduard Lindeman (Davenport and Davenport 1985). Lindeman went on to become a philosopher of adult education who further developed key elements of adult learning: self-direction, experiential, and problem-solving orientations (Davenport 1987). Later, Malcolm Knowles (1984a) established that andragogy centers on self-actualization; thus, a learning process involving a person's whole emotional, psychological, and intellectual being. Knowles' four assumptions about individuals as they become adults are 1) they become independent and self-directed learners; 2) they accumulate growing "lived experiences" throughout life that they then relate to new learning; 3) they are ready to learn and [are] oriented toward their own development rather than dependent on biological or academic demands, and 4) they immediately apply knowledge and are less future-oriented as it relates to learning, giving them a problem-centered rather than subject-centered orientation (Knowles 1975).

For many adults then, learning is transformational. This transformational learning is a deep process of meaning construction going beyond simple knowledge accumulation and information acquisition but is a meaning making process engaging a person's entire life. It fundamentally changes a person's worldview and life orientation through critical thinking and reflection and results in new ways of seeing the world. This is an emancipatory process. Transformational learning often leads to profound changes in our behaviors, thoughts, feelings, values, beliefs, and actions radically shifting a person's *being* in the world.

Following Knowles, Mezirow (1997) drew on the work of Freire (1972) and Habermas (1971) in the formulation of his adult education theory which said, among other things, that critical reflection triggers transformative learning by making meaning of life experiences and creating interpretations of them. According to Mezirow (1990), learning may be defined as "the process of making a new or revised interpretation of the meaning of an experience, which guides subsequent understanding, appreciation and action" (p.1). For most of us, if it happens at all, adult transformative learning is continuous but inconsistent. It may start at a particular, critical life crisis that then facilitates learning and transformation. Rohr (2011) calls this a "further journey."

DISORIENTING DILEMMA

This further journey is precipitated by what adult educators call a "disorienting dilemma" that propels the learner to think deeply and critically about life's assumptions and beliefs. It often changes their paradigms and alters their frames of reference about the world and their position in it (Mezirow 1997; Grabove 1997). Mezirow (1997) believed that this disorienting dilemma was triggered by a life crisis or major life transition like death or loss, tragedy, sickness, upheaval of life as usual—some necessary suffering or falling upward which propels adults to take a second journey in life very different than the first half of their lives (Rohr 2011).

Understanding this life upheaval is predominantly processed through rational and analytic means, though not exempt from spiritual or emotional processes as well. This critical reflection can drive an individual to make plans that redefine their lives and propel them to behave and act differently (Mezirow 1997; Grabove 1997; Freire 1970).

For some, incarceration is just such an experience and can serve as a powerful disorienting dilemma and catalyst for transformative learning. However, there should be no illusions that all incarcerated citizens experience this type of learning. Indeed, Rohr (2011) states that not everyone takes this second journey or engages in the kind of adult transformation that makes one grow, face themselves and their life, take on new habits and perspectives, and act in new ways.

Many members of our prison writing group are taking this second journey. They remind us that they do self-select to be part of the group and are determined to change. Writing is their tool for critical thinking and reflection and a way to process the transformation. What seems clear from speaking to the writers and reading their words is that incarceration can be a disorienting dilemma with potential for tremendous transformative learning. In the words of one student "prison saved my life" and in the additional words of Frankl, "In reality [prison], there was an opportunity and a challenge. One could make a victory of those experiences, turning life into an inner triumph, or one could ignore the challenge and simply vegetate" (2006, 93).

COLLECTIVE TRANSFORMATIVE LEARNING

It is perhaps appropriate at this juncture to explain that we do not understand transformational learning to be the only theory of the way that adults learn, albeit the field of adult education has been dominated by it. There is danger in viewing learning as solely an individual process of critical self-reflection and transformation (Newman 2014; Johnson-Bailey 2012), although it some-times is. Many other learning theories, particularly Freire's, goes beyond Mezirow's focus on individual transformation, and examines efforts toward social change with both scholars viewing critical reflection as integral (Taylor 1998 and 2007). Freire "sees its [transformational learning] purpose based on a rediscovery of power such that the more critically aware learners become, the more they are able to transform society and subsequently their own real-ity" (Taylor 1998, 17). This collective transformative learning is operative in prisons as it relates to both the institution and institutional racism inherent in the American prison system.

Prisons, for the most part, are horrible, tragic, and frightening institutions. Read any prison literature, and this fact will be confirmed. The prison experi-ence can be a very personal life crisis, but it may be that it is not only an indi-vidual journey or solitary transformation. From an American perspective, the mass incarceration of Black and Brown citizens is collective and calls for a collective understanding and experience of transformational learning because the history of racism resulting in an incarceration crisis scars an entire society regardless of color (VanThompson 2012). Transformational learning in prison frequently involves engagement of racial issues, racial history, racial dis-crimination, and racial identity as incarceration and race cannot be separated in America. Future chapters will engage this phenomenon. Therefore, it is not only the individual's responsibility to transform but also the responsibility of the collective society that needs transformative learning. This brings us to Critical Race Theory (henceforth CRT).

CRITICAL RACE THEORY

All the writers in the prison group mentioned at the opening of this chapter are men of color. Of course, this is unfortunately not a surprise. Not because Black and Brown men commit more crimes, but because of what CRT implies. CRT (Bell 1992) brilliantly purports that race is institutionalized in American society because of its horrific history of slavery.

Originally coming out of legal studies but now applied across academic disciplines, it is the perspective that law and legal institutions are inherently racist and as a social rather than biological construct, race is used by white people to support their economic and political advancement at the expense of people of color (Bell 1995). Applied to criminal justice, today's prisons are the evolution from: slavery, to the collapse of Reconstruction, to the racial terrorism of lynching, to convict leasing, to Jim Crow, to racial profiling, and finally to mass incarceration (Stevenson 2014). This evolution of car-ceral institutions plus educational segregation based on race demonstrate the validity and evidence of CRT as it is actualized in communities and exemplify what has been called the school to prison pipeline (Holzman 2017).

This connection between incarceration and education is another example of CRT in operation and apparent in the re-segregation of public schools across America. Currently, the US is now more segregated than before Brown vs. Board of Education, the landmark 1954 Supreme Court case in which the justices ruled unanimously that racial segregation of children in public schools was unconstitutional (Bell 1980). Due to institutional policies that distribute school funding and allocation based on property taxes, we are still not equal in our allocation of resources (Holzman 2017; Brown 2016). Richer communities, often white, secure higher taxes which then provide higher funding for schools. Poorer neighborhoods, often with high concentrations of people of color, collect lower taxes—hence the schools are funding at a substantially lower rate. White supremacy and white privilege are ever present in America as a result of our history, and whites often benefit from this interest convergence (Bell 1980).

Another example of CRT in practice is gentrification. Through far-reaching economic and zoning strategies, gentrification is transforming urban neighborhoods by economically pricing out the poor, and often people of color, from their communities, homes, and neighborhoods (Stigler 2016). The displaced simultaneously watch these neighborhoods improve in terms of the infrastructure—pothole repairs, more amiable police presence, less crime, better garbage collection, more fresh fruits and vegetables, and better transportation service. These gentrified neighborhoods are clean, trendy, and safe, having pushed the poor out while often destroying communities, cultural vitality, and neighborhood solidarity. Unless communities strategically plan with residents of color and make provision for low and middle-income housing to preserve the history and culture of communities, gentrification can be another form of oppression (Diaz 2017).

With a critical eye, CRT can be evidenced almost anywhere you go in America. The COVID-19 pandemic has highlighted racial disparities in both access to quality health care as well as the percentage of Americans who are essential workers and had to work during the pandemic exposing themselves to the virus. People of color, disproportional to their percentage of representation in the US population, have died and contacted COVID because of systemically poorer health care, and discriminatory access to quality education and job opportunities. This is an example of CRT actualized.

Institutionalized racism which CRT establishes is sometimes harder to identify and explain than overt acts of racism: hate speech, lynchings, white supremacist demonstrations, or church bombings. Institutionalized racism is more invisible and covert because it is ingrained in major systems of the police, schools, health care, housing, and employment. And as has been stated, in no other system is it more evolutionary and ingrained than in the prison industrial complex.

The United States is at the intersection of mass incarceration and the prison industrial complex coming out of the war on drugs. This war was primarily fought in poor neighborhoods and not in the financial capital of Wall Street (Alexander 2010) where it could just as easily have been waged. These intersecting policies imprisoned people of color disproportionally to that of whites. This is the institutional manifestation of CRT's presentation of white privilege and white supremacy operating to oppress people of color on a large scale in the US and will be referenced throughout this book (Matsuda 1987; Bell 1995).

With so many national disorienting dilemmas, COVID, George Floyd's murder at the hands of police, removal of the confederate flag; can we evolve as a collective of adults and as a nation? Perhaps we also have the collective ability, should we choose, to learn and transform together. Theodore Parker (1853), said, "The arc of the moral universe is long, but it bends toward justice." In that spirit, perhaps we can collectively learn to transform as a democracy—critically reflecting on our history, ethics, social interactions, policies—learning from our collective mistakes as a nation, in some instances with collective repentance, and collective transformative learning (Freire 1972; Horton 1998; Johnson-Bailey 2012). However, we must be willing to change and willing to learn from each other.

Juanita Johnson-Bailey (2012) cites Paulo Freire and his concept of con-scientization comparing it to a type of transformative learning that can happen in adult education with the poor and oppressed. Newman qualifies this comparison by stating that "there is a major divide between the two concepts [because] conscientization is about mobilizing learners to struggle against oppressive forces, and it encourages them to examine the ways those forces have worked on them. The learners are not to blame. The oppressors are" (Newman 2014, 348). Perhaps transformative learning, then, can and ought to be the experience of all—individually, collectively, victims and oppressors. Perhaps everyone has something to learn and something to teach.

INCARCERATED CITIZENS AS TEACHERS

And, so it is with the prison writing group, it is a privilege to learn with serious writers engaged in their craft. These writers are serious students of life, grappling with the disorienting dilemma of incarceration. The group learns from each other's lived experiences. What exactly are we learning or relearning? Perhaps we are learning to live in the present, to structure our days around writing and reading, to listen well and affirm others, to think and feel deeply, to take pain and let it transform us. These are powerful lessons.

DEFICIT PERSPECTIVE

The prison writing group took place in Queensboro Correctional Facility, a minimum-security state prison in New York City. The group met for three hours once a week over a five-month period in 2019. Participants were thirteen males from their early twenties to early sixties; the older men had spent decades in prison. One session after listening to the other twelve writers, one student writer said, "I am so impressed with all of you, I am not as advanced as you. You are amazing thinkers and writers. Everyone thinks the incarcerated are stupid, ignorant, and good for nothing but look at you—smart, serious about your writing, well-read, interesting in learning, feeling. It is such a stereotype about who we are." Unfortunately, this writer articulated a common perception of people who are incarcerated—dangerous, uneducated, inarticulate, and uninformed.

Unfortunately, throughout criminal justice literature, the incarcerated or formerly incarcerated are viewed from a deficit perspective—what they do not know, what they do not have, what skills they lack, and what they have missed. They are considered problems to be dealt with, people without the skills, resources, knowledge, employment, education, and stability to adapt to reentry and bound to return to prison. Also, although there are gaps in knowledge for those who did time, such as having a working knowledge of technology, current events, cultural capital, interpersonal communication skills, and conflict resolution, many have caught up on their reflection and thinking time, have devoted time to reading, invested in writing and spiritual formation, and learned to live in the present. Some have learned the value of community, family, authenticity, solitude, and forming a new identity. People of color have learned to live in their own skin, often embracing what Gaskew (2017, 1) calls "black cultural identity and privilege." Many come out of prison with a new sense of pride in their heritage and history, another skill set that the never-incarcerated may have lost sight of.

We want to be careful not to underestimate the impact of violence and post-traumatic stress disorder (PTSD) in prison environments. We further acknowledge the need for job placement and real financial support to aid in housing, healthcare, food, and child support upon reentry into society. These deficits are real. The needs are real. But along with those needs, the incarcerated and formerly incarcerated often bring an abundance of life skills honed through pain and struggle resulting in living gratefully, fully, disciplined, engaged with persistence, generosity, simplicity, and courage. These are gifts from the dark.

At this point, we want to make several disclaimers so that the reader will not think that we are talking about some type of confessional therapy. Newman (2014, 352) describes the danger of interpreting transformational learning noting that "there is an association with a confessional form of therapy in some of the adult education discourse. And this association is alive and well in adult transformative learning theory, lodged in the implication that our assumptions need to be transformed because they have become pathological, and are rendering our thinking and behavior dysfunctional."

Freire explains transformative learning this way: "We examine the encounter between the self and the social and material worlds. Consciousness [transformation] is a relationship. There is more. Encounters do not exist in a vacuum. They are mediated by all manner of context, phenomenon, and circumstance" (1972, 61). He argues that we construct ourselves "in word, in work, in action-reflection." This is much more than confession.

Having stated this, for the authors adult transformative learning informed by CRT is both individual and collective through reflection and action—praxis (Freire 1972). It straddles the borders of sometimes, yes—intense self-examination and repentance while understanding the larger social and historical dynamics that have impacted a person's incarceration. Chaney (co-author) presents this tension in his own auto-ethnography of his time in prison and struggling with drug addiction (Chaney and Schwartz 2017).

LEARNING FROM THE INCARCERATION EXPERIENCE

Newman (2014) asks the following questions as he discussed the aims of adult education: Do we look inwards, or do we reach out? Do we see education as therapy, or education as action? Do we focus on our faults, or build on our strengths? Do we examine the old as it is manifested in a few supposedly dysfunctional assumptions or out of shape frames of reference, or do we create the new in the form of a heightened consciousness? Perhaps the answers to these questions are not either/or but both/and. We make the case in this book that adults who are or who have been incarcerated are uniquely positioned to engage these questions and uniquely positioned to teach others.

In an age when, arguably, many Americans, particularly white Americans, are living longer, but not necessarily living better or happier (Barrett 2017) perhaps returning citizens have something to teach those who have not been physically incarcerated. This is the case we make in the remainder of this book through both historical and contemporary case examples. We begin with our present experience within the circle of writers at the correctional facility, who remind us to be present in the moment, to understand that there are many types of knowledge, and that feeling deeply and trusting others with your story is healthy and good. We are relearning that this binary between teacher and student is false; our students are often our teachers as any good teacher well understands.

According to Freire (1972) those who authentically commit themselves to the people must re-examine themselves constantly. To him, this conversion is so radical and does not allow for ambivalent behavior. Conversion to the people requires a profound rebirth. Those who undergo it must take on a new form of existence; they can no longer remain as they were. Several informal educators connect with Paulo Freire's metaphors drawn from Christian sources. The divide between teachers and learners is transcended. The educator for liberation dies as the unilateral educator of educatees to be born again as both the teacher and learner. An educator is a person who lives in the deep significance of Easter (Taylor 1993).

The authors cross this divide between teacher and student and incarcerated and non-incarcerated, and between individual and collective learning. The prison writing group partners, current inmates and soon to be returning citizens, are the eyes and ears for this chapter. They have read, given us feedback, set us straight, and done the member checking. Their peer review is invaluable and authentic and their lessons to us are potentially profound and transformational.

REFERENCES

Alexander, M. (2010). *The new Jim Crow*. New York: New Press.

Barrett, J. (October 12–14, 2017). We are living longer than ever. But are we living better? Boston: Future Forum. https://www.statnews.com/2017/02/14/living-longer-living-better-aging/

Bell, D. (1980). *Brown v. board of education* and the interest convergence dilemma. Harvard Law Review. 93:518–533.

Bell, D. (1992). *Faces at the bottom of the well*. New York: Basic Books.

Bell, D. (1995). "Who's Afraid of Critical Race Theory?". University of Illinois Law Review. 1995 (4): 893ff.

Brown, Emma. *The Washington Post*. May 17, 2016. On the anniversary of Brown v. Board, new evidence that U.S. schools are resegregating. https://www.washingtonpost.com/news/education/wp/2016/05/17/on-the-anniversary-of-brown-v-board-new-evidence-that-u-s-schools-are-resegregating/?utm_term=.94337b2b1e61

Chaney, J. R. (2017). Epiphany of a prodigal son: An autoethnography. In Chaney & Schwartz. *Race, education, and reintegrating formerly incarcerated citizens: Counterstories and counterspaces*. Lanham, MD: Lexington Books.

Chaney, J.R. and Schwartz, J. (2017). *Race, education, and reintegrating formerly incarcerated citizens: Counterstories and counterspaces*. Lanham, MD: Lexington Books.

Darkenwald, G. G., and Merriam, S. B. (1982). *Adult education: Foundations of practice*. New York: Harper & Row.

Davenport, J. III. (1987, March). A way out of the andragogy morass. Paper presented at the conference of the Georgia Adult Education Association, Savannah, GA.

Davenport, J., and Davenport, J. A. (1985). A chronology and analysis of the andragogy debate. *Adult Educational Quarterly*, 35 (3), 152159.

Diaz, R. (2017, October 11). Bronx Bureau President, Ruben Diaz interview at Joe Conzo: Born in the Bronx conference. LaGuardia Community College: NY.

Elias, D. (1997). It's time to change our minds: An introduction to transformative learning. *ReVision*, 20(1).

Frankl, V. (2006). *Man's search for meaning*. Boston: Beacon Press.

Freire P. (1972). *Pedagogy of the oppressed.* Harmonsworth, England: Penguin.

Gaskew, T. (2017). In Chaney, Schwartz, (Eds.) *Race, education, and reintegrating formerly incarcerated citizens: Counterstories and Counterspaces*. Lanham, MD: Lexington Books.

Grabove, Valerie. "The Many Facets of Transformative Learning Theory and Practice." In: *Transformative Learning in Action: Insights from Practice. New Directions for Adult and Continuing Education.* no. 74, edited by P. Cranton, pp. 89–96. San Francisco, CA: Jossey-Bass, Summer 1997.

Habermas, J. (1971). *Knowledge and human interests.* Boston: Beacon Press.

Holzman, M. (2017). In Chaney, Schwartz, (Eds.) *Race, education, and Reintegrating Formerly Incarcerated Citizens: Counterstories and Counterspaces*. Lanham, MD: Lexington Books.

Holmes, G. & Abington-Cooper, M. (2000). Pedagogy vs. andragogy: A false dichotomy? *The Journal of Technology Studies*. 26(2).

Horton, M. (1998). *The long haul.* New York, NY: Teachers College Press.

Johnson-Bailey, J. and Cervero, R.M. (2000). The invisible politics of race in adult education. In A.L. Wilson and E.R. Hayes (Eds.), *Handbook of Adult and Continuing Education* (147–160). San Francisco, CA: Jossey-Bass.

Johnson-Bailey J. (2012). Positionality and transformative learning: A tale of inclusion and exclusion. In Taylor E. W., Cranton P. & Associates (Eds.), *The handbook of transformative learning: Theory, research and practice.* San Francisco, CA: Jossey-Bass, 260–273.

Knowles, M. (1975). *Self-directed learning*. Chicago: Follet.

Knowles, M. (1984a). *The adult learner: A neglected species (3rd Ed.).* Houston, TX: Gulf Publishing.

Knowles, M. (1984b). *Andragogy in action.* San Francisco: Jossey-Bass.

Lindeman, E. C. (1925). *The meaning of adult education*. New York: New Republic (Republished in 1961 by Harvest House.)

Matsuda, M. (1987). "Looking to the Bottom: Critical Legal Studies and Reparations." Harvard Civil Rights-Civil Liberties Law Review. 22 (2): 323ff. ISSN 2153–2389

Mezirow, J. (1997). Transformative Learning: Theory to Practice. *New Directions for Adult and Continuing Education*, 74, 5–12.

Mezirow, J. (1990). *Fostering Critical Reflection in Adulthood: A Guide to Transformative and Emancipatory Learning.* San Francisco: Jossey-Bass.

Newman, M. (2014). Transformative Learning: Mutinous Thoughts Revisited. *Adult Education Quarterly.* Vol. 64(4) 345–355.

Parker, T. (1853). *Ten Sermons of Religion by Theodore Parker, Of Justice and the Conscience,* Boston: Crosby, Nichols and Company. p. 84–85.

Rohr, R. (2011). Falling upward: A spirituality for the two halves of life. San Francisco: Jossey-Bass.

Rugut, E. and Osman, A. (2013). Reflections on Paulo Freire and classroom relevance. *American International Journal of Social Science.* 2:2. p.23–28.

Shakur, A. (1987). Assata: An autobiography. Chicago: Lawrence Hill Books.

Stevenson, B. (2014). *Just Mercy.* New York: Spiegel & Grau.

Stigler, M. (2016). Arizona State University, ProQuest Dissertations Publishing. 10108088.

Taylor, P. (1993). *The texts of Paulo Freire.* Buckingham: Open University Press. https://www.worldcat.org/title/texts-of-paulo-freire/oclc/26307587

Taylor, E. W. (1998). *The theory and practice of transformative learning: A critical review* (In-formation Series No. 374). Columbus, OH: Center on Education and Training for Employment. (ERIC Document Reproduction Service No. ED 423 422

Taylor, E. W. (2007). An update of transformative learning theory: A critical review of the empirical research (1999–2005). *International Journal of Lifelong Education*, 26, 173–191.

Taylor, E. W., Cranton, P., and Associates. (2012). *The handbook of transformative learning: Theory, research and practice.* San Francisco, CA: Jossey-Bass.

Taylor, E. W., and Snyder, M. J. (2012). A critical review of research on transformative learning. In E. W. Taylor, P. Cranton, & Associates (Eds.), *The handbook of transformative learning: Theory, research and practice.* San Francisco, CA: Jossey-Bass, 37–55.

VanThompson (2012). In A new normal: Young men of color, trauma and engagement in learning. Schwartz, P. & Schwartz, J. (Producers) New York: City University of New York. https://www.youtube.com/watch?v=nD6r4CW_HeM

Chapter 3

Transformation: A Brave Act

To an outsider unfamiliar with prison, it is deceptively easy to underestimate prerelease self-reflection as a low-stakes endeavor. As new prisoners learn to navigate through the quagmire of their existence, each soon learns that within the institution there is method to the controlled madness that makes up the prison experience, and it is designed in many ways to obstruct transformation. This reflective learning often results in identity transformation and post-release reclamation despite acute internal or external obstacles. In truth, every man or woman daring to undertake transformative learning does so swimming upstream, facing formidable, complex institutional, and societal challenges.

PRISONIZATION

One of the most important aspects of prison management in the United States is the concept of *prisonization. Prisonization* is defined as a well-structured process of gradual individual and collective degradation implemented by the institution that pressures newly incarcerated individuals to accept and internalize prison culture. The term was originally coined by Donald Clemmer whose research claimed that the solidarity and influence of the prison culture inhibited prisoners from being rehabilitated. (Clemmer 1950; see also Siegal and Clemmons 2018) This inculcation and indoctrination to prison is in response to facility regulations and encouraging complete assimilation and institutional compliance to administrative mandates. These mandates include policies, philosophies, and strategies that are regularly explored by criminologists and law enforcement management as methodologies geared to enhance compliance and discipline. They are top priority initiatives in most institutions, routinely eclipsing in importance any governmental or community-sponsored programs fostering prisoner expressions of individualization or self-identity.

Outward manifestations of *prisonization* can be observed as new prisoners become acclimated to accepting state-issued institutional clothing, low quality meals, and minimal, often substandard medical care. There are restrictions on physical movement and social interaction, including recreational activities, visits to the commissary (prison store); separation from family, friends, and conjugal relations. Their new normal is the acceptance of severely limited or nonexistent access to amenities that free citizens take for granted. Each prisoner is, either through small incentives or with subtle or overt threats of coercion, expected to accept his or her role as part of a subclass, one that is for all purposes subordinate to the officers, staff, and visitors to the facility.

Except for classes and programs formally approved by the institution like cognitive behavioral therapy programs or moral reconation projects, (Federal Sentencing Alliance 2019) expressions of individuality are commonly discouraged. In fact, self-expression can even be perceived as a threat by discipline-oriented prison administrators. These policies are prevalent in high-security facilities, whose budgets are security and discipline-oriented. Except for substance abuse treatment and the aforementioned cognitive behavioral projects, these policies provide few programs using introspective and transformative activities leading to long-term rehabilitation.

Prisonization is a constant, ever-present process that is well documented through the implementation of the administrative control and inmate balance theories of prison management (Craig 2004). The administrative control method is popular in facilities with maximum security status. This management strategy emphasizes strict compliance with institutional regulations, often enforced with subliminal undertones of coercive force. While the administrative control method of prison management does not overtly ban expressions of individual growth that are the hallmarks of transformative learning, neither is it encouraged. Custody and control are the priorities. Underlying this theory is the belief that collective violence in prisons is caused by lack of strong security and mismanagement and lack of control by prison officials (Siegal and Clemens 2018).

On the other hand, transformative learners often find that institutions employing the inmate balance style of prison management are more open to growth opportunities. Prison proponents of this management style and theory believe that in order to avoid collective violence and prison disruption, a balance needs to be maintained between prisoners' freedoms and rights, security and control (Siegal and Clemons 2018). Prisons with this frame of reference tend to be receptive to the fact that some residents are more influential, creative, patient, intellectually gifted, stronger, or talented than others living together in the housing unit. Fully understanding that residents bring a variety of personalities and strengths to the institution, savvy officers and administrators effectuate informal negotiations with select residents securing their assistance in keeping the cell block or dorm clean and violence-free, thereby creating spaces more conducive to livable conditions.

DEPRIVATION AND IMPORTATION
MODELS OF PRISONIZATION

The extent that an individual internalizes *prisonization* is impacted by the corrections' management's efforts to encourage, either through normative, remunerative, or coercive means, compliance with prison rules. The newly admitted prisoner gradually accepts being denied access to ordinary privileges and courtesies taken for granted by free citizens, including the sudden and complete loss of privacy, and severe overcrowding of their new living quarters. There are two models of *prisonization* as it regards new prisoners: the deprivation model and the importation model (Thomas 1977; Cao, Zhaong and Dine 1997).

The deprivation model of *prisonization* suggests that the new prisoners' sudden loss of liberty, self-sufficiency, ability to access preferred foods, clothing, and services, and their inability to enjoy heterosexual relationships all have a significant impact upon decision-making and resulting behavior. Prisoners soon realize that expressions of autonomy that might include gambling, making phone calls at will, having an alcoholic drink (contraband), borrowing commissary from a neighbor, or being overly friendly with officers and staff can easily become dangerous behaviors within the netherworld of the prison experience. The deprivation model then forces many prisoners to express themselves through safer, non-threatening and administratively acceptable vestiges of individuality, particularly those that are officially sanctioned in some prison-based programs. Still, it is not uncommon to observe activities like the strategic and imaginative application of tattoos, as well as hair and beard stylings and other adornments worn by some prisoners to balance the incessant robotic drive toward sameness.

The importation model of *prisonization* acknowledges that newly admitted prisoners do not arrive in prison with empty psychosocial baskets. Each brings to the prison table a unique collection of habits, values, and learned behavior patterns, both positive and negative, that significantly impact their incarceration experience (Thomas and Foster 1973; Siegal and Clemens 2018). Depending upon whether one's lifestyle included parenthood, legal employment, gangbanging, street hustling, or caregiving, these factors all figure prominently in shaping the climate and dynamic of the institution, and with it the individual's prison experience. Those arriving with positive attributes like fortitude, persistence, and intellectual acumen are uniquely advantaged if in time they become blessed with an awakening to work on becoming their best selves. They may also may not be as susceptible to internalizing *prisonization.* And then again, there are those who are imprisoned unjustly and may already be their best selves. The prisonization process and the internalization is different for each prisoner.

THE INMATE CODE

Incarcerated citizens who no longer define themselves based upon the worst moments of their lives, the very criteria used by their correctional overseers, do so while learning to navigate a new culture which internalizes the infamous "inmate code" (Trammell 2009; Bronson 2006). This is a time-honored, well-documented, unwritten system of prisoner credos, existing simultaneously with the opposing culture of corrections and law enforcement. Each code is acknowledged by the other. Many male prisoners, especially those with weak or nonexistent ties with society at large, completely subscribe to the mores of the code, often using their guidelines to define status and self-worth. In addition to eschewing the rules of management who is seen as the "oppressor," "inmates" (the official term used by corrections staff for residents) are expected to adhere to the code solidifying inmate unity. Whether the prisoner is an incoming "fish," seasoned "convict," "gang soldier," "shot caller" (leader), bully, or "hustler" (successful provider within the underground economy of drugs and contraband), a prisoner faces severe consequences if any precept of the code is perceived to be violated by one's peers (Wellford 1967).

Precepts of the inmate code include never "ratting" on one's peers and never interfering with a fellow prisoner's business. Prisoners are expected to never trust officers and staff, or the things they stand for. Status and self-esteem are often then measured by activities within the correctional facility that are deemed objectionable, even abhorrent, by management standards of the prison system or the outside world (Akers, Hayner and Gruninger 1977). Even when programs are available, those invested in the code often ignore mechanisms that might cause them to question the validity of the lives they have lived up to that point, and how they identify themselves. The code is widely acknowledged as a legitimate vehicle that can foster much needed prisoner unity in times of legitimate objections to administrative inequities or civil rights violations (Thompson 2016). But persons who completely internalize the inmate code routinely reject the need or inclination to self-reflect upon the source or validity of their actions as they fall deeper into the chasm of institutionalization and *prisonization.* Upon release, these individuals often find themselves devoid of self-efficacy with no ability or inclination to reintegrate into the community as drug- and crime-free citizens. Long-term internalization of corrections bureaucracy and the inmate code without strong and consistent access to prerelease and/or reentry counseling, therapy and mentoring doom an individual to recidivism, new arrests, convictions, parole violations, and new episodes of incarceration. Such is the common mindset of the prisoner who proudly brands himself as a "convict." Firmly ensconced in all the variables of "jailing," he considers incarceration an intermittent occupational hazard of the antisocial lifestyle of the career criminal.

However, those having the courage to forge a new life pathway within this unforgiving environment of *prisonization,* deprivation, and the inmate code are challenging the ideologies that impact their prison survival and existence—an emotionally painful undertaking that must be approached with care and with extreme caution. These are the brave souls who address the disorienting dilemma of incarceration in a genuine effort to travel the daunting path toward transformative learning.

TRANSFORMING WITHIN THE INSTITUTION

Sometimes a prisoner's decision to redefine and reassess himself often begins within the confines of classrooms and institutional settings that are homes to prison-based programs. Prison volunteer instructors often experience intense intellectual and emotional energy despite the realization that students attend for different reasons, often simply to escape the boredom and monotony of prison living. Seasoned officers assigned to programs know all too well that gang-affiliated residents routinely seize upon the opportunity to exchange communications, transact, and distribute contraband while in class.

Others enjoy interacting with civilian volunteers who offer welcome connections to the outside world, however fleeting. Still others dutifully attend facility program offerings that will garner coveted certificates of completion that may curry favor with the parole board. Despite the mixed motives for attending classes, insightful instructors engaging students in assignments promoting critical thinking can witness the emergence of a participant undergoing wonderful identity metamorphosis. The fact that these inspired individuals navigate a host of formidable bureaucratic and pseudo societal quagmires to reinvent themselves in an unforgiving environment designed to resist deep change is, in the opinion of the authors, somewhat of a miracle.

SUBSTANCE ABUSE: THE GREAT
BARRIER TO TRANSFORMATION

Additional obstacles toward transformative learning, both internal and external, is alcohol and drug addiction. Imagine the number of men and women who bring such addictions into this schematic. A significant number of incarcerated men and women entering our nation's jails and prisons have extensive documented, histories of substance abuse (Fazel, Bains and Doll, 2006). Offenses listed as Index Crimes under the FBI's Uniform Crime Reporting program commonly have substance abuse as a prevailing factor (https://www. fbi.gov/services/cjis/ucr). For many, the incarceration experience then begins with the abrupt, dangerous, and agonizing period of unassisted substance withdrawal known as cold turkey. Once detoxified of all substances, a process that can routinely take several days, the individual becomes physically free of drugs.

A prisoner's mindset is crucial in determining which road the individual chooses—continued use or sobriety. During the pivotal early incarceration period, most institutions offer no treatment to introduce coping skills to counterbalance addictive personalities or to modify cognitive behavioral tendencies. Because most substance abuse treatment, as well as anger management, sex offender therapy and other treatment are routinely made available as parole eligibility time nears, the new and continuing prisoners are generally on their own. Once physically detoxified of the addictive substance, he/she is then confronted with hard choices.

The first choice is to learn how to remain drug free. The second choice is to learn how to exist as an incarcerated addict, including the ways and norms of the underground drug economy to acquire their substance of choice. This option is a dangerous undertaking that commonly includes circumventing officer searches, developing an underground hustle often in collaboration with gang activity to earn income to support one's habit, convincing loved ones to smuggle drugs in during visiting hours, or depositing funds into a drug dealer's commissary account. Amazing though it may seem, these harsh obstacles faced by an addicted prisoner often pale for many when compared to the intimidating realities of choosing to remain drug free and learning to live without being self-medicated while under the stress of incarceration.

This choice can be chilling as one's awakened mental clarity unleashes the ability to analyze the current state of their lives, as well as the awakening recognition of the devastating impact their choices often have had on victims and loved ones. This undertaking presents a myriad of daunting challenges and life-changing possibilities. Given the prevalence and availability of illegal drugs within correctional facilities, coupled with the extreme stress of prison, much credit must be given to the addicted inmate who decides that they have had enough. During this period of realization, a different kind of life becomes possible and the individual begins the painful process of self-reflection.

As mentioned previously, this self-reflective process includes a raw and often brutal assessment of the damage one's chosen lifestyle has had upon loved ones and innocent victims. This is a time when he or she comes to terms with the "why" of their current circumstance. One of the first points of clarity includes the individual's acceptance of the fact he or she is ultimately responsible for their conduct, notwithstanding the prevalence of real societal challenges that may include family-related dysfunctions and traumas, economic injustices, stigmas, and systemic racial disparities (Chaney and Schwartz 2017). Accepting one's role in the process of shaping one's life therefore becomes a prerequisite in tapping into previously dormant self-efficacy as well as inner courage, to manifest significant, lasting positive change.

TAKING RESPONSIBILITY

Coauthor Chaney's two-decade involvement with hard drugs resulted in a year of imprisonment on Riker's Island, another year inside a federal facility, and a three- to six-year New York State sentence received in 2000. In his autoethnographical chapter, "Epiphany of a Prodigal Son," (Chaney and Schwartz 2017); he candidly accounted the transformative process that began one evening inside a tiny dark cell in Attica prison during the summer of August 2001. Engaging in painstakingly slow and methodical self-evaluation, it had been the first time in years that he dared allow himself a true opportunity to reflect upon his regrettable past with mental clarity. His awakened conscience revitalized by positive values was consistently and sometimes viciously assaulted with memories of addiction-fueled incidents and his ill-advised decisions that resulted in considerable damage to friends, victims, and loved ones. He began to understand that his choices led to the inevitable demise and destruction of relationships, friendships, and to a once promising career as a young attorney.

He invested in self-reflection continuously for over a year. This process included evenings of meditation inside his cell and discussions with peers while in the prison yard. He memorialized his enlightened thoughts and observations in a journal that he eventually used to write his autoethnography (Chaney and Schwartz 2017). Looking back, he frequently wrestled with disturbing childhood flashbacks of traumatizing episodes of domestic violence brought about by his father's addiction to alcohol. He also found himself recalling, with amazing detail, his reactions to the plethora of racial microaggressions encountered while in high school and during his young, troubled professional life.

Chaney's assessment was a long and crucial process that, in time, led him to understand how he embraced addiction to mask deep psychological wounds and emotional scarring. Chaney also came to understand primarily through self-reflection that as forgiveness frees one's soul of bitterness, the only pathway to transformative personal growth, was accepting full responsibility for his past behaviors, good and bad. For the first time in his adult life he rejected the tempting choice to blame outside influences for his decisions. In doing so, he unlocked an untapped wellspring of transformative power and self-efficacy that enhanced his personal and professional life exponentially going forward, irrespective of a personal profile that included four felony convictions.

Years later as executive director of the Brooklyn District Attorney's Office's groundbreaking ComALERT reentry project, he observed scores of exceptional men and women taking similar steps while in prison, each finding courage to liberate themselves from destructive habits, thinking patterns, and values. In choosing to redefine themselves using new parameters of self-worth and success, each opted to defy prison norms and to empower themselves with psychological survival tools later needed to overcome post-prison societal stigmas. Like Chaney, these individuals embraced the task of becoming independent learners and living pursuant to a redefined, infinitely healthier system of values. For some, this process was nurtured as they achieved clarity and appreciation of their now coveted roles as parents of minor children; this was an especially powerful catalyst for incarcerated mothers. As with Chaney, their fires of growth and transformation happened through individual self-examination and acceptance of personal responsibility. Many also were supported in their growth through the positive reinforcement of mentoring.

PRE-AND POST-RELEASE MENTORING

Many of the brave figures highlighted in the authors' previous book, *Race, Education and Reintegrating Formerly Incarcerated Citizens*, have credited their decision to continue their transformative journeys because of the unflagging support and encouragement of strong positive role models, both within and outside the prison community (2017). Indeed, many incarcerated men shared that while growing up theirs was a single parent household, with the father often an absent figure, sometimes due to incarceration. Even when receiving the solid nurturing and love from their single moms, the continuous, often media-inspired promotion of values that glorify life of the streets, love of "the hustle" and "the game," became formidable and attractive obstacles for many peer status-driven young minds. The value systems held by some residing in socially and economically deprived communities regard incarceration as a perverse rite of passage into manhood. This hard truth includes the practice of otherwise law-abiding community members who, in the presence of juveniles, routinely laud the lifestyles of past and present high-profile criminals. The social damage of their illegal enterprises is conveniently ignored in place of the romantic myth of the anti-establishment rebel who adheres to no rules in pursuit of the "true" measure of one's status in the world—material wealth. These distractions can become formidable influences on young minds, especially on those with no access to healthy, positive family or community members offering support and guidance. Having no viable role models or positive structure in their formative years, many individuals, later incarcerated, are then enrolled in institutional classes and therapy sessions designed to re-habilitate. But in fact, these individuals were never afforded a true opportunity to habilitate, as it were, in the first place.

For some, then, the prerelease partnerships that prisons develop with non-governmental organizations treatment providers, workforce development trainers, colleges, and houses of worship become vehicles to engage with trained community members. These community members become mentors, bringing with them a different set of values. In recent years, faith-based organizations, in particular, proactively provide training sessions geared to provide emotional and societal support to these men and women (Chidi, De la Cruz, Richey and Albis 2017).

In addition to one-on-one mentoring, some incarcerated students have the opportunity to enroll in the all-too-few available academic projects like the Bard Prison Initiative or the Prison to College project offered by schools like CUNY's John Jay College of Criminal Justice where group and peer mentoring occur. Students are often surprised to discover that they have the intellectual capacity and enthusiasm to embrace the intellectual freedom that comes with independent and self-directed learning (Karpowitz 2017). Men and women after acclimating to the norms of prison, and after shedding the decimating effects of pre-incarceration addictions, whether to substances or lifestyles; often discover (or rediscover in some cases) their love of writing, reading, music, history, drawing, exercising, or spirituality. Choices like these underscore their need to embark upon new and wonderful journeys in their quest for personal growth and achievement, as well as for acceptance by society at large. These enlightened individuals are included among those who, in developing plans for discharge, often continue their education upon release with degree or certificate programs. Many also find the desire to give back to the neighborhoods they once damaged, making volunteer commitments and embarking upon careers in public service with governmental and community-based organizations. Many want to become mentors to others, especially those with a high risk of getting caught up within the criminal justice system. Later chapters in this book will delve more deeply into both educational and the giving back aspects of transformative learning.

For all brave souls' greater introspection, critical thinking and cognitive skill development, increase their arsenal of identity capital to maximize chances of successful reintegration. An interesting dynamic takes place, therefore, as part of any prerelease transformative development. The transformed individual finds oneself employing values, activities, and post-release planning consistent with the new and developing redefined self, all while carefully reconciling the journey in anticipation of conflicting, often dangerously applied policies and codes within the netherworld of the prison system.

RACE AND TRANSFORMATION

One would be hard pressed to ignore the very real challenges a prisoner faces while inside an institution that many consider designed for the mass incarceration of people of color. The highly acclaimed 2016 documentary "13th" produced by Ava Duvernay and Jason Moran offers a stark perspective of strategically implemented policies that, within a half century's time, targeted African Americans to become the largest prison population group in the United States. Currently, it is common to find the book, *The New Jim Crow*, the detailed accounting of the history of "legal" discrimination and segregation in the United States and its current impact upon African Americans as choice reading in prison cells as well as in college libraries. It is indeed an accessible classic reading on mass incarceration (Alexander 2010).

Because incarcerated individuals live this new Jim Crow, they daily observe its realities, accentuated by the decidedly lopsided racial ratios of officers on the prison payroll. Because the race of officers and staff in city and county jails tend to be representative of the community where the jails are located both racially and ethnically, mostly white officers from rural communities overwhelmingly predominate the overseeing of Black prisoners coming from large cities, serving state or federal sentences (Burton 2018; Thompson 2016). Consider, then, the possible reactions of imprisoned individuals whose reading choices might include one of the insightful literary selections of *The New Jim Crow* (2010) or Critical Race Theory (henceforth, CRT) pioneers Derrick Bell (Alexander 2016) or Richard Delgado and Jean Stefancic (2007). This reading fosters critical thinking around racism as a key and common component of the legal, economic, social, political, and other policies that people take for granted and accept as fair and reasonable while ignoring the subliminal disparities embedded within institutions like the criminal justice system. CRT also theorizes that because of America's history of slavery, race is a profound force and that mass incarceration is a manifestation of it today (Holzman 2017). This kind of critical inquiry can lead to an intellectual awakening for those most profoundly affected. In an article that explores CRT's relation to criminal justice, Delgado and Stefancic pose the scenario:

> A critically minded person might ask why our country tolerates a criminal justice that results in a prison population that is Black and Brown. Most people do not see that situation as problematic; they might say, "Well, each of them is in there because he or she committed a crime and was convicted." Fewer will ask about the racial cast of the system as a whole and what purposes it might serve (2007, 140).

The second half of this statement may not represent the mindset of everyone charged with the care, custody, and control of the prison population, but it certainly reflects the views of many professionals on the prison payroll. But in terms of prisoners, criminologist Tony Gaskew says that any prisoner seriously interested in transformation must grapple with what he calls Black Cultural Privilege which critically aligns with CRT. According to Gaskew, there is no transformation without the recognition of Black Privilege, and the critical recognition of the role of race in both incarceration and transformation (Gaskew 2014).

Another CRT concept that deserves mentioning here is the theme of interest convergence. This acknowledges the ancillary but very tangible rewards, often economic or status-oriented, received by whites in supporting policies and systems with both overt and hidden agendas. Sometimes when an oppressed population fights for a legitimate cause that is found to also provide a subliminal benefit to those of privilege and power the interest convergence will, CRT advocates state, find both groups in a supposedly united front albeit for entirely different purposes (Bell 1980). A more sinister example of this concept lies even closer to home for those who find themselves consumers of correctional services. Simply stated, full prisons represent economic security for facility officers and staff. Their interest in continuous employment offers a toxic convergence with their overt stance of being "tough on crime" and generally universalizing Black and Brown prisoners as incorrigible. As an inmate program associate, and years later as the New York state-appointed coordinator for the Brooklyn reentry task force, coauthor Chaney repeatedly heard laments from corrections personnel on the impact that closing a prison would have on jobs, the elimination of overtime pay needed for mortgages and paying college tuition for children of prison employees. Some expressed outrage about convicted prisoners taking advantage of tuition-free college

courses, ignoring or possibly fearing the evidence-based data proving education's effectiveness upon reducing recidivism, (see Chapter 8 in this book for
further details). For these reasons, the transforming prisoner can be seen by
facility personnel as both a short and long-term threat.

As these realities become apparent, both wisdom and courage are needed
for those individuals working toward transformation; they need to avoid the
attractive traps of blame and defiance offering quick justification for past
and possible future antisocial conduct. Not surprisingly, then, the majority of
those highlighted in the authors' prior and current texts are adults, possessing
minds unencumbered by controlled substances and biologically capable of
developing the cognitive schemata that is essential for permanent transformative growth. These are individuals able to accept responsibility for their own
individual errors, crimes, and behaviors while grappling and comprehending
the collective errors, crimes, and behaviors of a society bent on incarceration
of people of color. This nuanced and complex understanding of the world and
their own position and agency in it is a brave act.

REFERENCES

Akers, R., Hayner, N., and Gruninger, W. (1977). Prisonization in five countries type of prison and inmate characteristics. *Criminology*. https://doi.
org/10.1111/j.1745–9125.1977.tb00042.x

Alexander, M. (2010). *The new Jim Crow: Mass incarceration in the age of col-
orblindness*. New York: [Jackson, TN]: New Press; Distributed by Perseus
Distribution.

Alexander, M. (2016). The 21st Annual Derrick Bell Lecture on Race in American
Society. https://www.youtube.com/watch?v=znQ3CR———Kw

Duvernay, A. and Moran, J.. (2016). *13TH* Documentary. USA: Netflix.

Bell, D. (1980). *Brown v. Board of Education* and the Interest-Convergence Dilemma.
Harvard Law Review.Vol. 93, No. 3 (Jan. 1980), pp. 518–533.

Brooklyn Elected Officials Eps. 186 November 9, 2012. YouTube video BRIC tv
https://www.youtube.com/watch?v=HVqW62zRRno

Bronson, E. (2006). Medium security prisons and inmate subcultures: The "normal
prison." *The Southwest Journal of Criminal Justice* 3 (2): 61–86.

Burton, L. (January 2018). New York Times Reveals Racial Bias Rampant in Upstate
New York Prisons. *Prison Legal News*. Pg. 32

Cao, L., Zhao, J. and Dine, S. (1997). Prison disciplinary tickets: A test of the deprivation and importation models. *Journal of Criminal Justice*. 25:2, 103–133.

Chaney, J.R., and Schwartz, J., (2017). *Race, education and reintegrating formerly
incarcerated citizens: Counterspaces and counterstories*. Lanham, MD: Lexington
Books.

Chidi, U., De la Cruz, J., Richey, M. and Albis, K. (2017). Mentoring as a component of reentry: Practical considerations from the field. New York: The Council of State Governments Justice Center.

Clemmer, D. (1950). Observations on imprisonment as a source of criminality. *Journal of Criminal Law & Criminology*, 41:3.

ComAlert. http://brooklynda.org/re-entry-programs/

Craig, S. C. (2004). Rehabilitation versus control: An organizational theory of prison management. *The Prison Journal*. 84(4_suppl), 92S-114S. https://doi.org/10.1177/0032885504269394

Delgado, R. and Stefancic, J. (2007). Critical race theory and criminal justice. *Humanity & Society*, Vol. 31: 133–145.

Fazel, S., Bains, P. and Doll, H., (2006). Substance abuse and dependence in prisoners: A systematic review. *Addiction*. 101:(2), 181–191.

Federal Sentencing Alliance, (2019). The First Step Act of 2018 and prison reform. Florida. www.FederalSentencingAlliance.com

Gaskew, T. (2014). *Rethinking Prison Reentry: Transforming Humiliation to Humility*. Lanham, MD: Lexington Books.

Holzman, M. (2017). Schooling for prison, incarceration for poverty. In Chaney, J.R & Schwartz, J. (Eds.), *Race, Education and Reintegrating Formerly Incarcerated Citizens: Counterstories and Counterspaces*. Lanham, MD.: Lexington Press.

Karpowitz, D. (2017). *College in prison: Reading in the age of mass incarceration*. New Brunswick, NJy: Rutgers University Press.

Siegal, L. and Clemens, B., (2018). *Corrections today*. Wadsworth: Belmont, CA.

Thomas, C. and Foster, S. (1973) The importation model perspective on inmate social roles: An empirical test. *The Sociological Quarterly*, 14:2, 226–234, DOI: 10.1111/j.1533–8525.1973.tb00855.x

Thomas, C.W. (1977). Theoretical perspectives on prisonization: A comparison of importation and deprivation models. *Journal of Criminal Law and Criminology*. 68:1

Thompson, H. A. (2016). *Blood in the water: The Attica Prison uprising of 1971 and its legacy*. New York: Penguin Random House.

Trammell, R. (2009). Values, rules, and keeping the peace: How men describe order and the inmate code in California prisons. *Deviant Behavior*, 30:8, 746–771, DOI: 10.1080/01639620902854662

Wellford, C. (1967). Factors associated with adoption of the inmate code: A study of normative socialization. *The Journal of Criminal Law, Criminology, and Police Science*, 58(2), 197–203. doi:10.2307/1140837

Chapter 4

Understanding the Role of Race and Gender

"You go down there (courthouse) looking for justice, that's just what you'll find . . . just us" (Pryor, 1976). Said with humor, the famous quote does speak to this chapter. In our mission to locate and share examples of the men and women who experienced carceral metamorphosis to include in this book, it soon became apparent that people of color would play a preeminent role. The transformation process is an equal opportunity blessing earned and enjoyed by extraordinary men and women of all races who then share their gifts with the world. Having said this, it would be unrealistic, even irresponsible to ignore the research confirming that in the United States, prosecutorial and policing policies, as well as other economic and social factors, are significant contributors to the overwhelming presence of Black and Brown faces within the judicial system.

In 2020, Black men and women represent over 37% of all incarcerated individuals in the United States, though they comprise a mere 13% of the population overall (Sawyer and Wagner 2020). Many of our students and faculty colleagues participate in the 2020 Black Lives Matter movement demonstrations that have emerged in response to the atrocity of George Floyd's murder at the hands of rogue police in Minnesota. In so doing, many are likely unaware that their actions underscore that as recently as the 1990s, debates on issues of racial discrimination, in addition to economic or gender disparities, were legitimate factors when ascertaining the root causes of criminal conduct. Respected social scientists were content to present the American criminal justice system as an even playing field, with the individual's facility for self-control (or lack thereof) being the sole contributing factor as to whether he or she would be the subject of arrest, conviction, or incarceration (Cook 2016). More recent studies emerged that factored in social capital including race and gender that validated the importance of including both in any responsible discussion involving incarceration in America.

For criminologists, this includes examining how the legal system responds to individual offenders based on their social locations (Barak 2001). For example, Steffensmeier, Ulmer, and Kramer (2006) studied the interaction of race, gender, and age in sentencing decisions and discovered that outcomes are most punitive for defendants whose social locations place them at the margins of race, age, and gender systems—in other words, young Black men. The less transparent but equally decimating impact of administrative policies, privilege, economic, and other factors of race's role within the criminal justice system is seen through the lens of Critical Race Theory (CRT) (Delgado and Stefancic 2005).

CHALLENGES RELATED TO RACE AND GENDER

While some have begun to herald a gradual but important decline in the prison population in some states (Ghandnoosh, 2020), communities of color continue to be haunted by the sobering predictions of the 2019 Vera Institute study forecasting that one in five Black people born in 2001 will likely be incarcerated in their lifetime, compared to one in twenty-nine white people (Ghandnoosh 2020). Whether considering the economic policies that keep inner city schools in a perpetual state of disrepair and dysfunction leading to a disparate number of incarcerated dropouts of color (Holzman, 2017), or the findings revealed in corrections population assessments, it becomes all too apparent that race continues to be a key issue when discussing the state of 20th- and now 21st-century incarceration in America.

Noting that males consistently comprise at least 93% or more of the national prison population, these alarming forecasts are reflective of prison-centered studies that routinely combine men and women into their assessments. Case in point: the transformative journeys highlighted in the preceding chapters are predominated by men who chose not to define themselves by the yardstick often used by society: the worst moment of their lives.

Consider, then, that while the topic of incarcerated women within the annals of criminology and in academia began to receive some traction in the 1980s, it has been a painfully slow process. In fact, scholars concede that while the emergence of "critical criminology" represented a significant milestone in the study of criminal justice, it, too, had largely ignored the "social realities of gender" while spearheading proactive efforts to eliminate disparities involving economic privilege and race. In their article highlighting "androcentricism," authors Chesney-Lind and Chagnon confirm the prevailing view that while 21st-century criminological research now routinely include women as an important category. Previously, efforts to include their demographics have largely been superficial and one-dimensional (Chesney-Lind and Chagnon

2016). Acknowledging these glaring deficiencies, the advent of feminist criminology advocates a multidimensional analysis of our community's women within the system, especially our prison system, one that takes into account their experiences including racial marginalization, privilege, and victimization (Burgess-Proctor 2006). Feminist criminology considers how other factors of social, economic, and political inequality interlock with race and gender, in addition to the unequal distribution of power (Burgess-Proctor 2006). Feminist criminologists will provide fresh, realistic, and decidedly overdue approaches to research incarcerated women in America.

Literary offerings coming from incarcerated women often highlight the unique issues specific to gender previously minimalized, especially those impacting incarcerated Black females. These counterstories give strong, clear voice to arguably the most invisible and ignored population within. Often angry, often introspective, each individual who courageously chooses to express their deepest emotions and rage on paper often find that in doing so, they begin to see themselves, and help us to see themselves as well, in a new light. They challenge us to see them in full dimension, and not with a myopic view solely based upon their crime of conviction. Within the confines of some of the most inhumane and unforgiveable spaces on the planet, some of these women soon see that each word of their expression can be used to psychologically pave an avenue of clarity that leads the way to a glorious finding of transformation and power (Willingham 2011).

The 1990s War on Drugs, including the draconian Rockefeller Drug Laws in New York State, was responsible for raising the population of Black women by over 800%, by far the highest increase when studying females by race. Even with the introduction of alternative to incarceration programs like the highly successful Drug Treatment Alternative to Prison program (DTAP), Black women are less likely to receive these sanctions in response to their non-violent convictions as opposed to white females with similar convictions (Sentencing Project 2019). When considering the very special challenges faced by our mothers, sisters, and daughters while consumers of these correctional practices, their successful reintegration becomes unlikely, making their occurrence all the more impressive.

WOMEN IN JAIL

Consider, if you will, the fact that at the time of this book's publication in 2021, most of our nation's incarcerated 231,000 women and girls were serving time in county jails, not our state prisons (Kajsgura 2019). Designed for short-term and transient confinement, jails are typically grossly overcrowded, offering few if any resources fostering growth. In describing the harsh realities of New York City's Rikers Island, we note Assata Shakur's powerful and provocative accounts of fellow detainees inside the notorious "bullpen" awaiting arraignment:

> There are no criminals here at Riker's Island Correctional Institution for Women, (New York), only victims. Most of the women (over 95%) are black and Puerto Rican. Many were abused children. Most have been abused by men and all have been abused by the system. (1978, p. 9)

In emphasizing her point Shakur also offers that the majority of her bullpen companions are waiting to see the arraignment judge for drug-related matters, many connected as accessories to crimes committed by male partners.

In her provocative 2003 text "Are Prisons Obsolete?" Angela Davis credits Shakur for bringing to light key factors of racism, political repression, and male domination that may have otherwise been ignored (Davis, 2003). Years later, we find that the issues highlighted by both Shakur and Davis mirror the very same concerns that counselors and therapists continue to wrestle with today. These include incarcerated women who persistently battle with victimization; substance abuse; mental illness; domestic violence; lack of self-worth and misdirected self-contempt. These struggles are often the consequences of society's brutal demand that they accept their well-deserved marginal positionality as the product of their own design. Jails are by their very nature designed for a transient population and as such, one would be hard-pressed to find any serious efforts that invest significant tax dollars in jail-based activities or treatment leading to positive and sustained growth. One of the more saddening phenomena is that of the institutionalized woman who, through her seemingly perpetual grip upon a criminal lifestyle resulting in multiple and continuous short-term "skid bids," basically serves a life term on the installment plan. These are the women who, while in jail, never actually address the root causes of their incarceration but while there, have regarded the jail, fellow prisoners, and even their jailers, as home and a kind of pseudo family. In their prior work with community-based organizations including the Women's Prison Association, the authors routinely engaged women with histories of forty or more jail "skid bids." Well known to both organizational and jail staff, these "regulars" habitually make brief pit stops in between jail stints to participate in orientations making them eligible for metro cards to assist in transportation, emergency temporary housing, or grant-funded groceries. These are the incarcerated females highlighted in Shakur's re-telling of the fellow prisoner who, upon release, ensured that she would be rearrested and returned to Rikers, her "home," in time for the institution's annual Christmas party (Shakur 1978).

Studies have shown that incarcerated women overall and Black women in particular often find themselves in the vicious cycle of incarceration because of higher rates of drug use and drug dependency (National Institute of Drug Abuse 2020), often connected with domestic violence.

INCARCERATED MOTHERS

The authors consistently have discussions with resilient women who managed to successfully transition after release, and how each strove to reinvent themselves while incarcerated for the sake of their children. When these women succeed in breaking their psychological and social deprivation shackle to become a role model of love, resilience, and inspiration for their kids, the family unit can become infinitely stronger, reaping long-term benefits to their community. Sadly, the reuniting of the family unit does not always occur and mass incarceration's decimation of the Black family continues to tear a huge hole in the fabric of the morale and life quality within communities of color. Because households impacted by incarceration often consist of a single mother with fathers serving time, courts are traditionally reluctant to put mothers in prison (Clear, Reisig, Petrosino, and Cole 2017). Alarmingly, most women inside our jails and prisons are also parents who had custody of their minor children prior to incarceration. In addition to having to summon up the strength and resilience to survive the incarceration experience, incarcerated mothers also face the added stress of losing their parental rights forever.

For the pregnant mother who now finds herself behind bars, outcomes can become even more traumatizing. Many states require that babies born while the mother is in prison must be placed with a responsible family member or with a social agency within three weeks of birth, essentially destroying any chances of parental bonding, a devastating prospect for the new mother. If these children become part of the foster care system for an extended period of time during her incarceration, an incarcerated mother learns to serve time living with the constant fear that her children may one day be put up for adoption. Federal statutes like the Adoption and Safe Families Act specifically require the termination of parental rights for children in foster care for a specific period of time, making incarcerated mothers, without strong immediate family ties, all the more vulnerable.

For those pregnant incarcerated mothers with the good fortune to be eligible for housing in one of the few facilities with a nursery, they have the blessing of being able to bond with their newborn during the child's first year. The authors also had the privilege of meeting with new mothers participating in nursery programs at New York State's Bedford Hills maximum security facility for women, and during an international visit to Gulu Prison for Women in Uganda. Whether serving time in a local or international arena, the fate of an incarcerated mother's child or children typically takes precedence over all other concerns. Reestablishment of the parental bond becomes a primary motivation for many of these women, (and for many incarcerated fathers as well). Each works to develop a true and solid profile of a solid and responsible parent worthy of parental custody, thereby now being redefined as an asset to the community. Sadly, many incarcerated mothers simply lose hope in any effort to reclaim their children, often because of the subliminal message within the spirit of the aforementioned adoption laws, and in the lack of programming within most facilities, that perpetuate the stereotypical stigma that incarcerated mothers will always be unfit parents. Mothers determined to regain their rightful places as custodial parents upon release must, therefore, approach their undertaking with determination and passion, summoning up an unprecedented amount of resiliency to overcome both legal and societal obstacles.

THE GIFT OF RESILIENCY

In their prior roles as program administrators, the authors routinely celebrated news with female participants, witnessing a common confidence and strength of purpose as each would herald her post-release triumph of reaching a six-month milestone of sobriety; acquiring her GED, college degree, or trade licensure; finding housing to leave a toxic relationship or receiving a promotion at work. A brief overview of the typical female prisoner profile reveals that in significant ways, she has to overcome obstacles even more formidable and unforgiving than those of incarcerated men. Consider, for instance, the issue of sexual abuse and domestic violence. While it is a given that incarcerated men can be subject to sexual victimization, studies confirm that women more often find themselves the target of sexual abuse by officers, staff, and community volunteers working inside facilities. Angela Davis states the truth in her description of prison as "a space in which the threat of sexualized violence that looms in the larger society is effectively sanctioned as a routine aspect of the landscape of punishment behind prison walls" (Davis 2003, p.78).

Virtually all jails and prisons facilitate special orientations and training sessions for officers, staff, and volunteers that stress the consequences of entering a sexual relationship with a prisoner, male or female. Despite this training, corrections management has done precious little to understand the true impact of incarceration upon women whose history includes both sexual abuse and domestic violence. How much trauma does a woman experience when told to comply with a strip or body cavity search, or a shakedown of her cell, especially when carried out by a male corrections officer? To what extent do these regular occurrences place women on the path of recidivism after release, often because of turning to alcohol or drugs to self-medicate the resulting and lingering emotional pain, especially when we know that for these reasons female drug dependency is higher than with males?

Ironically, many of our incarcerated women who rely upon the facility for program guidance frequently find disappointment instead. With few exceptions, priority line items on corrections management spreadsheets support enhancing law enforcement and facility security, not job skills training, higher education classes or therapy. Facilities with workforce development programs for women often have limited offerings that showcase stereotypical jobs like secretarial training, often using equipment, especially computer hardware, that are past their prime or in significant states of disrepair.

A perfectly brewed storm of psychopathology can ensue for the unfortunate woman who, in an effort to "turn her life around," is assigned to participate in one of the numerous militaristic or confrontation therapy projects prevalent in some of our nation's prisons. Sometimes referred to as "shock incarceration," "boot camp" or "high impact," incarcerated women are often subject to extremely degrading and inhumane practices in the name of therapy or treatment. These types of programs are based upon the assumption that the woman is basically a lowlife that must be taken to task and humbled before the counseling process of rebuilding into a socially acceptable citizen can begin. Imagine, then, the plight of the incarcerated female victimized by domestic violence whose male abuser's habit was also to physically and emotionally assault his victim, then switch into the role of an apologetic and caring partner.

So many of the women who have returned home, earning their places in our communities as true role models and leaders, did so under these circumstances. In the case of incarcerated Black women who have been given the additional stigmatization of being sexually permissive, amoral, and unfit parents (Willingham 2011), they must delve so much deeper into their well of tenacity and resiliency to overcome these formidable obstacles. Racial oppression is a formidable foe. When an incarcerated Black woman finds the resiliency and self-efficacy to neutralize its effect as part of the transformation process, she must be considered, by any measure, extraordinary.

GIFTS OF SCHOLARSHIP AND ADVOCACY

In light of so many of the social and correctional policies, and even some research studies that continue to regard women as an "asterisk" in their overall planning, operations, and assessments, there is little wonder that so many of our imprisoned women write as a means of escape.

In a serious effort to effectuate much needed emotional healing, and to psychologically break from the torturous realities and monotony of jail life, many incarcerated females discover or re-discover the art of writing. Engaging in a creative activity that is solely their own, some write to build and maintain bridges with their families, friends, and significant others (Willingham 2011). Writing becomes a therapeutic activity that, in the courageous effort to document their personal inventory on paper, some begin to view themselves with fresh understanding and clarity. These self-assessments give them freshperspective to heretofore unrecognized influences that serve to reinforce destructive habits like drug addiction or acceptance of domestic violence victimization, as well as racial and gender disparities and societal marginalization.

The transformative process for incarcerated females, ironically, then often begins with the development of introspection through writing inside some of the most forbidding and regressive structures built by man. Michelle Jessamy, serving time for manslaughter and one of nine Black female writers whose work is featured in Wally Lamb's *Couldn't Keep It to Myself*, states: "The prison environment causes you to shut down and distrust other people, but writing has the opposite effect. By exploring my past through autobiographical fiction and sharing it with others, I am learning how to come to terms with the whys of my past actions and how to release my spirit from its prison" (2004, p. 265).

This phenomena, one that results in the self-gift of resiliency and rejuvenation is in itself remarkable, and arguably involves the creation of a magnificent gift to oneself that is later enjoyed by the community when, upon her release, a whole and healed citizen successfully reenters its ranks. The importance of this process becomes magnified exponentially, however, when the social, political, and economic significance of these powerful missives come to light when shared with the outside world. Known as counterstories, women who, for so long, have been shadowed by overwhelming studies of imprisoned males, seize the opportunity to use their writing to challenge and change the world's stereotypical notions of who prisoners actually are.

We have also seen that when a woman experiences enlightenment through a carceral epiphany, it often brings greater understanding of the external societal factors that are intricately connected to her current state of marginalization and oppression. Expressions of angst and rage at a system that many women identify as a major source of the problem, Carolina Soto represents so many of our incarcerated women who begin to see themselves, and the world, in a new and enlightened perspective, with their views often expressed through in their written work. Released from the US federal prison in Danbury, CT and now a participant of the authors' creative writing community workshop, she states:

> The main thing that people who leave prison have to teach us is that it is a system of institutionalized racism. The system is a slave system for workers who cannot or will not work for 11 cents an hour. That people who have a history of having their children stolen from them since slavery can survive a modern system that steals the mother, head of household, and puts her in a cage where she is forced to work for Americorp or full time and overtime to make 80 cents an hour making Dell computer parts or fiber optics for a war effort and survive have a lot to teach us about how capitalism works. How institutional racism destroys family and society. How survival is about community and in a place where you experience so much hate there is love. (C. Soto, personal communication, October 15, 2019)

When this process is undertaken by incarcerated Black females, their written expressions dare to challenge us not to look at them through the sullied lens of their convictions, but with the enlightened view that takes into account a host of individual, racial, and societal components that are distinctly different than that of their incarcerated white sisters. Assata Shakur's groundbreaking and masterful 1978 essay "Women in Prison: How It Is With Us," paved the way for the voices of incarcerated Black women to finally be heard and even more importantly, respected. Their work inspired scholarly discussion that gave rise to the study of Black feminism, with their experiences providing added impetus to the need to incorporate intersectionality to any valid study involving women in prison. Their powerful expressions soon became incorporated in the work of eminent scholars including Deborah E. McDowell and Patricia Hill Collins who discuss the rich qualitative findings therein when explaining her feminist theory, the "matrix of domination." Their stories and essays serve to add even more strength to Daly and Chesney-Linn's observations (2016) that the study of criminology has, until recently, involved a discipline based upon the limited experience of privileged white males in academia. Our incarcerated Black females include stories that only they can tell, those that even pose new sets of queries that can only be responsibly studied by academia with an intersectional lens. Overall, our nation's incarcerated women writers have contributed rich scholarship to the study of feminist criminology, including the creation of Black feminist criminology, arguably one of the most valuable and fascinating gifts from the dark that have blessed both academia and the world.

BLESSINGS FOR A HEALING NATION

During the creation of this book the global COVID-19 pandemic had begun in early spring 2020 to wreak havoc throughout America, especially inside American prisons and jails with the overwhelming number of victims being persons of color (Aviv 2020; Chammah 2020). By June 2020, daily protests over the perceived deliberate indifference by corrections officers and elected officials had begun to share headlines with those on the front lines of the Black Lives Matter demonstrations in response to the murder of George Floyd (Dreyer, Trent, Anderson, et al 2020). In immediate response to these atrocities, news footage began to televise or stream footage showcasing determined, articulate, and passionate activists irrespective of gender or color demanding equality and justice for all. Amid the madness of these challenging times, these images provide glimmers of hope that strategically implemented advocacy will heighten awareness of the continued disparities and oppression of our marginalized population groups.

As we take into account the extraordinary amount of political resources, stereotypical propaganda, and correctional policies used in keeping prisoners passive, voiceless, and ignored, the strength, tenacity, and courage of our incarcerated men and women who circumvent these odds cannot be overstated. Those first daring steps each incarcerated individual takes on the path toward transformative growth involves taking a serious look at themselves and their relationship with the world. For our incarcerated women and especially for our men and women of color this process, as 21st century criminology readily acknowledges, becomes infinitely more complex, challenging, and often fraught with raw emotion and rage. We know this now, and have begun to form more intelligent and informed opinions regarding the prison experience, in large thanks to those brave souls who share their experiences with us through their writing on the road of their transformative journey. Not surprisingly, now that they have returned home, these amazing men and women have become successful community leaders and role models. During their incarceration, they too became inspired by reading many of the powerful missives highlighted in this and other chapters. Vibrant, passionate voices of these women and people of color now add their valuable contributions to the front lines of advocacy with greater understanding and purpose. These valuable contributions are destined to be judged by history to be among society's most coveted gifts in its desperately needed effort to heal a nation, bringing equality and quality of life for everyone.

REFERENCES

Aviv, R. (June 15, 2020). Punishment by pandemic. *The New Yorker.* https://www.newyorker.com/magazine/2020/06/22/punishment-by-pandemic

Barak, G. (2001). Crime and crime control in an age of globalization: A theoretical dissection. *Critical Criminology* 10, 57–72 (2001). https://doi.org/10.1023/A:1013115820409

Burgess-Proctor, A. (2006). *Intersections of Race, Class, Gender, and Crime Future Directions for Feminist Criminology.* 1:1.

Chammah, M. (2020). Is COVID-19 falling harder on Black prisoners? Officials won't tell us. The Marshall Project. https://www.themarshallproject.org/2020/05/28/is-covid-19-falling-harder-on-black-prisoners-officials-won-t-tell-us

Chesney-Lind, M. & Chagnon, N. (2016). Criminology, gender, and race: A case study of privilege in the academy. *Feminist Criminology.*

Clear, T., Reisig, M., Petrosino, C., Cole, G. (2017). *American corrections in brief.* Boston: Cengage.

Cook, K. (2016). Has criminology awakened from its "androcentric slumber"? *Feminist Criminology.* Vol. 11(4).

Daly, K. & Chesney-Lind, M. (1988). Feminism and criminology. *Justice Quarterly,* 5:4, 497–538, DOI: 10.1080/07418828800089871

Davis, A. (2003). *Are prisons obsolete?* New York: Seven Stories Press.

Delgado, R. & Stefancic, J. (December 13, 2005). Critical Race Theory & Criminal Justice. Speech delivered at an inaugural colloquium at the Race and Criminal Justice Center, John Jay College of Criminal Justice.

Dreyer, B. P., Trent, M., Anderson, A. T., et al. (2020). The death of George Floyd: Bending the arc of history towards justice for generations of children. *Pediatrics.* doi: 10.1542/peds.2020-009639

Ghandnoosh, N. (2020). US prison decline: Insufficient to undo mass incarceration. The Sentencing Project: Washington D.C.

Holzman, M. (2017). Schooling for prison, incarceration for poverty. In *Race, education and reintegrating formerly incarcerated citizens.* Editors: Chaney, R. & Schwartz, J., Lanham, MD: Rowman & Littlefield.

Kajstura, A. (2019). Women's mass incarceration: The whole pie. Prison Policy Initiative. Northampton, MA.

Lamb, W. (2004). *Couldn't keep it to myself: Wally Lamb and the women of York Correctional Institution.* New York: HarperCollins.

National Institute of Drug Abuse. 2020, June 3. What are the unique treatment needs for women in the criminal justice system? Retrieved from https://www.drugabuse.gov/publications/principles-drug-abuse-treatment-criminal-justice-populations-research-based-guide/what-are-unique-treatment-needs-women-in-criminal-justice-system on 2020, July 14

Pryor, R. (July 25, 1976). *Was it something I said.* Comedy Album. Producer D. Banks. Reprise Labels.

Sawyer, W. & Wagner, P. (March, 2020). Mass incarceration: The whole pie. Prison Policy Initiative: Northhampton, MA.

The Sentencing Project. (2019). *Annual Report*. https://www.sentencingproject.org/
    wp-content/uploads/2020/03/Annual-Report-2019.pdf
Shakur, A. (1978). Women in prison: How it is with us. The Black Scholar.
    Sentencing Project (June 06, 2019) Incarcerated women and girls. https://www.
    sentencingproject.org/publications/incarcerated-women-and-girls/
Steffensmeier, D., Ulmer, J. & Kramer, J. (2006). The interaction of race, gender, and
    age in criminal sentencing: the punishment cost of being young, black, and male.
    Criminology. https://doi.org/10.1111/j.1745–9125.1998.tb01265.x
Willingham, B. (2011). Black women's prison narratives and the intersection of race,
    gender, and sexuality in US prisons. Critical Survey. Volume 3.

PART II

Learning that Transforms the Self

Chapter 5

Sitting with Yourself: Cells of Silence and Solitude

As early as the 1830s–40s, the American writer and philosopher Ralph Waldo Emerson thought about Anglo American prison reform and its relation to solitude and confinement. After his visits to the New Hampshire State Prison, he used the jail as a metaphor for modern man as a prisoner of a universal kind of captivity (Smith 2006). He wrote "I do not wish to remove from my present prison to a prison a little larger. I wish to break all prisons" (Sacks 2008, 93).

Emerson became an outcast in many circles after seemingly heretical statements he made at a Harvard Divinity School in 1838. "Tried and punished in the press, Emerson came to identify with the convict" (Smith 2006, 220). In this identification, Emerson "studied the art of solitude" and believed that the reformer like the prisoner must through solitary intellectual labor free himself from a "universal kind of mental captivity" and "conformity through silence and solitude" (Smith 2006, 217). Beyond Emerson, the concept of the healing and redemptive possibilities of solitude and silence have historically been associated with prisons.

HISTORICAL CONTEXT OF SILENCE AND SOLITUDE

Before the penitentiary as we know it today, there were dungeons, horrendous tortures, abandonment of criminals to penal colonies, public executions, monasteries and castles with areas designated for severe punishment. These dungeons of the 1700s lacked adequate food, sanitation, and medical care. They were overrun with violence most often placing men, women, and children in the same cells (History.com).

These inhumane conditions were not addressed until the late 1700s when the idea of the penitentiary developed; the penitentiary (from the word penance) was to be a place where repentance, and transformation occurred through solitary confinement, supervised labor, and religious instruction. A British philanthropist and social reformer, John Howard, who himself spent time in a European prison is usually credited with creating the idea of the penitentiary. Influenced by Howard, Americans adopted the penitentiary concept of reform rather than punishment. In 1790 an ecumenical group called the Pennsylvania Prison Society, which included many Quakers, (a Christian group devoted to social justice) gave birth to the penitentiary movement in America which would embrace solitary confinement. The Pennsylvania Prison Society was a group of reformers who wanted to change the horrendous dungeon prisons that existed at the time with humane accommodations and treatment. The work of the Quakers and the Society led to the creation of the Walnut Street Jail. When this jail became overcrowded, the famous Eastern State Penitentiary in Philadelphia was constructed. This would be known as the Pennsylvania Model of rehabilitation (Sullivan 2006).

This model included solitary confinement and was initially more humane, at least conceptually, than what we think of solitary confinement today—cells, which came from the monastic tradition were three times the size of prison cells today, often containing sky lights, gardens behind the cells, and the availability of the Bible. The goal was for the inmate to experience silence and solitude toward transformation. Gustave de Beaumont, a French magistrate and prisoner reformist, and Alexis de Tocqueville, a political scientist and diplomat, visited the American penitentiary system and recommended its application in France. "Thrown into solitude [the prisoner] reflects. Placed alone, in view of his crime, he learns to hate it . . . in solitude, where remorse will come to assail him" (Tocqueville and Beaumont,1831) was his perspective.

So, the Pennsylvania System and Eastern State Penitentiary in Philadelphia were the first experiments in solitary confinement in the United States in 1829. But as early as 1890, due to the expensive nature of this undertaking and its inability to adapt to the technology of the rising Industrial Revolution as well as overcrowding, the experiment failed; it was impossible to have adequate space for each prisoner and still be cost-effective. Additionally, very tragically instead of transformation, some prisoners went insane, committed suicide, or were no longer able to function in society (Medley vs. Colorado, 1890). For these reasons, the practice would be abandoned during the following decades and officially abandoned at Eastern State Petitionary in 1931.

In response to the Pennsylvania System, the Auburn or Congregate System was created in an Auburn, New York, penitentiary. This system included prison labor in groups during the day and solitary confinement at night; this was the forerunner of what is commonly now regarded as the prison industrial complex. Silence was always enforced, and any breach of silence would be punished by whipping and flogging. The penal approach was supposed to teach discipline, work, and skills while maintaining the benefits of silent repentance and obedience to authority. Auburn and Sing Sing (the "Big House") in New York utilized this more cost-effective congregate work setting with the prisoners learning vocational and construction skills, out of the cell during the day and back in their own solitary cell at night (Smith 2006).

Today, solitary confinement (also referred to as the hole, extreme isolation, the box, or the SHU, as in Special Housing Unit) is still used in prisons. Furthermore, another method used contemporaneously in military prisons and by terrorist groups with their captives involves the absence of silence. United States military kept Afghanistan detainees in dark prison-like caverns deprived of food and water, chained and unable to lie down with loud heavy metal and rap music blaring for weeks on end with no silence nor solitude (Sim 2007). Here, noise becomes a weapon.

As the remainder of this chapter maintains, solitude and silence are paradoxical. Silence and solitude in the form of solitary confinement became a cruel form of torture, not the penitent and transformative model that early prison reformers had hoped. Nevertheless, the concept and relationship between silence, solitude, reflection, penitence, and transformation has long continued to be explored.

DEFINING SILENCE AND SOLITUDE

We now know that solitary confinement can be a form of mental torture with individuals deprived of human communication where silence is enforced, not chosen. It is both undemocratic and immoral (Sim 2007). Paradoxically, it can also be said that some prisoners like Mandela, Martin Luther King Jr., and Malcolm X have heralded value and have amazingly found ways to create and nurture spiritual and intellectual enrichment despite these most oppressive conditions of confinement. Some priests who spent time in communist prisons behind the iron curtain also found solitary confinement to be the richest spiritual time with many blessings in their lives ("The Practice of Silence and Solitude" 2000"). Therefore, this choosing and seeking of silence and solitude that frequently occurs within prisons may not be a form of torture for everyone. Some will find it as a space for the development of spiritual and intellectual disciplines practiced habitually (Foster 1998).

Silence is the lack of sound or refraining from speaking –quiet, and the absence of all human-created stimuli or noise; thereby, a walk in nature could still be considered silence. Silence is the cessation of words. Only internal words are attended to, and one produces words through writing and journaling (McKay and McKay 2018). In contrast, solitude is the state of being alone, being by oneself, creating your own world with or without walls, or intimacy with oneself. It is a full and positive state different from loneliness, which is negative where one feels something is missing and feels isolated (Marano 2003). Solitude is being alone physically or alone even in a crowd. Solitude and silence are different disciplines but companions. In her well-researched book, *Quiet*, Susan Cain states that at least a third of us are introverts at heart, and we need and crave quiet and solitude. In fact, this is where we are energized and able to face the world (2012).

Richard Foster, a Christian theologian and author in the Quaker tradition, says "solitude is more a state of mind and heart than it is a place. There is a solitude of the heart that can always be maintained. Crowds, or the lack of them, have little to do with this inward attentiveness" (1998, 96). Therefore, silence is not a prerequisite to solitude. However, silence *does* seem to enhance the possibility for solitude. Solitude is intentional, an intentional withdrawal from others and engagement with others (McKay and McKay 2018). These twin concepts are alike in that they are both active and not passive. They provide space for contemplation and reflection, and sometimes transformation.

We live in a noisy world. Practicing silence by choosing to turn off our computer, cell phone, or television and turning to quiet, is an active choice. In actively practicing solitude by deciding to spend time alone, removing ourselves from community and fasting from media; we are making powerful choices. These twin disciplines have been praised by spiritual leaders, poets, philosophers, world leaders, and scientists alike. In this chapter, we speak about silence and solitude as companions.

ASSAULT ON SILENCE AND SOLITUDE

As Sim (2007) made clear in his book, *Manifesto for Silence*, there is global assault against silence with noise a prime feature of our culture. With increasing marketing and technology, noise is a matter of power, psychological/ physical health, and control. Imagine getting away for a peaceful dinner in a restaurant. How often is the noise level distracting and space for conversation and quiet hard to come by? There is always background noise. According to Sim, lack of silence affects our ability to concentrate, think, and relate to one another. He cites research to support the claim that noise pollution exacerbates: heart disease, mental health problems, hearing loss, job productivity, interpersonal conflict, spiritual well-being, and intellectual focus (2007).

Sim asserted that "silence is a threatened phenomenon" and that "the ability to think, to reflect and to create are all to a significant degree dependent on our being able to access silence and quiet on a regular, and reasonably predictable, basis" (2007, 1–2). He mounted a strong case from psychology, biology, and philosophy for the value of silence in modern life and his work was described in one book review as an "anguished defense of silence as a prerequisite of contemplation, critical thinking and character development and individuation" (Daniels 2008). Some people are afraid of silence to their own detriment, but silence has the ability to take us from our own contexts—social, intentional, political, and environmental—and make us think from variant perspectives. Noise and the lack of silence is the forgotten pollutant in today's world (Sim 2007).

Cain (2012) in her book, *Quiet*, argued that the introvert, as well as the extrovert, needs and craves quiet in their lives even in the company of others. Retreating to these twin disciplines gives us an emotional balance and equilibrium and feeds our brain. However, our society fosters noise, rewards extroversion, and creates less and less space for these disciplines. Nurturing solitude and silence, then, is a discipline and an art. In some cases, this is what the prisoner has mastered either through varying degrees of individual choice or through force and against his will.

PRISONERS—HARD FOUGHT
SOLITUDE AND SILENCE

Contemporary prisons are pressure cookers, frequently noisy and prone to conflict and violence. They are a "dangerous social world in which there is incredible pressure to establish and demonstrate manhood through aggressive behavior" (Phillips 2008, 9). Depending on the circumstances and the prison, prisoners often live in a small cell on a cell block with another cellmate. One prisoner called this "living in a closet with a stranger" (Phillips 2008, 7).

Some stay in open dormitories, often with well over a hundred beds separated by only a few feet. There is almost total lack of privacy with bathrooms being open with few or nonexistent partitions between toilets, showers, and urinals. The noise is endless and constant. In the words of one former female prisoner, "There was no quiet . . . you had to find the quiet" (C. Soto, personal communication, December 4, 2018). Based on statements like these, some may think it is ironic to say that we can learn from the currently and formerly incarcerated on how to engage in solitude and silence. But it is true. We can learn from them. They can be masterful teachers. To begin, the famous psychiatrist Viktor Frankl imprisoned in Auschwitz said this about solitude and prison:

> There were times, of course, when it was possible, and even necessary, to keep away from the crowd. The prisoner craved to be alone with himself and his thoughts. He yearned for privacy and for solitude. After my transportation to a

so-called rest camp I had the rare fortune to find solitude for about five minutes at a time behind the earthen hut where I worked and in which were crowded about fifty delirious patients, there was a quiet spot in a corner of the double fence of barbed wire surrounding the camp. I just sat and looked out the green flowering slopes and the distant blue hills of the Bavarian landscape, framed by the meshes of barbed wire. (2015, 48)

Because of their prison experience, prisoners and the formerly incarcerated often have an acute awareness of the human need for silence and solitude. As counterintuitive as it may seem, modern day prisoners, in some ways, find it easier to retreat into silence and solitude than those not physically imprisoned. Because technology, cell phones, and the internet are often limited or not permissible at all in prisons, prisoners have less stimuli to process. This is not to say that access to technology or the internet should not be accessible. This suggests that because there is so little immediate communication with the outside world, there is more opportunity for solitude and silence. Some prisoners choose to retreat to their cells for relative quiet and privacy when not working or engaged in prison activities. Others retreat within themselves, using head or earphones. Prisoners block out all manner of noise and chaos around them while reading a book, tucked away on a bunk in another world of solitude. This is how solitude is portable; it can be carried into the company of others (Smith 2006). That is how in the Auburn system, a 19th century penal method where prisoners worked together in silence during the day, with each confined alone at night, prisoners can be part of a working society of isolated prisoners in solitude while in a collective. Prisoners often learn how to be by themselves in their own world, often escaping through reading and writing.

The following example is a personal account from the coauthor, Chaney, illustrating this phenomenon:

I made some choices during my third and final period of incarceration. When I was transferred from a medium security prison dorm to the disciplinary SHU, then to a prison cell in Attica, I chose to live without the see-through portable black and white television offered to prisoners for purchase. I wanted to read, write, and most importantly think. I wanted solitude and silence. After three months, I decided that I could live without the television and that I was better off. I saw others utilizing the prison library to escape to silence and solitude, but I also saw men who seemed to have mastered the art of being solitary in a crowd. Because prisoners are often busy with work, classes or workshops during the day, the silence at night is particularly appreciated. I observed men creating spaces of silence and solitude for themselves and these appeared conscious choices to abstract themselves from others. Additionally, I found that men who were most able to create these spaces within themselves were most often better prepared to face re-entry; I observed this; I experienced it myself, and we often discussed it among ourselves.

TRANSFORMATIVE POTENTIAL OF
SILENCE AND SOLITUDE

Despite the underbelly of solitary confinement misuse, there is reason to believe that conceptually, and as a matter of choice, silence and solitude in prisons can be beneficial. However, this *voluntary*, as opposed to mandated, aspect cannot be emphasized enough. From both past and contemporary scholars and spiritual thinkers such as Parker Palmer, Richard Foster, Thomas Merton, Richard Rohr, and Henry David Thoreau; we have long understood silence and solitude to be spiritual disciplines to train the soul. Monastic literature describes the hermit's cell and in most all religious traditions silence and solitude is revered. We also now know from medicine and science and most recently from the study of Alzheimer's that the brain and body require regular doses of both. Incarcerated individuals choosing silence and solitude open the potential for the following adult transformative activities: study and self-examination, reflection and journaling, and prayer and meditation.

STUDY AND SELF-EXAMINATION

Study has an association with school, homework, and exams; in fact, study is key to adult education transformation. Research is clear that college courses, adult education courses (General Equivalency Diploma or GED, etc.) and job readiness courses are the ways in which prisons must move if they are to reduce recidivism and transform lives large scale (Chaney and Schwartz 2017). Adults, and in this case the formerly incarcerated, who engage in study for simply the absorption of knowledge (not test taking or grades) and to know the self are engaging in adult-centered learning at its best. The individual chooses what they will study, when, and how they will proceed—self-directed learning. Thought and action are inextricably connected. Study is also connected to the spiritual disciplines. According to Foster, study is integral to the transformation of the mind and spirit. "The purpose of the spiritual disciplines is the total transformation of the person. They aim at replacing old destructive habits of thought with new life-giving habits. Nowhere is this purpose more clearly seen than in the discipline of study. . . . The mind is renewed by applying it to those things that will transform it" (1998, 62).

Studying includes both reading and writing but is distinctive, more immersive, and broader. "Study is essentially disciplined reading" (McKay and McKay 2018). It involves research and deep thinking into context, history, life application, listening deeply, ongoing observation, and making connections. Some prisoners learn the art and skill of studying in prisons; some utilize the solitude of prison libraries and the cell; some teach others; some write often and read voraciously. These are skills to carry out into the world once released because it can be argued that life outside prison is over stimulated, noisy, and knows little of solitude and silence.

The study of self or self-examination is also where the concept of penance comes in—the examination of our sins, transgressions, our strengths, our weaknesses, our successes, and our failures. It is the study and examination of motivations, habits and behaviors, our fears, and our ignored desires. It is also the study of the self within the larger systems of society and a study of how we came to be who we are within the limitations, constraints, and freedoms of our families, neighborhoods, customs, societies, and institutions both good and bad. Mills calls this the *sociological imagination* (Mills 2000).

REFLECTION AND JOURNALING

Reflection and journaling are related to self-examination. Reflective practices have long been associated with adult transformative learning, journaling, keeping letters, and diaries. These traditions date back to ancient practices of 10th century Japan (Purcell 2018). These practices are also very common in prisons. Reflection is serious, often intense thinking and consideration of some idea or subject matter (Chaney and Schwartz 2017, 109). Reflection in physics is directional change of a wave front as it interfaces with two different media so that the wave front returns into the medium from which it began. A reflecting image from a mirror gives back by means of a reflecting surface an image to examine. It is this close examination of the image of one's life including behavior, habits, choices, situation, feelings, memories, thinking, and relationships that is the art of reflection. One way to record this thinking and feeling, however mundane, is through reflective journaling while in solitude and being silent (McKay and McKay 2018).

McKay and McKay go on to say that journaling is opening a door to the self, uncovering emotions and thoughts you did not know you had, knowing yourself, however painful and there is no right or wrong way to journal (2018). As one explores uncomfortable emotions, records thoughts, observations, feelings, experiences, and prayers there is potential for healing. Journaling also preserves memories, improves writing, sharpens senses, communicates with God, dialogues with others, finds comfort, and performs self-therapy. Science now recognizes the health benefits of journaling; it can decrease symptoms of asthma and rheumatoid arthritis, strengthen immune cells, and manage stress. According to Purcell, it is the cheapest therapy you will ever get (2018).

MEDITATION AND PRAYER

"We are all prisoners undergoing a life sentence, imprisoned by our own minds; We are all seeking parole being hostages of our anger, fear and desire" (Ariel and Menahemi 1997). Such are the words of the narrator in the powerful documentary, *Doing Time, Doing Vipassana,* from Tihar Jail located outside New Delhi, India. It is a relatively progressive prison complex and the largest prison in South Asia with over 10,000 prisoners. In Tihar, thousands of prisoners and their guards practice meditation known as Vipassana, a now scholarly recognized meditation system for reforming prisoners and preparing them for life outside prison (Ariel and Menahemi1997). Vipassana requires ten days and ten hours of silence and stillness a day based on the teachings of Buddha (Phillips 2008; Casarjian 1995).

This same method has been documented at W. E. Donaldson Correctional Facility in Alabama, a maximum-security prison where prisons report release from anger, resentment, bitterness, anxiety, fear, and traumatic memories through Vipassana meditation (Phillips 2008). Phillips documents the transformative emotional learning and healing that can happen using rigorous meditation practices through testimonies like Benjamin Harvey, a prisoner at Donaldson, who stated "This was a magnificent experience ... I didn't know how much anger, depression and hurt balled up inside. But the teachers told me, 'Don't run. Get to the root.' So, I stayed, and I worked, and by the eighth day all the garbage had come to the surface and I felt so much better" (Phillips 2008, 4). Meditation has been practiced in multiple religious traditions down through antiquity. Simply defined, meditation is a journey inside of yourself. It includes mindfulness, focused thought, clearing of the brain, to create an emotionally calm state.

Although prayer and meditation are similar, there are differences. Prayer often relies upon the sought-after silence and solitude of meditation. Unlike meditation, prayer is directed at a deity and goal oriented. One of earliest and famous prisoners to pray was the Apostle Paul in the New Testament in both Ephesians and Acts of the Apostles (the Bible, NIV 2011). He often referred to his chains and being a prisoner of Christ as well as in actual prison. As we have noted earlier, religion and thus prayer was a core of prison life. In Victorian prisons, religion was central, and the chapel was the site of prayer and silence. Early in prison history, attendance in chapels and prayer was mandatory, and it was not until 1976 that compulsory attendance came to an end for all prisoners in the United States. In today's prisons, chapels are often called prayer rooms and are multi-purpose rooms for a diversity of religions. They are often still used as places of privacy and quiet (Gilliat-Ray 2005). Another famous prisoner, theologian and German pastor, Dietrich Bonhoffer, imprisoned for one year under the Nazis for being a part of a plot to murder Hitler utilized time in prayer and writing before he died in prison. The seeking of solitude, silence, and prayer was integral to his prison time (Bonhoffer 1978).

THE FINAL WORD IN SUPPORT OF
SOLITUDE AND SILENCE

Perhaps it is the prisoner and returning citizen who can remind us of the value of solitude and silence in our crowded lives. Like the monk or solitary scholar, the returning citizen has had to grapple with fighting for and finding these spaces within an institution that has had an uneasy relationship with them. The final words on this topic come from returning citizen Michael Colbert; his words challenge us to rethink the role of silence and solitude in our own lives and how we make room and prioritize them. "I have run across countless men who were so gifted in their writing skills, geniuses in their minds, maybe because they had the time [and solitude] to sit and think, and sit and think" (Colbert M., personal communication, October 23, 2018).

REFERENCES

Ariel, E. and Menahemi, A. (1997). *Doing Time, Doing Vipassana.* India: Karuna Films.

Beckford, J.A. and Gilliat, S. (2005). *Religion in Prison: Equal Rites in a Multi-Faith Society.* Cambridge: Cambridge University Press.

Bonhoffer, D. (1978). *Prayers from prison.* Philadelphia: Fortress Press.

Cain, S. (2012). *Quiet: The power of introverts in a world that can't stop talking.* New York: Random House.

Casarjian, R. (1995). Houses of healing: A prisoner's guide to inner power and freedom. Boston: The Lionheart Foundation.

Chaney, J. R. and Schwartz, J. (2017). *Race, Education, and Reintegrating Formerly Incarcerated Citizens: Counterstories and Counterspaces.* Lanham, MD: Lexington Books.

Daniels, A. (2008, April). The Sound of silence [Review of the book *Manifesto for Silence: Confronting the Politics and Culture of Noise by Stuart Sim*]. New Criterion, https://www.newcriterion.com/issues/2008/4/the-sound-of-silence DLF.

TV (2010, May 5) Freedom Behind Bars: Meditation in Prison. Retrieved from https:// 2BM7i4v /binged.it/

Emerson, R. W. (1885). *Society and solitude*. Boston: Houghton, Mifflin and Company.

Emerson, R.W. (1993). *Self-Reliance and other essays*. Mineola, NY: Dover Publications, Inc.

Foster, R. (1998). *Celebration of discipline*. San Francisco: HarperCollins.

Frankl, V. (2015). *Man's search for meaning*. Boston: Beacon Press.

Gilliat-Ray, S. (2005). From "chapel" to "prayer room": The production, use, and politics of sacred space in public institutions. *Culture and Religion*. 6:2

History.com. Modern Marvels. *Prison History.* https://www.youtube.com/watch?v=FKiQi9OU2AU

Mandela, N. (2010). *Nelson Mandela: Conversations with myself.* New York: Farrar, Straus and Giroux

Marano, H. E. (2003, July 3). *What is Solitude?* Psychology Today. http://www.psychologytoday.com/us/articles/200307/what-is-solitude

McKay, B. and McKay, K. (2018, May 28). *The Practice of silence and solitude.* Retrieved from http://artofmanliness.com/articles/spiritual-disciplines-solitude-silence/ Medley vs. Colorado, 134 U.S., 160. (1890)

Mills, C. W. (2000). *The sociological imagination 40th ed.* New York: Oxford.

Muers, R. (2011). Book review QUAKER STUDIES 16/1 (2011) [135–140] ISSN 1363–013X

Phillips, J. (2008). *Letters from the dhamma brothers.* Onalaska, WA: Pariyatti Press.

Purcell, M. (2018). The health benefits of journaling. *Psych central.* Retrieved on November 28, 2018. From https://psychcentral.com/lib/the-health-benefits-of-journaling/

Quakerspeak. (2016, June 2). Did Quakers invent solitary confinement? Retrieved from: https://www.youtube.com/watch?v=KfMIA-B931s

Sack, K. (2008). Editor. *Emerson: Political writings*. Cambridge: Cambridge University Press.

Sim, S. (2007). *Manifesto for silence: Confronting the politics and culture of noise.* Edinburgh: Edinburgh University Press.

Smith, C. (2006). Emerson and incarceration. *American Literature*. 78:2.

Sullivan, L. (2006, July 26). Timeline: Solitary Confinement in U.S. Prisons. NPR https://www.npr.org/templates/story/story.php?storyId=5579901

The Practice of Silence and Solitude. (2000, June). Opusangelorum.org/oa_spirituality/six_traits_docs/Silenceandsolitude.html

Tocqueville, A. and Beaumont, G. (1831). Letter to the French Government on their visit to Eastern State Penitentiary.

Walsh, R. and Shapiro, S. (2006). The meeting of meditative disciplines and western psychology: A mutually enriching dialogue. *American Psychologist*. 61 (3): 227–239.

Watson, G. (1993). The bliss of solitude. *Sewanee Review*. 101:3.

Chapter 6

The Organic Intellectual

The familiar true story, *Prison Studies,* detailing how Malcolm X taught himself to read is often excerpted from his autobiography (1992) and used in adult literacy programs to encourage new adult readers. In his own words, Malcolm X dropped out of school in the eighth grade and was semi-literate. While in prison, he met other inmates who were well read and articulate, and he envied their knowledge. Subsequently, he sought to educate himself by copying the first page of the dictionary, rereading it, and then copying the second until he finished the entire volume in this manner. For months, he copied the entire dictionary thereby learning to read and expanding his vocabulary. This is adult self-directed learning at its best; he called it "home-made education" (1992, 197). Through this method he became a lifelong learner. He wrote:

> I suppose it was inevitable that as my word-base broadened, I could for the first time pick up a book and read and now begin to understand what the book was saying. Anyone who has read a great deal can imagine the new world that opened. Let me tell you something; from then until I left that prison, in every free moment I had, if I was not reading in the library, I was reading on my bunk. You couldn't have gotten me out of books with a wedge. . . In fact, up to then, I never had been so truly free in my life (1992, 198–199).

Malcolm X served seven years in Massachusetts prisons, two years in Charlestown and the last five years in an experimental prison in Norfolk with a large library. He utilized the prison library extensively, reading constantly, and became a student of history, philosophy, science (particularly genetics), and religion. He was particularly interested in the world history of Black civilizations.

Malcolm X's experiences of teaching himself to read then becoming a prolific reader, and his transformation into an intellectual began in prison. Although his educational journey is dramatic, it is not unusual in prisoners' experiences. Reading and writing in prison are widespread. To this point and from a practical perspective, there is convincing research to suggest that educating prisoners is both cost effective and reformatory (Bozick, Steele, Davis, and Turner 2018) Investment in more formal learning such as college courses, trade classes, General Equivalency Diploma or GED programs, English for Speakers of Other Languages (or ESOL), and adult literacy in prisons can reduce recidivism (Chaney and Schwartz 2017; Department of Justice Federal Bureau of Prisons 2016; Davis, Bozick, Steele, Saunders, and Miles 2013). In this chapter, we argue that in addition to being cost effective and lowering recidivism rates, educational pursuits such as reading and writing in prison is personally transformative. Malcolm X said it best:

> I have often reflected upon the new vistas that reading opened to me. I knew right there in prison that reading had changed forever the course of my life. As I see it today, the ability to read awoke inside me some long dormant craving to be mentally alive. I certainly wasn't seeking any degree, the way a college confers a status symbol upon its students. My homemade education gave me, with every additional book that I read, a little bit more sensitivity to the deafness, dumbness, and blindness that was afflicting the black race in America (1992, 206).

TRADITIONAL INTELLECTUALS AND ORGANIC INTELLECTUALS

In the thinking and language of Gramsci, Malcolm X became an *organic intellectual*. According to Gramsci, "All men are intellectuals, one could therefore say: but not all men in society have the function of intellectuals" (1971, 9). Gramsci makes a distinction between *traditional intellectuals*, who are often university professors and researchers and tend to cater to the larger neoliberal infrastructures (Zimmerman 2017) and organic intellectuals. Organic intellectuals do not rise from the university but from the sub-stratums of society: working class, lower-class communities and, even prison (Gramsci 1971).

Gramsci was imprisoned by Mussolini from 1926–1937 because he was a dissident intellectual who believed that hegemony was driven by the creation, dissemination, and adoption of ideology and that intellectuals needed to be the critical eye and voice in response to power. He was best known for his cultural hegemony theory which stated that capitalist ruling states institutionalize their power to control and create a hegemonic culture which maintains oppression and control of the masses. Cultural hegemony is often communicated through language—the stories we tell and the images we create to make sense of our world (Eaton 2018; Mayo 1999).

Gramsci's allegiance was to the factory worker, the unionist, the peasant, and prison educators. He believed that the intellectuals were the agents for social change (Mayo 1999). His prison writings articulated the role and responsibility of the intellectual in class struggles. Whether organic or traditional, intellectuals should be social activist scholars, who constantly struggle to transform minds and society through their intellectual work—the stories they tell and the images they communicate (Mayo 1999). For Gramsci the organic intellectual is committed to the marginalized and powerless and seeing intellectuals develop from these groups. Those intellectuals not from these groups assimilate with them and work reciprocally in collaboration. Gramsci (1971) saw the organic intellectual giving legitimacy to the work by telling counterstories (Chaney and Schwartz 2017), often opposing the dominant cultural narrative. Challenging dominant narratives through counterstory telling is a role of the intellectual, particularly the organic intellectual.

Furthermore, in a capitalistic society often one class exercises cultural and ideological dominance over the rest of society by the very consent of the exploited individuals. The hegemonic cultural ideology is created by those in power and "sold" as common sense (Gramsci 1971). In a contemporaneous context, Zimmerman (2017) says that this is what former United States president Donald Trump did; co-opted the working class and some aspects of the church in their own oppression.

Most scholars would agree that in the late 20th century, this hegemonic ideology as it relates to prisons and prison reform was made manifest in neoliberalist thought favoring the privatization of prisons over government control, individual responsibility contrasted to systemic responsibility, and deregulation (Clark 2016). To critique neoliberal hegemonic "common sense," the voice of the organic intellectual from the prison is what is needed (Zimmerman 2017).

THE PRISONER AS ORGANIC INTELLECTUAL

Malcolm X, the powerful and influential world leader of the Black Power Movement during the 1960s, was an advocate for the development of the intellectual while incarcerated. He was a spokesman for the Black prisoner who "symbolized white society's crime of keeping black men oppressed and deprived and ignorant, and unable to get decent jobs, turning them into criminals" (1992, 195). He became this public intellectual and revolutionary world leader in prison. Prison was his school; prison gave birth to this organic intellectual.

Like Malcolm X, Antonio Gramsci was a revolutionary thinker and activist. Conversely, Gramsci was already an intellectual before entering prison.

In fact, it was because of his intellectual pursuits that he was imprisoned. However, prison did provide the space to foster his writing and thought, producing the now classic *Prison Notebooks* (1971). Gramsci's writings, which are in the Marxist tradition, open areas of research and political thought around hegemony, historical contingency, human agency, the role of culture, civil struggle, and the role of the intellectual. His thoughts had wide repercussions across academic disciplines including, but not limited to media studies, political science, adult education, economics, sociology, linguistics, cultural studies, and critical theory (Gramsci 1971).

Beyond Gramsci and Malcolm X, one need only read the Pulitzer Prize winning book *Blood in the Water* to understand that the organic intellectual was well represented in the 1971 takeover of Attica Prison (Thompson 2016). The takeover was a response to deplorable and inhumane prison conditions, stoked by civil rights unrest across the country but most directly influenced by the Auburn Prison resistance (Thompson 2016). Attica's takeover happened suddenly in September of 1971. Thompson's book describes how 1300 prisoners at Attica Prison in Upstate New York organized to provide for basic needs, safety of both hostages and prisoners, medical attention, and elections that formed a representative democratic process with a committee led by organic intellectuals. The angry and disgruntled prisoners were able to talk through their concerns and demands; create an initial list of prison reforms needed; revise that list after consultation of a committee of outside consultants chosen by the prisoners, and maintain order and dialogue in the midst of a very dangerous and volatile atmosphere. In many instances, the prisoners of Attica were rational, deliberate, and strategic—very unfortunately, however, government and prison officials were not as thoughtful or deliberate. The takeover had the potential for peaceful resolution; sadly, that was not the case.

Nonetheless, several of Attica's prisoners demonstrated intellectual skills of negotiation, representative democracy, conflict resolution, and strategic planning that informed their activism. Unfortunately, they underestimated the lack of strategic planning, fear, and racism of the hegemonic prison officials and correctional officers, and government officials in particular New York Governor, Nelson A. Rockefeller and President Richard Nixon and the cultural ideology around prisoners and prisons at the time. Prisoners who were organic intellectuals played an early and stabilizing role in the takeover.

The leaders in the Attica takeover, Malcolm X, and Gramsci, in variant ways, demonstrate the power of the prisoner as an organic intellectual. In many cases, the returning citizen and prisoner scholar are the organic intellectuals in our historical era of mass incarceration in America. Traditional intellectuals can partner with returning citizens and support them to complete their college careers, create opportunities for informal adult education, legitimize their work and support their publishing, and start community-based organizations. These liaisons can also be used to protest prison injustices, develop scholarship programs for scholars returning from prison, use art as a vehicle of resistance, and develop collaborations between colleges and prisons where organic and traditional intellectuals work together.

Among the prison population, there is great eagerness for formal college and GED classes. The Bard College Prison Initiative (BPI 2019) illustrates the demand and hunger for intellectual pursuit. This initiative currently enrolls 350 prisoners in its Bachelors and Liberal Arts programs and has many more applicants for its degree-bearing courses in six New York State prisons (Karpowitz 2017). The goal of these endeavors is to reshape hegemonic ideologies around who prisoners are and who they are not with a critical stance toward mass incarceration.

THE MAKING OF THE ORGANIC INTELLECTUAL

There are five elements that contribute to making a prisoner an organic intellectual: time, choice, space, reading, and writing. The first two will only be discussed briefly as we delve into time and choice in other chapters. It is enough to say here that time is on the side of the prisoner. For the returning citizen, it is different. Unless they allocate time for continued intellectual endeavors, it will not be as easy as when they were imprisoned. This requires choice or the will to transform. When in prison, prisoners make choices to either "let the time do you, or you do the time." In other words, a prisoner may choose to use his or her sentence for intellectual pursuits, thereby developing a plan for self-directed learning. Once chosen, prison can provide space for devoted study.

THE MONK IN HIS CELL

Prisoners vary greatly in the amount of personal space allotted to them; this often depends on whether they are in minimum, medium, or maximum-security prisons. Furthermore, conditions of solitary confinement or isolation determine the amount of space and privacy allocated to the prisoner. Prisoners' experiences with privacy and personal space depend on whether they are in large dormitory rooms, have access to a library and/or outdoor spaces, have partitions between beds, have access to reading lights, and experience high noise levels. These elements impact the ability to concentrate often necessary for study. Having said this, some prisoners are able to carve out emotional and physical spaces for reading and writing.

Like Malcolm X, many prisoners create nearly monk-like attention to reading and writing while in prison. Historically monks have devoted multiple hours to writing and study in cells alone and with laser focus on their intellectual and spiritual work. In some ways a prison cell can be compared to medieval European monastery cells—Scriptoriums. Scriptorium literally means "a place for writing." As early as the 6th century, monks were devoted to writing and copying the Bible in these physical scriptoriums or, cell-like rooms, designed for quiet and concentration. It appears that scriptoriums were either solitary cells or collective rooms where monks sat at separate desks in silence (Janzen 2013). Much like the monk, incarcerated individuals may have this monk-like experience that promulgates the copious writing that so many produce. Many prisoners write novels, screenplays, volumes of poetry, memoirs, and letters while locked up. Once returned from prison, finding this existence back in society is a challenge for all writers.

WRITING INTO BEING

As well as reading, Gramsci wrote expansively and in a variety of genres. A description of his writing habits is contained in the large collection of his *Prison Notebooks* (1971):

> He wrote copiously, filling his notebooks systematically in a small, crabbed, curiously precise hand, transcribing quotations and practicing translations as well as developing his own thoughts. . . . He also wrote letters to immediate friends and relations. . . . These letters are an extraordinary document of human tenacity. (1971, xc)

Malcolm X was always orally articulate, using Black vernacular and the slang of the time. In prison, he embraced Islam and began to follow Elijah Muhammad, the Nation of Islam's founder. Malcolm X desired to communicate in writing with Mr. Muhammed but found it increasingly difficult, so he studied, and was eventually able to write daily to Mr. Muhammed (Malcolm X 1992).

After prison, there is indication that Malcolm X continued to write daily. He intended to publish a second book after his autobiography, but he died before he could achieve this goal. However, his travel journals were later published in his honor as "The Diary of Malcolm X" (Boyd and Al-Shabazz 2013). He wrote with a beautiful flowing handwriting—jotting down observations, interactions, reflections, and experiences during his two trips to Africa and the Middle East in 1964 as he had learned in prison.

The intense, therapeutic, and creative properties of writing in prison is perhaps articulated best by a former prisoner in Queensboro Correctional Facility in New York City who wrote for a prison college writing group and compares writing to a positive addiction. The former prisoner stated: "Writing is really a drug to me, and I believe I need rehab for this addiction. It's like I get a euphoric feeling every time I write. Those are the endorphins being released in my brain—feeling of ecstasy. I don't know what I would do without pen and paper, just thinking about that is real scary. . . . I need WA, Writing Anonymous, because writing is definitely my drug of choice!" (Black 2017).

THE ORGANIC INTELLECTUAL AND ACTIVISM

Prison is often a space where the organic intellectual is born giving way to the activist scholar. According to Edward W. Said, the public intellectual and founder of postcolonial studies, Malcolm X and Gramsci were both intellectuals and activists whose space of incubation and intense study was the dark gift of prison time. Organic intellectuals are active, involved, and agents of change (Said 1996). Malcolm X and Gramsci have had a powerful influence upon academics and activists going forward and much of what these two great thinkers became and the influence that they exuded was incubated, nurtured, and seeded in the prison experience. Said (1996) attributed much of who he became to his association with the work of Malcolm X among others.

Even though Gramsci died in prison at 46, and Malcolm X was assassinated in 1965 at 39, both had profound and far-reaching intellectual afterlives. Gramsci's *Prison Notebooks* was first published from 1948–51 and translated into French, German, and English. His main legacy was the development of the concepts of hegemonic thinking and hegemonic culture defined as the use of language and imagery to define common sense by those in power. In an age of social media, viral videos, global messaging, and mass higher education, and in the era of President Donald Trump, media vastly defines what common sense is (Eaton 2018). Gramsci's concept of invisible yet pervasive hegemonic culture seems more apropos than ever.

Malcolm X led the legacy of Black Lives Matter before there was movement. He fought injustices of all kinds but particularly as they engaged hegemonic concepts of racism advocating Black pride and Black culture. As an organic intellectual, he thought through his beliefs and was able and willing to change his thinking about whites, religion, and violence as protest. His writings and thinking on race, speaking truth to power, self-defense, and education left a legacy. His was a mind engaged and focused. Whether Gramsci and Malcolm X would have been as engaged intellectuals had they not gone to prison we will never know. However, we do know that the prison experience was impactful in nurturing their intellectual activism.

CODA

There are literally thousands of developing organic intellectuals in prisons across this country—perhaps even larger in number than in our colleges. We could have exemplified numerous others besides Malcolm X and Gramsci—but in many ways they are representative of what can and often does happen through the prison experience; suffering and the cell however unjust or ill-conceived can be excellent teachers. The final thoughts presented in this chapter are not fully developed but point to a way forward.

First, support for the prison organic intellectual in the forms of better prison libraries; space for study, reading lights, full expansion of the PELL grant (a federal grant awarded to students for post-secondary education at colleges, universities, and career schools); and most important GED and college classes, are both cost effective and humane. Second, support for the returning citizen to go to college is common sense. This support can be presented in the form of free tuition, re-entry college collaborations, or scholarships. Finally, partnering with prisoners and returning citizens should be the task of the traditional intellectual—allies with organic intellectuals for ongoing prison change. It is the intellectual's role "to speak truth to power" but this cannot be done effectively regarding mass incarceration in America without the input, collaboration, thinking, and leadership of the many organic intellectuals in prison and returning to society.

REFERENCES

American Friends Service Committee, (1955). Speak Truth to Power: A Quaker Search for an Alternative to Violence. USA.

Bard Prison Initiative (2019). https://bpi.bard.edu

Black, Y.N.N (2017), Highly intoxicated off writing. In *Transformative thoughts: Writings from prison.* J. Schwartz, Ed. LaGuardia Community College & Queensboro Correctional Facility. Unpublished.

Bonhoeffer, D. (1978). *Prayers from Prison.* Philadelphia: Fortress Press.

Bonhoeffer, D. (1997). *Letters & Papers from prison.* New York: Touchstone.

Boyd, H. and Al-Shabazz, I. (2013). *The Diary of Malcolm X.* Chicago: Third World Press.

Bozick, R., Steele, J., Davis, L. and Turner, S. (2018). *Does Providing Inmates with Education Improve Postrelease Outcomes? A Meta-Analysis of Correctional Education Programs in the United States.* Arlington, Virginia: Rand Corporation.

Chaney, J. and Schwartz, J. (Eds.). (2017). *Race, education, and reintegrating formerly incarcerated citizens: Counterstories and Counterspaces.* Lanham, MD: Lexington Books.

Clark, K. (2016). Prisons for profit: Neoliberal rationality's transformation of American prisons. Senior Independent Study Thesis. The College of Wooster. https://openworks. wooster.edu/independentstudy/7242/?utm_source=openworks.wooster.edu%2Fin dependentstudy%2F7242&utm_medium=PDF&utm_campaign=PDFCoverPages.

Davis, L., Bozick, J., Steele, J., Saunders, J. and Miles, J. (2013). *Evaluation the effectiveness of correctional education: A meta-analysis of programs that provide education to incarcerated adults.* Santa Monica, CA: RAND Corporation. http:// www.rand.org/pubs/research_reports/RR266.html

Department of Justice Federal Bureau of Prisons. (2016). *Bureau of Prisons Education Program Assessment, Final Report.* https://www.justice.gov/archives/ dag/page/file/914026/download

Eaton, G. (February 5, 2018). *Why Antonio Gramsci is the Marxist thinker for our times.* New Statesman America.

Gramsci, A. (1971). *Selections from the Prison Notebooks.* New York: International Publishers.

Harvey, D. (2007). *A brief history of neoliberalism.* New York: Oxford University Press.

Janzen, J. (January 25, 2013). *Pondering the Physical Scriptorium.* Medieval fragments. https://medievalfragments.wordpress.com/2013/01/25/ pondring-the-physical-scriptorium/

Karpowitz, D. (2017). *College in prison: Reading in an age of mass incarceration.* New Brunswick, NJ: Rutgers University Press.

Madhubuti, H. R. (2013). *Foreword: Intellectual, Activist, and Statesman.* In H. Boyd & I. Al-Shabazz (Eds.), *The Diary of Malcolm X: El-Hajj Malik El-Shabazz.* Chicago: Third World Press.

Mayo, P. (1999). *Gramsci, Freire & adult education.* London: Zed Books.

Said, E. (1996). *Representations of the intellectual: The 1993 Reith Lectures.* New York: Vintage Books.

Thompson, H. (2016). *Blood in the water: The Attica prison uprising of 1971 and its legacy.* New York: Vintage Books.

X, Malcolm and Haley, A. (1992). *The Autobiography of Malcolm X.* New York: 1st Ballantine Books Ed.

Zimmerman, A.S. (2017). The role of organic intellectuals in the era of a Trump. Berkeley Review of Education Call for Conversations: Education in the Era of Trump.

Chapter 7

Higher & Continuing Education:
Attracting the Best Students

A plethora of research is available on the benefits of prison education, particularly post-secondary education. These benefits include, but are not limited to, reduction of recidivism, access to good paying jobs, ability to support families, and secure stable housing. Approximately 64%, of American prisoners are eligible to enroll in college because they have a GED or high school diploma (Oakford, Brumfield, Goldvale, Tatum, diZerega, and Patrick 2019). Unfortunately, access to post-secondary education while in prison, whether trade schools or college, is very limited (Oakford et al., 2019). Even with the most recent Second Chance Pell Experimental Sites Initiative, initiated by the U.S. Department of Education in 2015 to give need-based Pell grants to people in state and federal prisons through partnerships with 65 colleges in 27 states (Schwartz 2019; Second Chance Act of 2007); only 12,000 incarcerated persons can be served per year. Between 4% and 9% of currently incarcerated persons in various American prisons receive a college or trade school completion certificate (Oakford et al. 2019). While the benefits of post-secondary education in prisons are well documented, with most of the current prison population being eligible, the United States has not had the inclination to provide this remedy until recently. This situation began with the public policy mistake of banning the Pell Grant to eligible incarcerated citizens as part of the 1990s tough on crime policies.

THE MISTAKE OF BANNING THE PELL GRANT

The Pell Grant was and is (except for most prisoners) a primary funding source for low-income students to attend college who otherwise could not afford it. It has been highly successful in helping individuals and their families move into the middle class through educational advancement over the 40 years of its existence. It started as the Higher Education Act of 1965 as part of the War on Poverty proposed by President Lyndon Johnson and passed by Congress. In 1972 this act was revised with the guidance of Senator Claiborne Pell of Rhode Island and reauthorized. In 1978 it was amended again, reauthorized, and renamed the Pell Grant after the senator who had worked to provide access to higher education for the country's low-income students. At its inception, people who were incarcerated were eligible and college courses in prisons were somewhat common (College Scholarships.org).

In 1994, however, prison students were excluded from eligibility as part of President Clinton's 1994 federal tough on crime bill. With this exclusion of the Pell Grant, prison college courses were nearly eliminated with but a few exceptions. Not only were grants eliminated, but ten billion dollars of taxes were budgeted to fund the construction of more prisons with potential grant money (Karpowitz 2017). According to Karpowitz, one of the early developers of the Bard College Prison Initiative:

Pell grants made a huge impact inside American prisons. Higher education quickly became the most efficient, affordable, and effective "program" in American corrections, consistently associated with the lowest rates of recidivism—meaning people who went to college while incarcerated almost never came back to prison again. It was stunningly cheap: at their peak, in 1994, such programs nationally cost a total of one half of one percent of all Pell spending. (2017, 6)

Despite its proven success in terms of rehabilitation throughout its long history, the Pell Grant was prohibited to those needing it most—America's incarcerated. While there were many reasons why lawmakers objected to the grant going to people in prison, most of them were directly linked with taxpayer dollars going to those who committed crimes instead of to the general population's own sons and daughters. However, this ban "flew in the face" of the abundant research that continues to support that college in prison has many benefits including saving the taxpayers money (Oakford et al. 2019; Pettit 2019). Providing college tuition is less expensive than incarcerating someone because there is a high chance that someone returning from prison with a college degree will be an active community contributor and taxpayer (Protopsaltis and Parrott 2017). While changes and amendments to the federal Pell Grant program continue to this day, its purpose remains steadfast, ensuring that higher education remains accessible to all students (Protopsaltis and Parrott, 2017).

RESTORING THE PELL GRANT

Restoring the Pell Grant to the prison population should be common sense given the evidence of its benefits. Pell Grants can increase employment and earnings for the formerly incarcerated, provide employers with workers who have the skills they are seeking, and can reduce prison spending by an estimated $365.8 million across the US each year (Petitt 2019; Oakland et al., 2019).

When the Pell Grant was taken away during the Clinton administration, some of the college programs, such as the Bard Prison Initiative and Hudson Link (Mercy College), were privately funded for years before the Obama administration worked to reinstate the grant. Doris Buffet (sister of Warren Buffet, an American investor, business tycoon, and philanthropist) was a constant donor and believer in the effects that the Mercy College program produced, as she witnessed in attending their graduation ceremonies every year. Harry Belafonte, Jamaican-American singer, songwriter, activist, and actor is another supporter. With the removal of the Pell Grant, this alternative support came from private donors, foundations, and colleges (personal correspondence, Dario Pena, April 24, 2020).

Currently there are efforts in Congress to move toward grant restoration. One such effort is the Restoring Education and Learning Act (henceforth, REAL). REAL was introduced on April 9, 2019, by a bipartisan group of US senators including Brian Schatz (D-Hawaii), Mike Lee (R-Utah), and Dick Durban (D-Ill.). This act was supported by bipartisan representatives in the House as well as several hundred organizations as diverse as the Association of State Correctional Administrators, American Correctional Association, American Council on Education, and the Law Enforcement Action Partnership (Office of US. Senator Brian Schatz, 2019) (S. 1074–116th Congress, 2019–2020).

As mentioned previously, the Second Chance Pell Experimental Sites Initiative, often referred to as the Second Chance Pell Pilot Program for Incarcerated Individuals (SCP) began in 2015 and restored grants to select incarcerated students. By the fall of 2017, 4,900 prison students were enrolled in college programs. This was a small percentage of the eligible prison population but a promising start to reinstatement of the Pell (Bolden 2018). In December 2020 an encouraging legislative breakthrough occurred as part of a $23 billion COVID-19 relief package, that will restore Pell grant funding eligibility for more of our incarcerated men and women, including persons with drug-related convictions (Murakami 2020). After 26 years Congress lifted the prohibition of the Pell grant to state prisoners (Green 2020; Stratford 2020).

Chapter 7

ADULT BASIC EDUCATION (ABE) AND HIGH
SCHOOL ATTAINMENT PROGRAMS

Although the majority of people in prison are eligible for college, approximately 36% of the population still have less than a high school education attainment (Oakland et a.l, 2019), are in need of adult literacy, English for Speakers of Other Languages, and high school graduation or equivalency programs. Research indicates that these programs and classes are operational in correctional facilities throughout the US prison system, although their quality and the prisoners' abilities to avail themselves of these programs are uncertain, as only a small proportion of prisoners engage (Brazzell, Crayton, Mukamal, Solomon and Lindahl 2009; Cullen, Jonson and Eck 2012; May and Brown 2011). Evidence also suggests that the reach of some programs within prisons is limited and has not kept pace with mass incarceration (Patterson 2019). However murky the data, one thing is clear: there is low participation in these classes. According to Brazzell et al., (2009), only 2% of adults in state and federal prisons participate in Adult Basic Education (henceforth, ABE) classes. Greenberg, Dunleavy, and Kutner, (2008), found that on average 19% of incarcerated adults earned a High School Equivalency (HSE) certificate while in prison, and an additional 5% were enrolled in classes. This is consistent with data from the GED Testing Service.

In terms of participation in GED programs, the three providers of the US tests of General Education Development (GED, High School Equivalency Test (HiSET), and Test Assessing Secondary Completion (TASC), with the exception of the GED Testing Service, do not report publicly on recent correctional facility testing and pass rates (Patterson 2019). However, in 2011, the GED Testing Service did report that 75,000 incarcerated individuals took the GED test in 1,730 state, federal, and for-profit correctional facilities in 2010 (Patterson and Song, 2011). As of 2016, more than 48,000 incarcerated adults took GED tests in approximately 1,100 correctional facilities (Bledsoe 2017; Patterson 2019). Using the 2016 numbers, we know that, during that time, approximately 6% of those in prison needing high school took the exam for it.

While evidence continues to grow that engagement in correctional education at any level reduces recidivism (Patterson 2019), one must ask why there are low participation rates among prisoners in ABE and GED testing? According to Patterson (2019), there are many reasons. They include lack of interest, lack of funding, lack of awareness of programs among prisoners, not seeing connection to life on the outside, dependence on correctional staff for scheduling and support of participation, and dependence on volunteer teachers.

Although this issue is not the premise or focus of this book, the tepid promotion of educational programs in prison, for whatever reason, seems incon-
gruent with the mounting evidence of the value of those engagements for both
recidivism and quality of life in and after prison (Chaney and Schwartz 2017).
Perhaps more research and intervention is warranted in this area.

BEYOND RECIDIVISM: WHO MAKES
THE BEST COLLEGE STUDENT?

Daniel Karpowitz, a former director and teacher with the Bard College
Prison Initiative, one of the most successful and rigorous liberal arts college
programs in select American prisons, explores in his 2017 book, *College in
Prison: Reading in an Age of Mass Incarceration*, the arguments against providing college to prisoners. These arguments include, but are not limited to,
why should law-abiding, hard-working people pay for their children's education and someone who's committed a crime get it for free? Surely, those who
play by the rules should be rewarded, not those who do not. Prisons are a form
of punishment meant to prevent people from committing crimes again. One
wonders why college is offered to a few prisoners when colleges themselves
are steeped in institutionalized inequality and white privilege. Surely, it is too
little too late. He goes on to write that some critics of college in prison do
not object to drug counseling, job readiness, job training, moral reconation
therapy, and cognitive behavioral therapy but to a liberal arts education there
is objection (Karpowitz 2017, 14). A college education with its study of literature, philosophy, languages, and the arts appear to be designed for rich Whites
not prisoners who are disproportionally Black and ties into the racialization
of the criminal justice system.

These criticisms and objections are reflected in the "educational" components of the reform efforts of The First Step Act of 2018. This Act focuses
on individual transformation of prisoners rather than structural rehabilitation
of flawed prison systems. The emphasis is on therapeutic solutions rather
than full-scale education and employment rehabilitation. So how widespread
and institutional The First Step Act achievements become remains to be seen
(Clark and Ross 2019).

While Karpowitz recognizes the evidenced reduction of recidivism argument in favor of college in prison, he does not emphasize this because he
believes that a liberal arts education in and of itself can be transformative
and thereby the very foundation of a working democracy. For him, this is the
reason college in prison is so important (2017). The authors concur.

The main transformative change needed is the entire institution of the
prison and its role, presence, mission, and structural operations in the United

States. Nevertheless, as we continue to maintain throughout this book, individual transformation and transformative learning often occurs within a "rich" set of circumstances, disorienting dilemmas or life experiences and one of those can be prison. Beyond reduced recidivism is the transformative learning that is intrinsic to the prison experience, particularly the college or educational pursuits while there.

TWO DEGREES AND SHAKESPEARE

The authors met Dario Pena several months before his release; he had spent twenty-five years in prison for second degree murder. While serving his sentence he completed a Bachelor's Degree in Social and Behavioral Science from Mercy College in 2016, as well as a Master of Professional Studies from New York Theological Seminary in 2017. These degrees may eventually enable him to become employed as an adjunct professor at a local college. But perhaps even more impressive than his degrees are his artistic achievements as an actor and writer. While incarcerated Dario performed in a Sing Sing production of West Side Story (Hodara 2007) and in 2009 played Macbeth in a Big House—Sing Sing Prison production of Shakespeare's classic tragedy (Sabo and McShane 2009). The production was produced through Rehabilitation through the Arts (henceforth, RTA), a privately funded program and at that time, Macbeth was its 22nd production. RTA was founded by Katherine Vockins at Sing Sing Correctional Facility in Ossining, New York, in 1996. Today, it provides artistic classes and productions in the visual arts, theatre, dance, music, and writing in five men's and women's medium and maximum security prisons in New York. RTA is also the lead organization for a collaborative of global non-governmental organizations (NGOs) involved in the arts in prisons (RTA—https://www.rta-arts.org/about-us).

Theatre in prison has a long history and spans many countries with a variety of approaches (Balfour 2004). But what all these prison theatre programs have in common is the goal of addressing human basic needs of self-expression; emotional intelligence, identity development; rehabilitation, critical thinking; self-reflection; and transformative learning (Balfour, 2004; Heard, Mutch, Fitzgerald and Pensalfin 2013).

While prison theatre takes many formats, work with Shakespearean texts have shown promise, particularly internationally, in prisons showcasing a range of theatre projects. Shailor (2011) researched the Shakespeare Project at Racine Correctional Institution, a medium-security prison in Wisconsin in partnership with the University of Wisconsin-Parkside. The study found the project had significant impact for participants who utilized performance as a vehicle for transformation. According to Shailor (2010), the Shakespearean characters are like a mask that make it safe to express aspects of yourself that were otherwise too painful. While not therapy, it can be therapeutic. According to Lovascio (2020):

> The convicts' meeting with Shakespeare is a utopian flash of light, as Shakespeare becomes a privileged vehicle for the exploration as well as the expression of inner freedom in a very peculiar environment, in which every action is severely controlled. Specifically, the rehabilitative and regenerating function of theater seems simultaneously to carry disturbing retributive overtones, since this reawakening contact with art leads some of the inmates fully to realize the extent of what they have lost. (http://www.borrowers.uga.edu/784103/show)

Dario, in playing Macbeth at Sing Sing, described the connection between his character and himself this way, "The character just jumped out at me; I could identify" (Sabo and McShane 2009). This kind of identification and therapeutic reflection through the arts is as valid as programs of cognitive behavioral therapy and moral reconation work. This kind of work includes the lowering of recidivism but reflects transformative learning far beyond simple numbers and statistics.

While completing his final months in prison, Dario was a part of the authors' prison writing group and at that time reviewed and critiqued some of the chapters in this book. His helpful feedback, deep thinking, acute listening, and keen insights were indicative of the transformation he had undergone; a transformation he attested to through his writing and conversations (D. Pena, personal correspondence, March 28, 2020). Since completing his degrees, Dario is now investigating college adjunct teaching positions in philosophy.

OBSTACLES TO COLLEGE ADMISSION
AFTER INCARCERATION

For formerly incarcerated citizens who choose to attend college there are unique obstacles. Colleges generally want to attract the best students. That is the job of admissions administrators: deciphering who will best succeed and graduate, resulting in research and accomplishments that will then reflect favorably on the university. Additionally, there is an attempt to "weed out" those students who will not succeed, who will reflect badly on the university, and who they perceive might possibly harm its community. When "weeding out" such prospective students, formerly incarcerated citizens are at a disadvantage, particularly Black applicants with a felony record. This is true for all universities but especially for Ivy League and elite colleges (Stewart and Uggen 2020). Recent research confirms that a felony record does not completely disqualify a person's college access, but it can be a serious barrier (Stewart and Uggen 2020). Stewart and Uggen conducted a recent modified experimental national audit to learn whether and to what extent criminal records affect admissions decisions. A portion of the findings are included here:

> Nearly 72 percent of colleges require criminal history information during their application processes, which indicates that an applicant's criminal history could be a significant impediment to achieving the benefits associated with higher education. . . .... Thus, the benefits of higher education may not accrue for students with criminal records. . . .The increasing scrutiny of criminal records in college admissions is especially consequential for groups most subject to the criminal justice system, particularly young Black males. (2020, 1–2)

These findings are troubling to say the least but not insurmountable. The same researchers suggest that universities reexamine college admissions policies and procedures and their impact for reentry and racial progress, as well as the underrepresentation of students of color on college campuses. These findings also have impact on the college "Ban the Box" movement, (a collective effort to prohibit colleges from asking about a person's criminal history on a university application) and its implementation nationwide (Stewart and Uggen 2020).

THE BEST SCHOLARS

These admissions obstacles for returning citizens unfortunately fly in the face of a vital premise of this book, that the prison experience can be transformative and a unique forum to create scholars. Previous chapters highlight the habits and experiences that make organic intellectuals. Among these are silence and solitude, intensive reading and writing, the mind/body connection, engagement with the arts, critical thinking, flow, and emotional intelligence. These experiences and disciplined outcomes are the very attributes needed to be a successful student in higher education. They also signal what psychologist and researcher, Carol Dweck, calls the growth mindset.

For decades at Stanford University, Dweck and her colleagues have looked at the mindset that make successful college students. They determined that a growth mindset as opposed to a fixed mindset makes the difference. People with a growth mindset believe that their talents and intellect can be developed through hard work, strategic planning, and feedback from others. This view creates a love of learning and a resilience that can overcome obstacles and setbacks (Dweck 2016). This growth mindset sounds very much like transformative learning through the incarceration experience.

It may seem incongruous but some returning citizens may be among the best equipped individuals for college classrooms. They may be the most able bodied to tackle deep work, critical thinking, empathic comprehension, and make strong cohort bonds needed for graduate work and research in academia. Not all returning citizens, surely, but maybe more than a few.

In closing, rather than viewing the incarceration experience as a failure, deficit, potential danger; the experience, as we have already demonstrated, can and does prepare select individuals to be disciplined, deep, critical readers and writers with an often strong inclination toward empathy and community. Among the best applicants for college may very well be the returning citizen who has chosen transformation and possesses a growth mindset. Any university classroom might well benefit from these scholars' insight, learning, study habits, resilience, and presence.

REFERENCES

Balfour, M. (Ed.) (2004). *Theatre in Prison: Theory and Practice.*Intellect Books, Bristol.

Bledsoe, J. (March 2017). Corrections testing update. Retrieved from https://gedtestingservice.com/in-session/Corrections-testingupdate_Mar17/#more-1495

Bolden, A. (June 2018). Second Chance Pell Experimental Sites Initiative Update. Vera Institute of Justice Update. https://www.vera.org/publications/second-chance-pell-experimental-sites-initiative-update

Brazzell, D., Crayton, A., Mukamal, D., Solomon, A., and Lindahl, N. (2009). *From the classroom to the community: Exploring the role of education during incarceration and re-entry.* Washington, DC: The Urban Institute.

Chaney, J. R. and Schwartz, J. (2017). *Race, Education & Reintegrating Formerly Incarcerated Citizens: Counterstories & Counterspaces.* Lanham, MD: Lexington Press.

Clark, D. and Ross, J. (November 24, 2019). The First Step Act promised widespread reform. What has the criminal justice overhaul achieved so far? MSNBC News https://www.nbcnews.com/politics/politics-news/first-step-act-promised-widespread-reform-what-has-criminal-justice-n1079771

College Scholarship.org http://www.collegescholarships.org/grants/pell.htm

Cullen, F. T, Jonson, C. L., & Eck, J. E. (2012). The accountable prison. *Journal of Contemporary Criminal Justice*, 28(1), 77–95.

Dweck, C. (2016). *Mindset: The new psychology of success.* New York: Random House.

Green, E. L. (December 21, 2020). Financial aid is restored for prisoners as part of the stimulus bill. *New York Times*.

Greenberg, E., Dunleavy, E., & Kutner, M. (2008). Literacy behind bars: Results from the 2003 National Assessment of Adult Literacy Prison Survey Chapter 4: Education and job training in prison. *The Journal for Vocational Special Needs Education*, 30(2), 27–34.

Heard, E., Mutch, A., Fitzgerald, L. & Pensalfin, R. (2013). Shakespeare in Prison: affecting health and wellbeing. *International Journal of Prisoner Health*. Vol. 9: No.3.

Hodara, S. (2007, May), For Inmates, a Stage Paved With Hope. The New York Times.

Karpowitz, D. (2017). College in Prison: Reading in an Age of Mass Incarceration. New Brunswick, NJ: Rutgers University Press.

Lovascio, D. (2020). "Da quando ho conosciuto l'arte, 'sta cella è diventata 'na prigione": Cesare deve morire and the unsettling self-(re-)fashioning power of theater. Borrowers and Lenders: The Journal of Shakespeare and Appropriation. http://www.borrowers.uga.edu/784103/show

May, D. C., & Brown, T. (2011). Examining the effect of correctional programming on perceptions of likelihood of recidivism among incarcerated prisoners. *Journal of Social Service Research*, 37, 353–364.

Murakami, K. (December 22, 2020). Congressional Deal Would Give Higher Ed $23B, Inside Higher Education Congressional Deal Would Give Higher Ed $23B [insidehighered.us2.list-manage.com]

Oakford, P., Brumfield, C., Goldvale, C., Tatum, L., diZerega, M. and Patrick, F. (2019). Investing in futures: Economic and fiscal benefits of postsecondary education in prison. New York: Vera Institute of Justice.

Patterson, M. (2019). Incarcerated adults with low skills: Findings from the 2014 PIAAC prison study. COABE Journal: The Resource for Adult Education. Special Edition Prison Literacy. Pgs. 14–24.

Patterson, M. B., and Song, W. (2011). GED testing in correctional centers. Washington, DC: American Council on Education. Retrieved from https://www.researchgate.net/publication/321635403_GED_R_Testing_in_Correctional_Centers

Pena, D. (2020). Nostalgia. Unpublished.

Pettit, E. (2019). Ending ban on Pell Grants for prisoners is said to yield cascade of benefits. The Chronicles of Higher Education. https://www.chronicle.com/article/Ending-Ban-on-Pell-Grants-for/245481

Protopsaltis, S., and Parrott, S. (2017). Pell Grants—a key tool for expanding college access and economic opportunity—need strengthening, not cuts. Center for Budget & Policy Priorities. Washington, DC.

REAL Act. Senate Bill 1074. (2019) .https://www.congress.gov/bill/116th-congress/senate-bill/1074?q=%7B%22search%22%3A%5B%22S.+1074%22%5D%7D&s=1&r=1

Sabo, R. and McShane, L. (May 26, 2009). Shakespeare comes to Sing-Sing prison for all inmate version of MacBeth. *Daily News*: New York.

Schwartz, N. (May 21, 2019). Ed Dept expands Second Chance Pell Grant program for people in prison. Education Dive. https://www.educationdive.com/news/ed-dept-expands-second-chance-pell-grant-program-for-people-in-prison/555220/

Second Chance Act of 2007: Community Safety Through Recidivism Prevention, 110 Congress of the United States. Pub. L. 110–199.

Shailor, J. (2011). Humanizing Education Behind Bars: The Theatre of Empowerment and The Shakespeare Project. In S. Hartnett (Ed.), *Challenging the Prison-Industrial Complex: Activism, Arts, & Educational Alternatives*. Chicago: University of Illinois Press. pp. 229–251.

Shailor, J. (2010). Prison Theatre and the Promise of Reintegration. In Shailor, J. (Ed.), *Performing New Lives: Prison Theatre*. London: Jessica Kingsley Publishers. pp. 180–196.

Stewart, R. and Uggen, C. (2020). Criminal records and college admissions: A modified experimental audit. *Criminology*. 58:1 Pages 156–188.

Stratford, M. (December 20, 2020). Congress clinches deal to restore Pell grants for prisoners 26 years after ban. Politco.com.

Chapter 8

Exercising Body and Mind: Habits and Flow

Much of this book thus far focuses on the development of the mind and emotions through the prison experience—fasting, prayer, quiet, solitude, reading, writing, meditation, study, and deep mental work. This chapter shifts its focus to the body and its connection to the mind, as well as the choices some prisoners make to transform their bodies while incarcerated. The body-mind connection explores the complex interplay between the physical, mental, and emotional, and their interactive influence. In this chapter, a brief history of research around the mind-body connection is presented before revisiting the prison experience by examining the stories of three recently released long-term prisoners. One gentleman now makes a living on his prison transformation; the others reflect on the role of exercise and body building in prison and upon returning home. The chapter concludes with how the theories of habits of mind and flow present themselves in the prison experience.

THE BODY-MIND CONNECTION

For centuries and before modern science, philosophers and physicians alike recognized how the mind influenced the functioning of the body and vice versa. From Greek and Roman antiquity, the history of medicine documents the close relationship between emotions, the body, and disease (National Library of Medicine 2020). Hippocrates (ca. 460 B.C.–ca. 370 B.C), who medical professionals consider the Father of Modern Medicine and from whom the Hippocratic Oath is based, professionalized and secularized the field of medicine and believed in the strong connection between physical, emotional, mental, and spiritual health (Online Liberty Library 2020). Plato, who was an athlete as well as philosopher, urged temperance in exercise but stressed the importance of it for developing the mind. Throughout his writing, he promoted a balance between the mind, body, and psyche and stated this balance should be an ideal to strive for (Plato 1943).

During the European Renaissance (1350–1550) Paracelsus (1493–1541), a Swiss medical doctor, alchemist and philosopher, promoted a holistic approach to treating disease, not merely treating the infected part of the body but the whole being. He stated, "A man who is angry is not only angry in his head or in his fist, but all over . . . all the organs of the body, and the body itself, are only form-manifestations of previously and universally existing mental states" (WRF, Retrieved March 26, 2020). This type of thought continued the perception that the mind and body cannot be separated.

In the 17th century, Western thought made a turn from the integrated view of the mind and body to reconceptualizing them as separate and distinct. Rene Descartes claimed that "there is a great difference between mind and body, inasmuch as body is by nature always divisible, and the mind is entirely indivisible . . . the mind or soul of man is entirely different from the body" (Descartes, (1974), VII 86–87: CSM II 59). In later centuries, the notion of the disembodied mind flourished. From it, western thought developed two basic ideas: reason is disembodied because the mind is disembodied and reason is transcendent and universal (Descartes 1991).

In more modern times this dualism would be questioned. Sigmund Freud was one of the early psychodynamic researchers whose theories took the body into account when initially studying the link between physical and psychological dimensions of hysteria (Barth 2014; Smith 1999). In 1937 based in part on the work of Freud, Joseph Pilates an inventor, physical fitness trainer, and founder of Pilates in New York City, published his book, *Your Health*, where he wrote about achieving a balance of mind and body and the natural development of a connection between the two (Pilates and Robbins 2011). Originally from Germany, Pilates was a sickly child. This experience led him to develop training methods based on physical workouts and body healing. In 1945 Pilates wrote *Return to Life* where he analyzed the stresses of modern life. Pilates was ahead of his time in thinking, writing, and experimenting with the mind-body connection, wellness, the benefits of mind-body exercise, and functional exercise (Pilates 1945).

Into the 20th century, researchers studied the mind-body connection and scientifically demonstrated complex links between the two. With the advance of neuroscience in the 1960s initially out of Harvard, Massachusetts Institute of Technology (MIT), and Stanford scientists studied the cellular, functional, behavioral, and medical aspects of the nervous system and brain activity. The study of the brain crosses multiple fields, such as mathematics, linguistics, engineering, computer science, chemistry, philosophy, psychology, and medicine and led to extensive empirical evidence confirming the body-mind connection (Markic 2013). Today this interdisciplinary body of work is most often referred to as cognitive science with neuroscientists focusing on the biological aspects of the brain. On the other hand, psychologists, anthropologists, and philosophers examine learning, decision-making, and perception in behavioral and human evolutionary contexts while computer scientists simulate and model the functions of the brain. These are variant fields of focus but are overlapping and interdependent (Markic 2013).

In the early years of neuroscience and before cognitive science development, scientists, although not dualists like Descartes, still did not think that the body influenced the brain and thinking in any major way. However, in the 1980s and 90s, through the works of Varela (Varela, Thompson, and Rosch 1991), a biologist, philosopher, and neuroscientist; and Lakoff (2012), a linguist and other interdisciplinary scholars, the theory of embodied cognition or the embodiment of cognition took hold. Varela clarifies embodied cognition this way:

> By using the term embodied we mean to highlight two points: first that cognition depends upon the kinds of experience that come from having a body with various sensorimotor capacities, and second, that these individual sensorimotor capacities are themselves embedded in a more encompassing biological, psychological and cultural context. (Varela, Thompson and Rosch 1991, 172–173)

This means that thinking and learning are dependent and connected deeply to our physical bodies and its functioning. Therefore, a person's physical body plays an integral role in one's cognitive processing (Wilson and Foglia 2017) and is relevant to transformative learning.

EMBODIED COGNITION, EXERCISE, AND THE PRISONER

This body-mind connection is well established from neurological research and cognitive science, and the use of exercise as an intervention to improve health of both the mind and body is well documented. However, this kind of research in the context of prisoners and prisons is less robust. Nevertheless, the research that does exist is consistent with that of free populations. A summary of that literature is highlighted below.

Busby and Kremer (1994) examined the relationship between exercise and mood state in a study of thirty-six high-security inmates, aged 35–55 years, in Northern Ireland. Daigle, Leger, Lamoureux, Mercier, Gauvin (2003) studied the effect of a structured exercise regime on the mental health of thirty-eight inmates within a psychiatric prison setting in Canada. Ozano (2008) investigated the role of physical education, sport, and exercise in a female prison, and Cashin, Potter, and Butler (2008) looked at hopelessness among prisoners in prisons and the effects of exercise on diminishing it.

A 2015 study conducted in an Italian prison tested the effect of physical exercise on the psychological well-being of prisoners. It also looked at which mental disorders were most impacted positively by physical activity (Battaglia, Di Cagno, Fiorilli, Giombini, Borrione, Baralla, Marchetti, and Pigozzi 2015). In an Ireland prison, O'Toole, Maguire and Murphy, (2018) explored whether an exercise referral program was effective in health promotion for male prisoners with mental health symptoms. The researchers reported significantly positive results for these programs contributing to new knowledge regarding Irish male prisoners' mental health and embodied cognition. A study of children under the age of 18 incarcerated in England and Wales concluded that sports and physical exercise can confer significant psychosocial benefits toward post-release rehabilitation and reintegration when coupled with other psychosocial and social support and provisions (Parker, Meek, and Lewis 2014).

As stated previously, the research on this connection is insufficient but encouraging. There is need for a better understanding of embodied cognition, the mind-body connection, and physical exercise or activity in prison and upon release through continued scholarship. However, from the literature that does exist, the findings seem clear: there is psychological benefit in terms of prisons mental and emotional well-being when the mind body connection is supported through exercise regimens and programs for all age populations. The following narratives exemplify this phenomenon in personal terms especially looking at re-entry.

CONBODY

Coss Marte was sent to prison in 2009 for running a network of cocaine dealers. Today he is a successful entrepreneur and CEO of CONBODY, a prison-style fitness boot camp that hires formerly incarcerated individuals to teach fitness classes.

Marte grew up on the Lower East Side of New York City during the 1980s and began selling drugs at age thirteen. By the age of nineteen he had twenty employees working for him, and he was making 2 million dollars a year selling crack and cocaine. At age twenty-three, he was busted by the FBI, and Marte was sent to prison. In prison, health officials told him that he would probably die while in prison as he was overweight and had extremely high blood pressure and cholesterol levels. This was Marte's disorienting dilemma plummeting him into major transformative learning for both his body and mind. It was in prison that he decided to do something about his health and proceeded to put himself on an exercise regimen through which he would lose seventy pounds in six months. By simply using the walls and floors, no expensive machines or equipment was needed to see results. Marte's cramped cell had no elbow room, so he worked his triceps with dips (exercises that use the arms to lift the body up and down), hands on his bed and feet on the toilet. Marte began running twenty laps around the prison yard daily then included other forms of exercise like pushups, sit ups, kicks, squats, and shoulder presses using only his body weight.

As he lost the weight and toned his body, he thought of the benefits for other prisoners. He then organized a prison yard boot camp conducting these intense military-like exercise drills with other prisoners. Even in solitary confinement, he maintained his exercise routine using the cramped space, cot, wall and toilet to brace his exercises. Marte then developed unique paired exercises which compensated for the lack of gym and weight equipment, training other prisoners in the routine.

Once released, after failed attempts at securing employment, Marte received start up business support from a non-profit organization and started CONBODY, a prison-style group fitness program modeled after his prison experience. It is a no frills, no equipment, rigorous workout program designed specifically for young professionals. It is located on the Lower East Side of New York, the exact location where he used to sell drugs (https://conbody. com/). CONBODY founded in 2014 now has a second "cell" on Fifth Avenue in Manhattan. Marte wrote a workout book that tells his story and the story of the organization (Marte 2020). The program locations replicate a correctional facility as you enter through a steel cell-style door and workout in dim lit and dark prison-like cells, the very kind of place where Marte transformed both his mind and his body. But the most significant part of the program is that all classes are taught by the formerly incarcerated. In fact, no one is hired unless they have been to prison. The hour-long unglamorous and no-nonsense prison workout taught by formerly incarcerated teachers attracts many clients and a great deal of press attention.

According to Marte, the real mission of CONBODY is prison reform and transforming how people perceive the formerly incarcerated while bridging a gap between the new gentrifying community, young professionals, and formerly incarcerated individuals. Marte understands his market. By hiring former prisoners as trainers and refusing to put locks on lockers because trust of everyone is paramount at CONBODY especially trust for returning citizens, Marte is giving back to other returning citizens and his community in new ways, while also challenging stereotypes. He is a frequently sought-after featured public speaker on Ted Talks and regularly asked to talk about both CONBODY and his own mind/body transformation through the prison experience at colleges, community centers, and public health forums.

HABITS OF BODY AND MIND

Marvin Wade was released from prison in late 2019 after serving twenty-five years and is now successfully negotiating his return to family and society. The authors met him in their prison writing class. Aside from being a prolific short story author while locked up, he also maintained a regular and rigorous work-out schedule during his twenty-five years and came back with a well-toned and healthy body. In speaking with Wade, he explained that before going to prison he had always taken care of his body and that while he was in prison he continued to work out as well as eat the best he could despite the prison meals being high in carbohydrates and lacking in fresh fruits and vegetables. He relied on his family bringing good food and sharing with other prisoners food they could prepare from the outside to stay healthy and maintain a regular exercise regimen. The key was to make sure they were getting enough protein, a challenge in prison.

While healthy nutrition was an ongoing challenge, the structure of his days supported his meditation and writing as well as his physical workout. Wade explained that he was not alone in this endeavor but that numerous prisoners chose to build their bodies and that the structure of the prison days often leant themselves to such development. In Marvin's own words:

> In prison most of our movement is controlled by outside forces. Exercising is one of the only activities that gives one a sense of control and power of self as well as discipline. I always believed exercising contributes to better mental health. Exercising gives structure, a positive structure within, which helps immensely in dealing with the chaotic structure behind the wall (M. Wade, personal communication, March 8, 2020).

He also reported that some prisoners built their bodies to protect and defend themselves while inside, but others chose for health and personal reasons to care for themselves.

Wade has a good family support system, but has also developed, through his life and years in prison, a sound and balanced connection between the body and the mind. Indeed, he appears to have acquired effective habits of mind. Costa and Kallick (2000) have written extensively about sixteen habits of mind often present with transformative learning whether it is physical or cognitive. These habits are: persistence, communicating with clarity and precision, managing impulsivity, gathering data through all senses, listening with understanding and empathy, creating, flexible thinking, responding with wonder, metacognition, taking responsible risks, striving for accuracy, finding humor, questioning, thinking interdependently, applying past knowledge to new situations, and openness to learning (Costa and Kallick 2000). When choosing to transform one's body in prison, that decision requires a certain amount of persistence, managing impulsivity, imaginative approaches, humor, interdependency, and an openness to learn. And from what we know of embedded cognition, the actual biological benefits of prison exercise benefit the way people feel, interact, take risks, question, gather information, and apply knowledge. Wade has integrated these habits and appears centered in his relationships and interactions with others. He is testament to this phenomenon in part due to his prison experience. He is not alone; other returning citizens come home with well-disciplined bodies and minds ready to contribute to their communities as well.

Habits of mind are patterns of intellectual behaviors demonstrated consistently over time leading to effective action, decision-making, or resolution of conflict. It is a disposition toward behaving intelligently when faced with a disorienting dilemma. As stated earlier in this book, prison is a disorienting dilemma and in response some prisoners attend to their bodies through disciplined and persistent exercise and attention to healthy eating within the confines and severe limitations of prison.

Sylvester "Sonny" Jackson is another case in point. He was released from prison in 2019 after several stays. He is a senior citizen with stage 4 cancer, currently in remission but still receiving chemotherapy. During his last period of incarceration he entered prison with this diagnosis. The relationship between his body and mind was integral to his survival. Sonny managed to eat as healthy as possible through the kindness of other prisoners who would share outside food with him to supplement the inadequate prison meal offerings. Paying attention to his body, attending to sleep, advocating for medical treatment, writing his poetry, and keeping connections to loved ones was an ongoing battle.

Sonny continues to face this physical crisis with the habits of both humor and a sense of awe and wonder. Each day since his release, he wakes early (often because of pain) makes himself a cup of coffee, sits with Bentley—his cat, writes poetry, and watches the sun rise. He has learned to live well in the present moment. Now free, he is even more acutely aware of the need for a healthy mind-body connection.

During the 2020 Coronavirus pandemic which required quarantine and mandatory confinement in New York City, Sonny stated that he knew how to live through the solitary living and social distancing because he had learned effective habits of mind in prison that could be applied to the new crisis (S. Jackson, personal communication, March 27, 2020).

FLOW IN PRISON—IS HAPPINESS POSSIBLE?

A previous chapter examined the concept of "deep work" within the prison setting. A related concept is flow theory developed by American-Hungarian psychologist Dr. Mihaly Csikszentmihalyi who is considered the founder of positive psychology. Csikszentmihalyi first became interested in what is now famously identified as flow theory and its relationship to happiness during World War II in Europe. He observed how some people who in the very worst and horrific of situations of war were able to maintain joy. He wondered what made select individuals able to enjoy life regardless of external circumstances and what habits cultivated and maintained their integrity and joy under demise (2008).

After extensive research mainly with athletes and artists, Csikszentmihalyi identified states of body and mind when humans feel most alive, fully engaged in an activity, and acting under their own internal control despite circumstances. He found it happened most often in intense sports and bodily engagement like dance or singing, but also during concentrated reading, conversation, or writing. During flow a person forgets time, lives in the present, fully concentrates, is completely engaged, not worried about failure, is focused on restricted stimuli but finds pleasure just in the activity itself—autotelic. It is a state where the body and mind are fully engaged and connected, and where an individual can express who they are through what they do and are in harmony with their environment. Flow is also associated with high degrees of happiness in everyday life for most populations (Csikszentmihalyi 1990).

However, little research on flow theory and the prison experience has been done. This begs the question: is flow possible in prison? Csikszentmihalyi would probably say "certainly so." The authors believe that they have seen flow present in their prison writing groups and through anecdotal reports of the formerly incarcerated. And the authors hypothesize that flow in the prison experience is operative with select prisoners who have cultivated habits of mind through exercise and working out as well as intensive writing and reading. Additionally, as exemplified in Chapter 1 of this book, prison literature alludes to flow and even to the possibility of happiness during the flow experience in prison throughout history. More immediately, Marvin, Sonny, and the authors can attest to this possibility. In this regard, Marvin expressed the following reflection: "The flow theory was also interesting to me. Exercising, eating healthy, writing and meditating gave me peace, joy and happiness. You can find all these things behind the wall amid the chaos" (M. Wade, personal communication, March 30, 2020).

More formal research in this area is certainly needed. Even so, despite structured discipline and repression which characterizes the prison environment, select individuals choose to enter the flow experience often through bodily exercise and regain internal control of their lives creating the possibility of a measure of happiness despite the repressive external environment that is prison. If this is true and every indication is that it is, then returning citizens have much to teach the general population. Once out of prison, these prison habits can be transferred to freedom and become paradigm shifts during reintegration into society. One advantage that individuals who have experienced incarceration have is that they learned (often imposed) structure. They learned how to enter flow and maintain some measure of happiness. The lessons of flow learned in prison can be revamped and used in freedom. We have caught encouraging glimpses of this phenomena in Marte, Wade, Sonny, and other returning citizens as it relates to the body-mind connection.

REFERENCES

Barth, F. D. (2014). The Body-Mind Connection. In *Integrative Clinical Social Work Practice*. Essential Clinical Social Work Series. Springer: New York, NY.

Battaglia, C., Di Cagno, A., Fiorilli, G., Giombini, A., Borrione, P., Barralla, F. Marchetti, and Pigozzi, F. (2015). Participation in a 9-month selected physical exercise programme enhances psychological well-being in a prison population. *Criminal Behavior and Mental Health* 25: 343–354.

Busby, G. and Kremer, J. (1994). Physical exercise and mood state in a long-term prison population. British Psychological Society's Annual Conference, Institute of Education, London.

Cashin A., Potter E., and Butler T. (2008). The relationship between exercise and hopelessness in prison. *Journal of Psychiatric and Mental Health Nursing* 15, 66–71

Costa, A. & Kallick, B. (2000). Habits of Mind: A Developmental Series. Association for Supervision and Curriculum Development: Alexandria, VA.

Csikszentmihalyi, M. (2008). *Flow: The Psychology of Optimal Experience*. Harper & Row: New York.

Csikszentmihalyi, M. (1990). Flow: The psychology of optimal experience. *Journal of Leisure Research*, 24(1), pp. 93–94.

Daigle C., Leger L., Lamoureux D., Mercier, D., Gauvin, L. (2003). Physical Exercise and Mental Health in a Psychiatric Prison Setting. Available at http://www.csc-scc. gc.ca/text/rsrch/regional/ summary9820e_e.shtml

Descartes, R. (1974–1989). *Ouevres de Descartes*, 11 vols., eds. Charles Adam and Paul Tannery, Paris: Vrin.,

Descartes, R. (1991). *The Philosophical Writings of Descartes*, Vol. 3: Correspondence, trans. By John G. Cottingham, Robert Stoothof, Dugald Murdoch, and Anthony Kenny. Cambridge: Cambridge University Press.

Lakoff, G. (2012). Explaining Embodied Cognition Results. *Topics in Cognitive Science*. Vol. 4:4. Pg. 773–785.

Markic, O. (2013). The Philosophical Framework for Understanding Neuroscientific Research. *Interdisciplinary Description of Complex Systems*. 11(4): 351–362.

Marte, C. (2020). *CONBODY: The Revolutionary Bodyweight Prison Boot Camp, Born from an Extraordinary Story of Hope*. New York: St. Martin's Griffin.

National Library of Medicine (NLM). (retrieved, March 26, 2020). History of Medicine Division (HMD), Emotions and Diseases in Historical Perspective https://www.nlm.nih.gov/hmd/index.html

Online Liberty Library, (2020). Hippocrates. https://oll.libertyfund.org/pages/hippocrates-c-460-377-bc

O'Toole, S., Maguire, J. and Murphy, P. (2018). "The efficacy of exercise referral as an intervention for Irish male prisoners presenting with mental health symptoms," *International Journal of Prisoner Health*, Vol. 14 No. 2, pp. 109–123. https://doi.org/10.1108/IJPH-12-2016-0073

Ozano, K. (2008). The role of physical education, sport and exercise in a female prison Thesis: University of Chester   http://hdl.handle.net/10034/84838

Parker, A., Meek, R. and Lewis, G. (2014). Sport in a youth prison: Male young offenders' experiences of a sporting intervention. *Journal of Youth Studies*, 17:3, 381–396, DOI: 10.1080/13676261.2013.830699

Plato. (1943). *Plato's The Republic*. New York: Books, Inc.

Pilates, J. (1945). *Return to Life Through Contrology*. Miami, FL: Pilates Method Alliance, Inc.

Pilates, J. and Robbins, J. (2011). Your Health. Presentation Dynamics https://presentationdynamics.net

Smith D.L. (1999). Freud and the Mind-Body Problem. In *Freud's Philosophy of the Unconscious*. Studies in Cognitive Systems, vol. 23. Springer, Dordrecht.

Varela, F., Thompson, E. and Rosch, E. (1991). *The Embodied Mind: Cognitive Science and Human Experience*. Cambridge, MA: MIT Press.

Wilson, R.A. and Foglia, L. (2017). "Embodied Cognition," *The Stanford Encyclopedia of Philosophy,* Edward N. Zalta (ed.). https://plato.stanford.edu/archives/spr2017/entries/embodied-cognition/.

WRF. (2020). Paracelsus, Physician and Philosopher. https://www.wrf.org/men-women-medicine/paracelsus-physician-philosopher.php

Chapter 9

Emotional Intelligence and the Prison Experience

Susan Rosenberg was a United States political prisoner for sixteen years, spending time in some of the country's toughest maximum-security prisons. During those sixteen years, she fought for her sanity and emotional stability. She wrote:

> Daily life was a kind of nothingness alternating with verbal abuse. There was absolutely nowhere to go; it felt like death. All that lay in front of me were the ruins of my life. I was losing everything—dreams, visions, and hopes, my routine and my family, and even my favorite color, favorite food, and favorite season. I began to understand that the very small things, the details that are different for every individual, that make up the identity of each person, but that I had paid little attention to on the outside, get stripped away in prison until the days seem like hours and years like days (Rosenberg 2011, 62).

In the 1970s Rosenberg was involved in radical activism in feminist causes. She was imprisoned in 1984 as a young adult for non-violent crimes in her personal and collective struggle against racism, sexism, and military involvements around the world. In 1971, Attica prisoners protested prisoner abuse and prison corruption. The New York Attica prison uprising of 1971 is a tragic study of the historical corruption and violence in our incarceration system, the rewriting of history, the lengths government will go to protect its own, and the nature of cover-ups. Both Rosenberg and what would come to be known as the Attica Brothers are the study of adult transformative learning, emotional trauma, and the fight by the most marginalized of individuals to be treated as human beings.

ROSENBERG AND THE ATTICA UPRISING

Both Rosenberg on an individual level and the Attica Brothers on a collective level give voice to the impact of emotional trauma as a result of time in prison. They speak to the sometimes gift of emotional intelligence as a result of the carceral experience. Rosenberg was active in many radical movements including the Puerto Rican Independence Movement, the Black Liberation Army, the Weather Underground, and protests against the FBI's COINTELPRO program of the 1960s and 1970s. She was given a 58-year sentence until President Clinton commuted her sentence in 2001. She was accused but never convicted of aiding Assata Shakur's prison escape and driving a getaway car in the 1981 Brinks robbery in which two police officers and one security guard were killed (Rosenberg 2011).

During the sixteen years of her imprisonment, she was held in various facilities. At Lexington Federal Correctional Institution, one of the locations where she was held, she was one of the first two prisoners to be placed in a High Security Unit (henceforth, HSU), a subterrain basement with no windows, natural light, or exercise facilities, no phone calls, few books, no visitors, and constant video surveillance. She felt buried alive. Designed for complete sensory deprivation, the walls were painted white so that it affected eyesight, and often the ability to read. Besides the 24-hour video surveillance there were daily strip searches, which sometimes included sexual violation by guards. Guards woke prisoners up every hour or half hour in order to induce sleep deprivation. All her actions and reactions were recorded and monitored as a type of psychiatric experiment. This inhumane treatment was a human rights violation and a form of international torture in an American prison (Rosenblum 1989). The purpose of HSU was control of high profile prisoners deemed a threat to society but in actuality it created emotional trauma, grief, pain, damage, hopelessness, and depression so that Rosenberg and other female political prisoners would renounce their political beliefs. Rosenberg speaks of the emotional trauma and her overcoming and eventual transformation to a life of work, family, and activism.

> To survive it, to hold fast, to keep a part of one's self free from that process of disintegration takes an enormous effort. But people do it. I did it; I resisted one moment at a time. All my life I had responded to injustice by asking how do I live with this and how can I do something about it . . . Now I am consumed by the business of living. I am for the most part intact. I have a new life, including a family and work that has value. (2011, 367)

As Rosenberg's emotional trauma, resistance, and eventual emotional healing captures one woman's internal struggle; the Attica prison uprising of 1971 is a case study in *collective* resistance and emotional trauma in response to injustice. The catalysts for the uprising were the prisoners' recognition of their own basic emotional and physical needs and how these human needs were being abused, neglected, and unmet in the early 1970s Attica was extremely overcrowded and deplorable living conditions. The Auburn prison protests, an uprising that preceded Attica's were, for the most part, non-violent protests to prison environments that were emotionally unsafe.

> Every month, prisoners would receive one bar of soap and one roll of toilet paper, which meant that men were forced to limit themselves "to one sheet per day." The state's food budget was insufficient to meet the minimum dietary standards as determined by federal guidelines. The reality was that many men at Attica went to bed hungry... being able to buy deodorant was no luxury since these men were allowed only one shower a week and were given only two quarts of water a day. With this water prisoners were expected to wash their socks and underwear, shave, brush their teeth, and clean the cell to a correction officer's exacting standards. . . . Attica's men spent fifteen to twenty-four hours of every day in their cells . . . crammed into each tiny cell was a bed, a toilet, and a basin, which left barely enough room for a man to move around. Most of the men were allowed thirty-one to one hundred minutes a day in one of the prison's four exercise yards. . . . No newspapers, very few books to share, and nothing at all to read in Spanish . . . there were scores of rules governing the daily behavior, on the whole, petty and thus netted men frequent punishment. Breaking rules usually resulted in a man facing "keeplock"—a slang term for being confined to his cell, twenty-four hours a day, for an indefinite number of days. (Thompson 2016, 8–9)

Amidst these dire conditions and in response to them, dissent and tension began to rise. Prisoners attempted to write letters and express their legitimate gripes to the commissioner of corrections. Reasonable demands collectively articulated by the prisoners made clear that basic emotional as well as physical needs at Attica were not being met. The specific demands included the following: better and timely medical care; competent psychiatric staff; Spanish-speaking correctional officers and counselors; fresh fruits and vegetables; warm clothing and sanitary conditions; minimum wage for prison work; a narcotics treatment program; religious freedom; removal of screens in visiting rooms; expansion of work release; more frequent parole board reviews; Black culture courses; recreation and artistic programs; an improved law library and new Spanish library; and protection from reprisals (Thompson 2016, 23).

The prisoners of Attica, including Susan Rosenberg, are representative of how under conditions of extreme emotional duress human beings are capable of transformative emotional learning—a facet of adult transformative learning. The deliberate choices by both Rosenberg and the Attica Brothers to respond, cope, organize, resist, and move forward beyond trauma point to the link between emotional learning and mental cognition, leading to the resiliency of the human spirit.

EMOTION AND EMOTIONAL
INTELLIGENCE DEFINED

Emotion is extremely difficult to define and is often described differently between disciplines. However, for purposes of this chapter we rely on Boler's work on feeling, power, and emotion (1999). Megan Boler, in her seminal work in the 1980s and 1990s on the politics of emotion and emotions and education, presented a socially produced and constructed notion of the term (Boler and Zembylas 2016). Boler defines emotions as an experience both individualistic and collective "embodied and situated within culture, social class, race and gender. Emotions are in part physiological or sensational but also cognitive shaped by beliefs and perceptions" (Boler 1999, xvi). Boler maintains that there has been a longstanding historical and cultural association of women with emotions that almost excludes men (Boler and Zembylas 2016). Within the last several decades, this emphasis on women and emotion has changed and the study of emotion has become more gender inclusive, multi and interdisciplinary.

Symptoms including increased heartbeat, adrenaline, headache, tension in the neck or stomach, euphoria intertwined with cognition, are each influenced by emotion. As stated previously, historically emotion and cognition have been viewed as two separate processes. Now, because of neuroscience brain research we know this not to be the case. In the past two decades, there has been a plethora of research connecting cognition and emotions revealing that they are interdependent (Ledoux 1998).

Boler (1999) also challenges long-held beliefs and polarities of emotions including private vs. public; feminine vs. masculine, individualistic vs. collective, and guilt vs. innocence. She cautions against using emotions as social control both at the individual and collective levels. She also identifies the "feeling power" behind social justice movements like the feminist movement, civil rights movement, and the Attica protests.

With recent advances in cognitive science and behavioral psychology and following the early 20th-century mental-hygiene movement, the discourse of emotional intelligence was developed (Goleman 1995; Boler 2004). Howard Gardner (1983) explored emotional intelligence (henceforth, EI) among his work on scientific, creative, technical, musical, kinesthetic, and mathematical intelligence. In brief, EI is the ability to negotiate and understand interpersonal and intrapersonal relationships; the ability to greet conflict well; monitor and discriminate our feelings and the feelings of others; guide our thinking and actions based on analysis of feelings, and be emotionally resilient. For further clarity, EI allows us to confront our affective relationships with ourselves and others with insight, patience, and imagination (#TheSchoolOfLife). It often develops with age and experience and meets the classical criteria to be categorized as an intelligence (Mayer, Caruso and Salovey 1999). There is also recent evidence to suggest a correlation between low emotional intelligence and criminal behavior (Sharma, Prakash, Sengar, Chaudhury and Singh 2015). As with other intelligences, EI is learned through experience, modeling, or direct instruction. It is worth reiterating that EI is not inborn but learned; therefore, emotional education is necessary (Salovey & Sluyter, 1997).

The concept of EI has its critics. Boler and Zembylas (2016), for example, sees the neuroscientific accounts and research of emotion as potentially dangerous and risky as it places emotions in biology rather than socio-cultural context.

Notwithstanding and taking Boler's concerns about controlling emotions and decontextualizing them from cultural and social norms into account, the authors still believe the work on EI has relevance for addressing emotional education and the prison experience.

EMOTIONAL EDUCATION IN PRISON AND AFTER

In chapter 2 the authors discussed the disorienting dilemma toward transformative adult learning that prison often is. This includes emotional learning and transformation not separated from cognition. Suffering and trauma of the type experienced by Rosenberg and the prisoners of Attica can be unsolicited teachers, and it is perhaps a sad paradox that we learn from suffering. To be sure, to suffer is integral to human development as documented throughout classic and contemporary literature from Herodotus, the Bible, Hesse, Shakespeare, Frankl, Dostoevsky, Ticht Naht Han, and Angelou. In fact the Bible, as exemplified in the Old Testament book of Job, implies that the development of wisdom favors those who have suffered over those who research, analyze, or speculate about it (Held Evans 2018). "From this book [Job] above all others in scripture [Bible], we learn that the person in pain is a theologian of unique authority" (Davis 2001,122).

We now know that our brains have plasticity; they grow and change throughout life. Suffering can have an impact on the growth of one's brain (Gilbert 2012; Doidge 2007). Undoubtedly, some individuals suffer more than others.

PTSD AND THE PRISON EXPERIENCE

In the past, post-traumatic stress disorder (henceforth, PTSD) was mainly identified with returning military soldiers and called shell shock or combat fatigue (U.S. Department of Veterans Affairs 2018). However, we now know that PTSD is present in the general population, particularly in neighborhoods plagued by violence and poverty, most notably among Black males (Van Thompson and Schwartz 2017). PTSD among sentenced prisoners is also higher than within the general population (Goff, Rose, Rose and Purves 2007; Baranyi, Cassidy, Fazel, Priebe and Mundt 2018). Indeed, returning home from prison has been compared to returning from war:

> War is hell, and war seems an appropriate metaphor for the depressing state of formerly incarcerated men of color who return from [prison]. These men might be called the collateral damage of a war caused by history and failed policies. They continue to be punished by barriers to reentry into society and education. (Miller, Mondesir, Stater and Schwartz 2017)

Not unlike war, PTSD from the prison experience develops after going through or watching a shocking, scary, or dangerous event. But it can also be due to ongoing, daily exposure to danger or potential danger and stress as in being in a war zone or a prison. More specific causes are experiencing or witnessing physical and sexual assault or witnessing someone being killed or seriously injured coupled with ongoing anxiety, sensory deprivation, verbal abuse, loneliness, and unresolved grief (Elements Behavior Health 2017). Symptoms of PTSD include, but are not limited to, drug and alcohol abuse, depression, mood swings, and inappropriate interpersonal communication affecting employment and personal relationships (The 4 Most Common Causes of PTSD, n.d.). Understanding that prisoners are at great risk for PTSD provides an opportunity to address and treat this disorder and for them to reflectively examine these emotions.

RACIAL TRAUMA

From a Critical Race Theory (henceforth, CRT) framework, it is impossible to talk about PTSD and trauma without addressing racial trauma. Because a disproportionate number of prisoners and returning citizens are persons of color, its discussion is therefore applicable. To date, racial trauma or race-based stress is not listed in the *Diagnostic and Statistical Manual of Mental Disorders* (*DSM-5*) (2013). The difference between PTSD and racial trauma is that generally, racial trauma is an ongoing and constant exposure to microaggressions (Miller 2009; Comas-Diaz 2016). Microaggressions, first identified and classified by Derald Wing Sue, are ongoing and often unintentional subtle comments or behavior directed at historically marginalized individuals that communicate a derogatory or hostile message to the recipient (Sue 2010). Recipients may feel dismissed, hurt, and angry but do not know how to address these feelings, or as is the case in prison, are unable to respond for fear of punitive repercussions and further discrimination, abuse, and torture.

As CRT frames race in America, race is institutionalized and permeates all of society, interactions, and institutions; prisons and educational institutions are no exceptions (Chaney and Schwartz, 2017). Subsequently, racial microaggressions are often culturally determined and executed within racist societies. Response to ongoing racial trauma requires an enormous amount of emotional labor, a term originally coined by Hoschschild (2012) which centrally involves responding with the appropriate feelings to a constrained workplace environment. This generally includes the inducement and suppression of emotions to sustain appropriate outward countenance producing the proper state of mind in others (Hoschschild 2012). Applied to the prison experience, it is the ongoing effort and control of emotions under extreme stress and trauma. More will be addressed about emotional labor further on in this discussion. But emotional labor relates in part to Boler's (1999) collective emotion and pedagogy of discomfort.

BOLER'S PEDAGOGY OF DISCOMFORT

Boler's Pedagogy of Discomfort (1999) may seem an odd leap for the study of emotion in the prison experience as most of her ground-breaking work applies to traditional higher education, classrooms, and schooling in the U.S. Additionally, much of her research and that of her colleague, Michalinos Zembylas (2015) centers on non-prisoners of dominant culture—White students. Some scholars argue that pedagogy of discomfort in classrooms is designed for white students of privilege, not marginalized individuals who are often aware of issues of systematic dominance and oppression (see MacDonald 2018).

However, as the authors have maintained throughout this book, the prison experience itself is often schooling of a sort and the site of collective and individual critical inquiry and transformative adult learning. Therefore, Boler's Pedagogy of Discomfort applies. Pedagogy of discomfort builds from Foucault's (1994) ethic of discomfort which suggests the transformative and proactive potential of discomfort. It is a space to critique ourselves, our assumptions, beliefs, and relationships from the place of uncomfortability both on a personal and an interpersonal level. According to Boler (1999), emotions are disciplined, suppressed, or ignored throughout our educational journeys and in our institutions on both individual and collective levels. Classrooms, then, should be spaces to explore the social control of emotions as well as sites of social and political struggle. The authors maintain that prisons, as spaces, should also be regarded in this way.

Pedagogy of discomfort distinguishes itself from emotional literacy or emotional intelligence perspectives in that the latter two movements are reluctant to question the systems of privilege and institutionalized oppression which are often catalysts for emotional responses. Therefore, individuals who engage in a pedagogy of discomfort toward adult transformative education are critically examining their own personal, emotional responses (anger, guilt, shame, boundaries, etc.) considering both their own emotions and actions and the actions of larger institutional and systemic injustices. This examination was certainly true of both Rosenberg and the Attica prisoners.

At the heart of pedagogy of discomfort is affective learning through critical inquiry. This is not the suppression of emotion but the embracing, understanding, and using of emotion for transformational and social justice learning that foregrounds an understanding of emotion as critical analysis. It has the potential to break with inscribed habits, personal assumptions, values, perceptions, and beliefs within a socio-historical framework (Gaskew 2014). Where can this happen? If not in a classroom, it can and often does happen in the cell, in prison groups, through reading, meditation, and support groups.

Again, a disclaimer seems needed. This is in no way to suggest that the outcome of violence in prisons of any sort—physical, psychological, emotional is ever "ethical violence" because it somehow leads to adult transformative learning. But we do argue that repeatedly returning citizens and prisoners have testified to Foucault and Boler's assertion that discomfort and dwelling in discomfort allows for individuals to become "ambiguous selves" from which to grow and examine themselves, others, and society (Foucault 1994; Boler and Zembylas 2016) and that cognition and emotional pain and empathy can be strong teachers once emotional labor and emotional learning are embraced.

EMOTIONAL LABOR VS. EMOTIONAL LEARNING

The carceral experience requires heavy emotional labor. Emotional labor is the putting on a face (the "ice grill"), controlling your feelings, masking your reactions, and "sucking up," that is expected in prisons every time an individual is faced with offensive, violating, and uncomfortable situations. There is an expectation by prison authorities that a prisoner be polite, controlled, obedient, and submissive (Wilkinson 2018; Hochschild 2012). As mentioned earlier in this chapter, the term emotional labor first came from an analysis of controlling feelings and performing appropriate gender-related emotions in the workplace by Hochschild (2012). If the workplace requires high levels of emotional labor, then the prisons and streets require much more. Prisons are places where not only emotion must be controlled and suppressed but it is also monitored, judged, and punished. The ability to perform high levels of emotional labor are required both during and after one's prison sentence. This is taxing, exhausting, and unhealthy; therefore, emotional *learning* and education *are* required.

Emotional learning contrasts with emotional labor. The latter infers coping, negotiating, suppressing, adapting, and controlling emotions to appropriate social and cultural contexts. Whereas emotional learning is an integration of emotion with cognition to make meaning and use emotional intelligence to grow, develop, change both the self and the environment. Actively engaging with those feelings facilitates individual and collective transformation.

Anger management training is often the core of such emotional education programs incorporating self-awareness, self-management, social aware-ness, relationship skills, goal-oriented behavior, personal responsibility, decision-making, boundary setting, conflict resolution, and optimistic think-ing into the training. Frequently this type of training is utilized in prison and re-entry programs.

However good this kind of emotional skill building is, it falls short of emo-tional learning often because of its sole emphasis upon the personal short-comings of the individual. It places the "problem" solely with the individual and his lack of emotional and social control and the need to control and man-age emotions. This speaks to Boler's (1999) fears of emotional intelligence and mental health hygiene being understood as merely another form of social control. This is a valid concern.

Therefore, we expand the definition of emotional learning, to include the aforementioned areas related to anger control and management, but to the following as well: identifying structural oppression often manifested in microaggressions, Black cultural privilege (Gaskew 2014), healing from trauma, seeking mental health counseling, self-care, the healing power of collective agency, and creation of new social capital and social networks. Emotional learning must be situated in both an acceptance and understand-ing of an individual's personal responsibility and accountability, plus the collective and societal responsibility and accountability to all human beings. Emotional learning, then, is emotional acceptance through the understanding of individual experience and structural and cultural experiences. Emotional learning or education is hard work and often a cognitive decision to connect body and mind, embrace feelings, understand emotion and utilize silence, solitude, and the organic intellectual (see Chapters 5 and 6, respectfully). It requires humility and self-reflection that accepts personal responsibility for wrongs committed manifested in acts of forgiveness, restitution, reconciliation, and apology when called for. But it also understands when shame, guilt, and acceptance of blame are inappropriate, and draws on love for self and strong ego, a firm understanding of history and social dynamics of oppression to appropriately apportion responsibility. The integration of these polarities is an overarching theme of this book.

One more disclaimer here, within prisoners and among returning citizens as well as those who have never been imprisoned, there are genuine mental health concerns that need ongoing professional treatment and medical attention from competent psychiatric professionals. In fact, an indication of emotional health is an ability to admit and recognize the need for professional mental health and trauma counseling, and to seek this support. However, we do not elaborate on this here as it is not within the scope of this book.

What we are referencing is emotional learning that examines an individual's own feelings, reactions, and motives and how they influence how they think or act. This is reflexivity; the ability to stand back and examine our emotions. Based on our ability and capacity to be reflective, the degree of emotional learning will be determined.

Regarding this frame of thought, recent research findings indicate that following EI competencies deter recidivism. Such competencies as the identification of one's own thinking errors, delaying gratification, mastering self-management through new prosocial thinking habits, pre-release decision-making and planning for success, mastering failure and disappointment, motivation to desist criminal activity, patience, being careful of others, seeking humility (Waleed 2017), and acting on and within our habitus or embodied history (Bourdieau 1980) can be extremely positive.

The previous chapters of this book have highlighted tools that engage reflexivity and support emotional learning: silence and solitude, books, think time, counseling, prayer, exercise, meditation, education classes, and goal setting. Chapters 2 and 3 emphasized that choosing bravely is a prerequisite to transformative learning of any kind, in this case, emotional integration.

One tool among them, writing, should be reiterated as it frequently is cited by returning citizens and prisoners as therapeutic (Schwartz, 2010). Beyond being a tool somewhat easily accessible in prisons, writing in Rosenberg's words "became the mechanism to save my own sanity" (2007).

For several years, the authors of this book have facilitated two writing groups: one in prison and one for returning citizens in the community. Participants attest to the therapeutic nature of writing. Writers vary in the genre they write but almost all agree that writing provides an avenue to explore feelings, to bond with others, and allow their voices to be heard.

Part of healing is to be heard, not dismissed, to be understood and express feelings. Writing can do all of this. And writing in a group can provide an amazing counterspace (Chaney and Schwartz, 2017) for writing into being and emotional learning. Writing into being is the act of giving voice to one's experiences, validating those experiences, reflecting on one's identity in light of those experiences, and acting on this new knowledge of self. It is an act of transformation learning. In these groups writing is not used as therapy but nonetheless it produces therapeutic results. For some, writing becomes a positive addiction replacing old addictions (Black 2018).

THE DARK GIFT OF EMOTIONAL PAIN AND EMPATHY

It follows then that emotional pain has the potential to be another dark gift of the prison experience. Some people embrace this unsettling gift born of suffering well while others do not. Not all people affected by the criminal justice system grow emotionally, but many do. There are enough examples to suggest that if suffering is embraced there is the potential for emotional education by grappling with failure and disappointment, grief, loneliness, guilt, shame, self-control, forgiveness, and repentance. As discussed earlier in this book, prison and re-entry can serve as spaces to reflect on emotional relationships, navigate fears, master failings, understand childhood experiences, make and keep commitments, create appropriate disclosure and boundaries, discern the cause of emotions, and develop empathy. This self-work and interior thinking can lead to claiming an identity beyond that of "formerly incarcerated," toward self-directed learning. The authors can attest to knowing and befriending many individuals who through and despite their experience in prison, have engaged in emotional education and self-work toward emotional transformation. They are frequently deep souls, acquainted with grief who know how to laugh and appreciate life.

Prisoners and returning citizens who have "dealt with their stuff" who have chosen awareness not avoidance through critical inquiry of their pain, shame, anger, guilt, anxiety, and confusion frequently experience transformative learning demonstrated by healthy emotional intelligence. This self-investigative work is on both a personal/soul level and a structural/collective level. As a result, these individuals often possess a depth of empathy, insight, tolerance, and wisdom that can only be unearthed by those who have suffered deeply and survived with relative emotional health. Davon Harris a poet, writer, and college graduate sums up this awareness nicely in the following prose-poem entitled "Maintaining Hope in the Can" (2019):

See I been trying to maintain hope in the can

Sitting in here jammed
Waiting for my parole hearing so I could put on a good show for the man
And maybe. . . Just maybe. . .
He'll use his pale hands to sign and stamp. . .
Then the pig will stroll on by with key in hand and let me out of this concentration camp
See they laughs when I make that reference
Talking some shit bout we get 3 meals a day
A hot and a cot plus all our bills are paid
See you pig motherfucker what you don't understand is that I understand. . ..
There are numerous ways to kill a man
You aint gotta throw me in no goddamn fire and burn me to ashes
Or. . .
Tie me to a tree and whip me until I get lashes. . .
I'm hip to your game. . .
Like why you call me by a number instead of my name. . .
I know your aim. . .
Shoot to kill. . . But not in the physical. . .
Kill my spirit and kill my pride. . .
The judge slammed that gravel and sentenced me to death. . .
But what he don't know and you don't know is I's alive
I didn't die
I chose to grow. . .
Elevated my mind while your 100 feet walls tried to keep me blind to the world. . .
But I could see past your walls. . .
To be honest I could see clearer than before. . .
Now just the thought of returning here sends chills up my spine. . .
A13208 on the Pack up!!!!
Hold on I think that number is mine. . .

This is an example of the gifted wisdom of the traumatic prison experience. Once chosen this emotional education has the potential to be a gift to others. Susan Rosenberg and other Attica prisoners have given others this gift. The Attica prisoners, including but certainly not limited to Big Black and David Brosig (two prisoners who suffered severe trauma but fought and won lawsuits for all Attica prisoners) (Thompson 2016) survived to tell their stories, shine the light on grave institutional evils, obtain some monetary restitution, and garner their collective emotion for change. These examples speak profoundly to the resiliency of the human spirit and certainly to the gift of emotional learning from the place of suffering.

REFERENCES

Baranyi, G., Cassidy, M., Fazel, S., Priebe, S. and Mundt, A.P. (2018). Prevalence of posttraumatic stress disorder in prisoners. *Epidemiology Review.* 40(1):134–145.

Black, Y.N.N. (2018). *Addicted to writing.* In Schwartz, J. Transformative thoughts: A collection of writing from QCF. New York: Unpublished.

Boler, M. (1999). *Feeling Power: Emotions and Education.* New York: Routledge. Print.

Boler, M. (1999). *Feeling power: Emotions and education.* New York: Routledge.

Boler, M. (2004). *Teaching, learning, and loving: Reclaiming passion in educational practice.* Routledge: New York.

Boler, M. & Zembylas, M. (2016). *Interview with Megan Boler: From "feminist politics of emotions"to the "affective turn."* In Zembylas, M. & Schutz, P. (Eds.), *Methodological advances in research on emotion and education.* New York: Springer.

Bourdieu, P. (1980). *The logic of practice.* Stanford, Stanford University Press.

Chaney, J.R. and Schwartz, J. (Eds.). (2017). *Race, education, and reintegrating formerly incarcerated citizens.* Rowman & Littlefield: Lanham, MD.

Comas-Diaz, L. (2016). Racial trauma recovery: A race-informed therapeutic approach to racial wounds. In A.N. Alvarex, C.T.H. Liang, & H.A. Neville (Eds.) *Cultural, racial and ethnic psychology book series. The cost of racism for people of color: Contextualizing experiences of discrimination* (pp. 249–272). Washington, DC, US: American Psychological Association.

Davis, E. (2001). *Getting involved with God: Rediscovering the Old Testament.* Plymouth, UK: Cowley Publications.

Diagnostic and Statistical Manual of Mental Disorders (DSM-5). (2013). Washington, DC: American Psychiatric Association.

Doidge, N. (2007). *The brain that changes itself: Stories of personal triumph from the frontiers of brain science.* Penguin Books: New York.

Doidge, N. (2016). *The brain's way of healing: Remarkable discoveries and recoveries from the frontiers of neuroplasticity.* Penguin: New York.

Elements Behavior Health. (2017, October 2). Prisoners at Higher Risk for PTSD. Trauma & PTSD. https://www.elementsbehavioralhealth.com/trauma-ptsd/prisoners-higher-risk-ptsd/

Foucault, M. (1994). "For an Ethic of Discomfort." In *Essential Works of Foucault, 1954–1984.* Edited J.D. Faubion. Vol. 3, 443–448. New York: The New York Press.

Gardner, H. (1983). *Frames of mind: The theory of multiple intelligences.* New York: Basic Books.

Gardner, H. (2006). *Multiple intelligences: New horizons.* New York: Basic Books.

Gaskew, T. (2014). *Rethinking prison reentry: Transforming humiliation into humility.* Rowman & Littlefield Publishers: Lanham, MD.

Gilbert, P. (2012). *Human nature and suffering.* New York: Psychology Press.

Goleman, D. (1995). *Emotional intelligence.* New York: Bantam Books.

Goff, A., Rose, E., Rose, S. & Purves, D. (2007). Does PTSD occur in sentenced prison populations? A systematic literature review. *Criminal Behavior Mental Health.* 17(3):152–162.

Harris, D. (2019). Maintaining hope in the can. Unpublished prose-poetry.

Held Evans, R. (2018). *Inspired: Slaying giants, walking on water, and loving the Bible again.* Nashville, TN: Nelson Books.

Hochschild, A. (2012). *The managed heart: Commercialization of Human Feeling.* University of California Press: Berkeley.

Ledoux, J. (1998). *The Emotional Brain.* New York: Touchstone.

MacDonald, H. R. (2018). A pedagogy of discomfort: A qualified defense. Dissertation M.A. Queens University: Kingston, Ontario, Canada.

Mayer, J., Caruso, D. & Salovey, P. (1999). Emotional intelligence meets traditional standards for an intelligence. *Intelligence,* 27(4), 267–298.

Miller, B., Mondesir, J., Stater, T., & Schwartz, J. (2017). Returning to school after incarceration: Policy, prisoners, and the classroom. In J.R. Chaney & J. Schwartz (Eds.), *Race, education, and reintegrating formerly incarcerated citizens: Counterstories and counterspaces.* Lanham, MD: Rowman & Littlefield Publishers.

Miller, G.H. (2009). The trauma of insidious racism. *Journal of American Academy of Psychiatry Law.* 37(1), 41–44.

Rosenberg, S. (2011). *An American radical: Political prisoner in my own country.* Citadel Press: New York.

Rosenberg, S. (2007). Words Under Confinement, part of the PEN World Voices Festival.

Rosenblum, N. (1989). (Producer) Through the Wire Documentary. United States: Daedalus Productions Inc.

Salovey, P., and Sluyter, D. (Eds.) (1997) *Emotional development and emotional intelligence: Educational implications.* New York: Basic Books.

Schwartz, J. (2017). Writing into being and post incarceration. In J.R. Chaney & J. Schwartz (Eds.), Race, education, and reintegrating formerly incarcerated citizens: Counterstories and counterspaces. Lanham, MD: Rowman & Littlefield, Publishers.

Schwartz, J. (2010). Engaging out-of-school males in learning. Unpublished doctoral dissertation. Rutgers University, New Brunswick, New Jersey.

Sharma, N., Prakash, O., Sengar, K., Chaudhury, S. and Singh, A. (2015). The relation between emotional intelligence and criminal behavior: A study among convicted criminals. *Industrial Psychiatry Journal.* 24(1): 54–58.

Sue, D. W. (2010). *Microaggressions in everyday life: Race, gender and sexual orientation.* Hobokon, NJ: John Wiley & Sons, Inc.

#TheSchoolOfLife. What is emotional intelligence? https://www.youtube.com/watch?v=LgUCyWhJf6s

The 4 most common causes of PTSD (n.d.) Retrieved from https://vantagepointrecovery.com/ptsd-causes/

Thompson, H. (2016). *Blood in the water.* New York: Vintage Books.

U.S. Department of Veterans Affairs. (2018). VA research on Posttraumatic Stress Disorder (PTSD). https://www.research.va.gov/pubs/docs/va_factsheets/ptsd.pdf

Van Thompson, C. and Schwartz, P. (2017). A new normal: Young of color, trauma and engagement in learning. In J.R. Chaney & J. Schwartz (Eds.), *Race, education, and reintegrating formerly incarcerated citizens: Counterstories and counterspaces.* pp. 95–106. Lanham, MD: Rowman & Littlefield Publishers.

Waleed, C. (2017). *What aspects of emotional intelligence help former prisoners make decisions to desist crime?* Dissertation, Ed.D. 333

Wilkinson, S. (2018). December 24, 2018. Why was everyone talking about emotional labour in 2018? http://www.bbc.co.uk/bbcthree/article/5ea9f140-f722-4214-bb57-8b84f9418a7e

Zembylas, M. (2015). Pedagogy of discomfort and its ethical implications: The tensions of ethical violence in social justice education. *Ethics of Education.* 10:2. pp. 163–174.

PART III

Learning in Relation to Others

Chapter 10

The Black Family and the Incarceration Experience

Because mass incarceration continues to disproportionally affect Black communities in America, we begin this chapter with perhaps the most infamous report on the Black family: Daniel Patrick Moynihan's (1965) *The Negro Family: The Case for National Action*. In retrospect, this report is an indictment of American history and oppression, structural racism, and discrimination as well as the breakdown of the Black family and its impact upon incarceration and the community. Unfortunately, this internal government document became known solely for its pathologizing of the Black family, and its deficit perspective of the single-parent female run household, and not for the other, more palatable, portions of the report (Coates 2015).

There is a running debate on the beliefs, influence, career, and motivations of Moynihan by distinguished scholars. Moynihan was an influential voice who facilitated a fray of controversy around the American Black family, and ultimately influenced the thinking behind mass incarceration as we know it today (Weiner 2015; Coates 2015).

MOYNIHAN AND THE MYTH OF BLACK FAMILY PATHOLOGY

Daniel Patrick Moynihan was himself from a broken home, his father having left his mother when he was ten years old. Born in Oklahoma, he was raised in a poor household by his mother in New York City. As a young man he was a longshoreman on the docks in Manhattan. He attended City College of New York before enlisting in the Navy, which later enabled him to attend Tufts University for bachelor's and master's degrees, and then a doctorate at the London School of Economics. He later served in the Kennedy, Johnson, and Nixon administrations and was an ambassador, senator, sociologist, and itinerant American intellectual (Patterson 2010; Coates 2015).

Moynihan's initial goal in writing his Black family report was to garner support to address social problems including poverty, education, unemployment, and healthcare and to persuade the Johnson White House that racial equality would not be achieved solely by civil rights legislation. Unfortunately, Moynihan's report is remembered and vilified for its focus on his choice of the word *pathology*. Regrettably, this choice overshadowed his valid point that decades of injustice, slavery, and the interconnectedness of institutionalized racism within the nation's education, healthcare, employment, housing, and criminal justice systems were responsible for breakdown of the Black family, including the destruction of its patriarch. Moynihan expressed it this way:

> What then is the problem? We feel the answer is clear enough. Three centuries of injustice have brought about deep-seated structural distortions in the life of the Negro-American. At this point, the present tangle of pathology is capable of perpetuating itself without assistance from the white world. The cycle can be broken only if these distortions are set right (Moynihan 1965, 30).

Sadly, this message was unheard, likely due to the report's contradictions and ambiguities with an over-emphasis on family structure which seemingly blurred the report's true message and goals. Some people understood the report as advocacy for new race-based economic policies addressing inequalities, but others used it to rationalize a racist view of the Black family. These latter individuals argued a "pull yourself up by the bootstraps" perspective reinforcing racist stereotypes of loose family morality, single-parent families, welfare mothers, Black family pathology, and eventually Black criminology. Emphasis was drawn away from addressing systemic racism to instead focus on the family.

Things may have been different had the report excluded terms with negative connotations like *pathology*, which decades later are still entangled with Black family discourse and the criminalization of young Black men. It may have been better received had it included specific solutions addressing system changes. Perhaps then the true aims of the Moynihan report might not have been lost and interpreted from a framework of Black family pathology, leaving the Black family to fend for itself (Coates 2015).

CONTINUING THE FALSE NARRATIVE

Whatever Moynihan's intent, the report bolstered the view of Black Americans as a race prone to crime. This is not a new narrative to the American consciousness, but one socially constructed and perpetrated since slavery and the Fugitive Slave Act of 1850. This erroneous narrative of tangled pathology was particularly attached to the Black man, Black criminology, and extended to the Black family (Kendi 2016).

William Ryan, Boston College scholar and author of *Blaming the Victim* (1976), one of Moynihan's biggest critics charged Moynihan with blaming the very people who were victims of ongoing racism. This framing of urban Blacks, particularly as coming from dysfunctional families ultimately bolstered thinking that encouraged the formation and enforcement of tough-on-crime policies like the Rockefeller drug laws; racial stereotyping; stop and frisk; and the continued criminalization of the Black man (Coates 2015; Greary 2015).

In 1996, another report continued this narrative and extended it to the criminalization of young, Black males using the term *super-predator. Body Count: Moral Poverty. . . and How to Win America* by William J. Bennett, from the Office of National Drug Control Policy in the Bush administration; John P. Walters, Council on Crime in America and John J. Dilulio, Jr., professor of politics and public affairs at Princeton, who offered a very serious and depressing analysis of the growing crime problem in America at the time. The three authors cited "moral poverty" as the basic cause of violence and drug abuse, defining moral poverty as the absence of loving, capable, responsible adults who can teach children right from wrong. They rejected the premise that hardship, poor schools, and institutionalized racism drive crime. They bemoaned the neglect of children, taking the position that many parents did not want them and did not want to raise them; that schools do not want to educate them; and that government support was too stretched to provide adequate assistance.

According to Bennett, Walters, and Dilulio, this creates what the report notoriously called *super-predators:* kids aged thirteen to sixteen who apparently have no conscious as they kill, rob, or rape. They are so dangerous and unattached from their feelings that rehabilitation is not possible. This term has most often been associated with urban Black youth. *Super-predator* conjured images of welfare mothers, single-parent families, and absentee fathers. Both the Moynihan and the Bennett, et al. reports supported the notion that the Black man and thus the patriarch, is either absent, damaged, dangerous, violent, and ultimately a threat to white society. This dangerous and distorted portrayal of the Black man and family can be seen acted out in law enforcement activities that also include racial stereotyping and dispari-ties connected with "stop and frisk" policies. These, in addition to "driving while black" incidents, and police brutality, all lead to the disproportionality of incarcerated Black men. Sadly, manifestations of this false and unfortunate narrative run deep within the American psyche through history to this day (Kendi 2016).

INCARCERATION'S STAMP ON THE FAMILY

Beyond how mass incarceration came about and was conceptualized through reports like Moynihan's, there is no question that the incarceration experience takes an economic, emotional, and psychological toll upon families. Families affected by incarceration are less likely to own homes, cars, or bank accounts, all of which are key indicators of economic stability and social mobility (Turney and Schneider 2016). Research has shown cases of family homeown-ers taking out second and sometimes even third mortgages to cover retainers for lawyers representing a recently arrested son or daughter. Citizens return-ing home after incarceration often experience job insecurity and inability to complete educational degrees, frequently resulting in being economically limited to living in disadvantaged neighborhoods (Coates 2015).

While a loved one is incarcerated, urban families wishing to visit must travel long distances to rural white communities where a majority of state prisons are located. These trips can be long and expensive. Phone calls are also expensive and families who regularly add funds to a loved one's prison commissary account often do so with considerable economic strain. In so doing, there is sometimes fear that a prisoner will be extorted for the money families send. Families worry and suffer continuous anxiety about their loved one's safety and health. Some family members feel like they are in prison along with their incarcerated loved one (Coates 2015).

Access to adequate ongoing healthcare has dramatic effects on suscepti-bility to diseases as seen with the COVID-19 virus pandemic of 2020, and its unequal representation among people of color and in prisons, adds to physical, emotional, and economic costs. Relational tolls include the loss of relationships with a spouse, partner, or estrangement from children. A father's current incarceration may increase the likelihood of a mother having a child with another partner, causing reduced parental attention, time, and monetary support for all the children. Additionally, these circumstances can increase family stress, conflict, and general instability (Cancian, Chung, and Meyer 2016).

One study suggests that young children under ten years old with incarcer-ated fathers experienced more behavioral disturbances such as acting out or depression when compared to peers whose fathers are not in custody. Incarceration has long-lasting, intense and painful ramifications for families and children. These ramifications are all too real but should certainly never be confused with pathology.

COUNTERSTORY

It was 9 am on a brisk January morning near the rear exit of New York State's Queensboro Correctional Facility in Long Island City, New York. A woman in perhaps her mid-60s was pacing the sidewalk across the street furtively glancing at the prison door. Half a dozen cars were idling nearby, each with one or two occupants. This was a Wednesday when a group of prisoners would be released, some after many years of incarceration. One of the authors walked over and began a conversation with a lady who they now know is Mrs. Wade, waiting to greet her son, Marvin, returning home to his family after 25 years. She was ready to receive her son and so was the family. Granted there would be obstacles, many previously mentioned; they drew upon an ever-present wellspring of familial love and support, and the rich cultural legacy that embodies the Black family.

Marvin too was readily armed with what Gaskew calls Black Cultural Privilege (BCP), although he would not call it that. Marvin had mentally prepared himself for his return, physically, emotionally, and spiritually. He would lean on his family, and they would in turn encourage, support, and fortify him during his return journey.

BLACK CULTURAL PRIVILEGE, NOT
BLACK FAMILY PATHOLOGY

Without ignoring the suffering of the family, specifically the Black family, but embracing the relationship between suffering and transformation Tony Gaskew, noted criminal justice professional and scholar, aptly describes the pervasive American myth and narrative attached to the Black family:

> the socially constructed label attached to the black male is so powerful and pervasive in its historic ugliness that it many times consumes the separate and unique voices of not only incarcerated black women, but those of any race or ethnicity, making the subjugation of the black male the most accurate reflection of how the United States defines the concept justice. (2014, 6)

Notably, Gaskew does not stop there; he creates a counterstory to this deficit narrative of the Black man and family. He calls this counterstory, Black
Cultural Privilege (henceforth, BCP) in his body of work:

> a physical, mental, and spiritual awareness connects the rich diverse history of
> an African past with the ever-evolving journey into the legacy of the collective
> lived black American experience. It's an unconscious bond that exists among
> a people whose roots share an indestructible cultural DNA that has only been
> strengthened by four hundred years of direct and structural violence, acts of
> slavery, the black codes, and Jim Crow . . . it is a narrative that rests on the foun-
> dational cultural pride of unparalleled transformational survival skills. It allows
> a black male [family] to know that despite the four hundred years of structural
> injustices perpetrated by white supremacy, [they] will survive and succeed in
> life because it's in [their] cultural DNA to do so (Gaskew 2014, 68).

BCP says that the Black man and the Black family are not a pathology despite
a history of oppression that in many ways did attempt to destroy it. Instead,
there is reason to celebrate the Black family's historical and social heritage of
survival and thriving through suffering and oppression whether in the form of
slavery or mass incarceration.

Based on bell hook's work on radical pedagogical engagement (1994)
which is transformative learning at its best, Gaskew submits five tenets to
this transformative learning: 1. owning your own truth, 2. understanding your
connective history and BCP, 3. learning to process the criminal justice system, 4. knowing the true victims of a Black counter-culture, and 5. exploiting
your duty to remain free and to start making your own life choices. According
to Gaskew, when armed with these tenets, returning citizens are prepared for
re-entry (Gaskew 2014).

Owning one's own truth or taking personal responsibility and exploiting one's duty to be free and making choices or choosing to transform are
addressed in other chapters of this book. Tenets three and five are examined in part in chapter 5 on the organic intellectual. While understanding
one's connective history and cultural achievements emphatically applies to
the black family and its impact upon its incarcerated men and women the
strength, resilience, faith, and community acquired through suffering is a gift
to all peoples.

When celebrating the amazing resiliency and world contributions of a
people whose history of oppression and struggle are well-documented and
continue to the present day, we are not only celebrating the accomplishments of the Black family, but of the universal family of man. All of us, no
matter our race or ethnicity, can learn from the gift of BCP as it exemplifies
the stellar scope of what each of us can possibly accomplish in the face of

seemingly insurmountable odds. After all, every person on the planet shares at least 99.9% of the same DNA (Chial 2008). That is the ongoing premise of this book; most of us have not had the experience of incarceration, and yet we can still glean from the experience of those who have. One can only wonder how many more readers who have not shared the Black experience might nonetheless self-identify with BCP had Gaskew considered naming the intriguing concept something more universal.

THE BLACK FAMILY: MATRIARCHAL STRUCTURE

E. Franklin Frazier was the first Black president of the American Sociological Association in the late 1940s, himself a scholar on the Black family not without controversy. Through his career, a number of scholars, mostly Black, accused him, like Moynihan, of pathologizing the Black family, although other scholars did not agree with this assessment of his prolific work and writing (Semmes 2001; Browning, Miller and Spruance 2001). Frazier recognized the matriarchal structure of many Black families as the result of experiencing slavery but viewed it from a vantage point of strength not deficit. African American female headed households demonstrated self-sufficiency, resilience, and resourcefulness in surviving and caring for children in the absence of fathers and husbands (Hill 1971; Hill 1993). This kind of strength is still demonstrated by women facing the absence of sons and fathers through mass incarceration. Black families were and are diverse in their structures and leadership rather than monolithic and nuclear (Hill 1971; Hill 1993; Frazier 1939). Critical to family instability were the external factors of racism and economic integration not the matriarchal structure of the family. This structure is evidence of survival over oppression and resiliency, not pathology (Frazier 1939).

SPIRITUALITY AND RELIGION

No conversation about the Black family, and in particular those touched by incarceration, can be had without recognizing the role of religion and spirituality. Nearly all Black men and women carry within some system of core religious or spiritual beliefs that provide a foundation of inner strength. If not an experience inspired by traditional houses of worship, then an internalized sense of spirituality is tapped for power and strength, particularly in times of crisis. Spiritual lifestyle and orientation, and unfaltering faith frame their lives and is embedded in the African psyche (Littlejohn-Blake and Anderson Darling 1993). This tradition is primarily from American Christianity and

African religions germinated during slavery. African Kwanza celebrating heritage, unity, and culture with the principles of self-determination, collective work and responsibility, cooperative economics, purpose, creativity, and faith embody characteristics consistently underscored in research studies focusing upon the Black family.

Restorative movements within criminal justice draw from Biblical and spiritual foundations already in place within the Black family. Three themes of restorative justice are (1) repair harm done by crime, (2) encounters with victims and perpetrators together, and (3) transformation of people, relationships, and communities. Forgiveness, repentance, restoration and transformation are all spiritual principles found in most religions and spiritual traditions (Center for Justice and Reconciliation 2020).

FLUIDITY AND SENSE OF COMMUNITY

Beyond diversity of family structure and religion, another ever-present characteristic is the culture's willingness to absorb others into the household or kin structured network through informal adoptions, grandmothers, and close relations or friends among family members, especially in crisis. There is an openness to calling on relatives for support, guidance, and reciprocity; there is an elasticity and flexibility that often embrace others beyond the nuclear family. This is generationally learned, coming from decades of understanding that there is always room at the table (Littlejohn-Blake and Anderson, Darling 1993).

There is also fluidity of roles within the Black family, seen in children raising siblings; grandmothers and grandfathers raising grandchildren; eldest sons taking on the role of heads of households; mothers working two and three jobs; and fathers whose primary family tasks include taking on domestic responsibilities. This fluidity of roles is developed out of economic necessity and structural racism as well as faith and a strong sense of community and interpersonal responsibility—"it takes a village to raise a child" and "I am my brother's keeper" (Littlejohn-Blake and Anderson Darling 1993). This view defines the family broadly to include the community. A strong sense of community responsibility can be particularly seen in returning citizens who develop strong attachments within and outside prison walls upon coming home, not unlike veterans. The strong sense of community responsibility combined with Black religious traditions spawns active faith-based social services in Black communities and the strong feeling of responsibility for impoverished and under-served neighbors. One historical example was the Great Migration between 1916 and 1970 when 6 million African Americans from the rural South migrated to the urban Northeast, Midwest, and West for employment, resulting in escalating populations in these areas. Churches forged partnerships with emerging civil rights groups including the National Association for the Advancement of Colored People (NAACP) and the Urban League to help newly arrived Black migrants establish community roots within the cities (Harris 2005). Powerful Black ministers engaged in political activities and social justice activism. This well-documented practice and cultural legacy of democratic activism and agency is intricately woven into the context of the Black family, in sharp and deep contrast to Moynihan's deficit model.

SOCIAL JUSTICE ACTIVISM

The Black family's rich cultural legacy is frequently manifest in community and social justice activism, particularly around jail and prison reform. Social activism intertwined with religious calling and connected to Biblical imagery of freedom from slavery and God delivering His people in the Spirit of Moses and delivery from Egypt. "Black churches were born out of political and social resistance, with enslaved African Americans organizing around a theology that God would deliver them from their oppression" (Eligron 2018). Nat Turner and the slave rebellion, Sojourner Truth and the Underground Railroad, Martin Luther King, and the Civil Rights Movement are among the most familiar examples. This is a logical extension of the Black family's involvement in nurturing and protecting its community. The Black church continues to the present day to be a formidable force for social activism as exemplified by Jesse Jackson, Al Sharpton, Jeremiah Wright, Michael Eric Dyson, and Charles E. Black to name just a few. The family, the church, and social activism are culturally intertwined.

CODA

The men and women making up the American Black family represent the primary racial group within a decidedly broken criminal justice system that has disproportionally imprisoned a people that history has fortified with a rich legacy of struggle and triumph. Those holding the family together while in prison, the roles of faith and community responsibility; flexible and fluency in adopting "nontraditional" family roles; and social activism through both educational scholarship and community are all powerful cultural and social capital that many incarcerated citizens tap into during their period of transformation, and later share widely with the world. Combined with tools of restorative justice, these assets are infused with transformative virtues that commonly include forgiveness and repentance, resilience through struggle, and inspiration. These are gifts applicable to all people. They were oftentimes created and/or nurtured through a long history of unspeakable tragedy and oppression. And yet, the myriad of historical and familial profiled examples of perseverance, love and triumph, can now be offered by the Black family as powerful gifts to any person or community on the planet seeking to survive, thrive, succeed, and contribute in the face of extreme disparity and oppression.

Race is a social construct. It is not real in biological or scientific sense, but painfully and tragically real in its social and societal consequences (Dyson 2017). Despite mankind's use of race to construct and facilitate diverse forms of evil including severely damaging the infrastructure of the Black family, it continues to survive, thrive, and share its lessons, talents, and enhanced value systems. Thankfully, this phenomenon includes pre-incarceration infusions that resurrect hope, positive values, and civic responsibility to the many men and women whose lives become impacted by the criminal justice system, enabling them to reintegrate as assets to the community.

REFERENCES

Bennett, W. J. Dilulio, J. and Walters. J. (1996). *Body count: Moral poverty and how to win America's war against crime and drugs*. New York: Simon & Schuster.

Browning, S., Miller, R. and Spruance, L. (2001). Criminal Incarceration Dividing the Ties that Bind: Black Men and their Families. *Journal of African American Men*. Vol. 6, No. 1, pp. 87–102.

Cancian, M., Chung, Y., and Meyer, D. (2016). Fathers' imprisonment and mothers' multiple-partner Fertility. *Demography* 53, vol. 6, pgs. 2045–74.

Center for Justice and Reconciliation. (2020). http://www.pficjr.org/

Chial, H. (2008). DNA sequencing technologies key to the Human Genome Project. *Nature Education* 1(1):219.

Coates, T. (October, 2015). The Atlantic. The Black Family in the Age of Mass Incarceration. https://www.theatlantic.com/magazine/archive/2015/10/the-black-family-in-the-age-of-mass-incarceration/403246/

Dyson, E.M. (2017). *Tears We Cannot Stop: A Sermon to White America*. New York: St. Martin's Press.

Eligron, J. (2018, April 3). Where Today's Black Church Leaders Stand on Activism, *The New York Times*. https://www.nytimes.com/2018/04/03/us/mlk-church-civil-rights.html Center for Justice and Reconciliation. International Prison Fellowship 2020.

Frazier, E. F. (1939). *The Negro family in the United States*. Chicago: University of Chicago Press.

Gaskew, T. (2014). *Rethinking prison reentry*. Lanham, MD: Lexington Press.

Greary, D. (September 14, 2015). The Moynihan Report: An Annotated Edition. *The Atlantic.* A historian unpacks The Negro Family: The Case for National Action on its 50th anniversary. https://www.theatlantic.com/politics/archive/2015/09/the-moynihan-report-an-annotated-edition/404632/

Harris, F. (2005). Black churches and civic traditions: Outreach, activism, and the politics of public funding of faith-based ministries. In *Black Churches and Local Politics*, Editors Smith R. and Harris, F. Lanham, MD: Rowman & Littlefield.

Hill, R. B. (1971). *The strengths of Black families.* New York: Emerson Hall.

Hill, R. B. (1993). *Research on the African American family: A holistic perspective.* Westport, CT: Auburn House.

hooks, bell (1994). *Teaching to Transgress. Education as the practice of freedom.* London: Routledge.

Kendi, I. (2016). *Stamped from the Beginning.* New York: Nation Books.

Littlejohn-Blake, S. and Anderson Darling, C. (1993). Understanding the strengths of African American families. *Journal of Black Studies.* Vol. 23, No. 4 (Jun., 1993), pp. 460–471.

Moynihan, D. P. (1965). The Negro family: The case for national action. https://liberalarts.utexas.edu/coretexts/_files/resources/texts/1965%20Moynihan%20Report.pdf

Patterson, J. (2010). *Freedom is not enough: The Moynihan Report and America's struggle over Black family life—from LBJ to Obama.* New York: Basic Books.

Ryan, W. (1976). *Blaming the victim.* New York: Vintage Books.

Semmes, C. (2001). E. Franklin Frazier's theory of the Black family: Vindication and sociological insight. *The Journal of Sociology & Social Welfare.* 28:2.

Turney, K. and Schneider, D. (2016). Incarceration and household asset ownership, *Demography* 53, vol. 6 (2016): 2075–103.

Turney, K. (2017). The unequal consequence of mass incarceration for children. *Demography* 54, 361–389 DOI 10.1007/s15324-0160543–1.

Weiner, G. (2015). *American Burke: The Uncommon Liberalism of Daniel Patrick Moynihan.* Laurence: University Press of Kansas.

Chapter 11

The Prison Experience and Technology

There is no disputing that we are in a transformational shift in the way we process information due to the growth of the internet and the global village as McLuhan had predicted as far back as the 1960s. As of 2021, there is a global digital population of 4.7 billion users. According to the Pew Institute, nine out of ten Americans are online, an increase of approximately 40% since 2000 (Smith 2017). This phenomenon includes four key trends: 81% of all Americans own smartphones with 96% owning a cellphone of some variety; 81% of households have broadband service; seven in ten Americans use social media; and half of Americans own tablets and e-readers. Three in ten American adults report being "constantly online" (Perrin and Kumar 2019; Smith 2017). This has only increased with the COVID-19 pandemic. Even before the pandemic, substantial usage change had happened since the year 2000, with all ages included in this transformation from small children to senior citizens (Perrin and Kumar 2019; Smith 2017). There is no turning back the clock, nor should we want to. There is much to applaud in these advancements.

While this transformational learning shift is occurring, there lies another phenomenon: decarceration coupled with the aging of state prison populations (Carson and Sabol 2016). After decades of mass incarceration the growth has waned, and since 2008 there has been a gradual decrease in incarceration rates (Gramlich 2018). In the past, longer sentences and reductions in discretionary parole led to a higher proportion of prisoners over 55 years of age (Aday 2003). This means more mature, newly released citizens are returning to our communities with no exposure to this new technology, resulting in no skill development in this area. This chapter argues that this lack of exposure and skills is both an asset and liability—a paradox of sorts. Before exploring this paradox, a brief overview of technology and prisons is provided for context. This summary is not meant to be comprehensive but introductory.

TECHNOLOGY AND PRISONS

According to Christopher Grew, CEO and Founder American Prison Data Systems, "There's a lot of hesitancy to provide technology to people in prisons. . . . Prisons are a lot more comfortable buying pepper spray than they are in investing in technology" (Martinez 2016).

> Unfortunately, . . . some social issues have been positively addressed by the investment in technology: access to healthcare and the democratization of education are two examples [But] technology in the service of prison reform seems to lag behind. United States prisons rely on outdated methods for both inmate tracking and management as well as rehabilitative use of technology to improve and enhance prisoners' lives both in and once they are outside of prison. (Martinez 2016, 1)

Perhaps some of this lag is due to exploitation by tech companies like Global Tel Link (GTL) which provides phone, tablets, and video kiosks to prisoners mostly to communicate with their families on the outside. As in the case of landline phones, people are charged a fee for calls. Until recently, these types of fees have been costly and exploitative of prisoners and their families (Martinez 2016). Despite past exploitation, new solutions to better the lives of guards, prisoners, and society are imminent and needed. Educating with technology toward the goal of rehabilitation and preparation for re-entry seems to be gradually gaining momentum, though it is sorely behind the major progresses of technology in society. Access to technology in prison education programs varies from prison to prison and is not widespread with isolated experiments in online learning programs (Morris 2015).

Clearly there are security and societal boundary considerations when implementing technology, especially interactive media like the internet into the prison system. And perhaps technology in correctional education will need to be more self-contained than interactive, or monitored more closely in its interaction with the outside world. Nevertheless, the potential advantages to both prisons and prisoners are without question—video visitation, faster processing of legal matters, expanded educational opportunities are but a few examples. Currently, however, very few prisoners have access to technology and will only have access once they return to society.

PUNITIVE TECHNOLOGY—E-CARCERATION

One area where there is more rapid movement in the use of technology is electronic monitoring and high-tech tools and algorithms used as solutions to mass incarceration. While the rate of prison growth is dropping, electronic monitoring is growing. Digital jails, as they are called, mirror the punitive conditions experienced in prison but instead shift the site of imprisonment to homes, especially Black and Latinx households for whom the monitoring is used more frequently. Generally, it is used for parole or probation, and pre-trial release (Kilgore, Sanders and Hayes 2018).

Electronic monitoring and house arrest are often used with pre-trial risk assessment tools that still maintain the old racial biases. This ongoing social and racial control through technological advancement has sometimes been referred to as the Newest Jim Crow (Alexander 2018). There has been a 140% increase in the use of electronic monitoring in the past decade (MediaJustice, 2019). According to Kilgore, Sanders and Hayes (2018), electronic monitoring is an extension of incarceration that limits freedom and potential success while on parole. There is no research to date to prove it works; it does not save money, and the rules and regulations are inconsistent and vague surrounding its use. It expands the reach of the surveillance state.

After prisoners have done their time, they should be free. They should not be subjected to electronic shackles, or punitive electronic devices (Kilgore, Sanders and Hayes 2018). Furthermore, these digital prisons do not appear to support rehabilitation but have the potential to impair chances for employment, the number one need of returning citizens after obtaining housing. Instead, individuals are held captive in their homes, making participation in employment, education, medical services, social service opportunities, and family and religious events difficult if not impossible. The use of digital ankle bracelets is particularly troubling because it restricts mobility. Digital prisons can limit a person's participation in caregiving, increase the risk of domestic violence due to crowded and stressful living environments, heighten racial disparities in the system, and apply user fees that are difficult for the poor to manage. Meanwhile, there is no evidence that digital prisons improve court appearance rates (MediaJustice #NoDigitalPrisons 2019).

This use of technology has also created a new market niche for two companies: Apax and Attenti. These companies push for technological incarceration as it is economically beneficial for them (MediaJustice #NoDigitalPrisons 2019). As decarceration and ending cash bail rise to prominence on the criminal legal agenda, electronic monitoring has gained favor as an alleged alternative to incarceration (Kilgore, Sanders and Hayes 2018; Alexander 2018).

With this troubling context in mind, this chapter focuses on the complex paradox surrounding the absence of technology in the lived experience of many prisoners amidst the proliferation and prominence of technology and the cultural shift in the ways in which humans process information.

TECHNOLOGY AND HOW IT IS
CHANGING THE WAY WE THINK

Children as young as two years old are using mobile devices with ease. This phenomenon has led to a generational shift in the way we process information and is recognized as a cognitive style. Technology and media of all varieties has changed the way we live, socialize, do business, and think (Hayles 2007) for those who have access.

From brain research we know that media-rich environments rewire children's brains differently than adults who have not grown up with media-saturated conditions (Hayles 2007). Scientists call this new rewiring of the brain and subsequent processing of information and attention, *hyper-cognition*. The trend toward hyper-cognition is accelerating with every new generation (Hayles 2007). This is different than multi-tasking which is alternating between different tasks, often quickly (Rubinstein, Meyer and Evans 2001). Hyper-cognition is a process of retraining the brain and retraining the neural circuitry (Carr 2010). Generations of young people have grown up with media. The average time young people spend with media is 6.5 hours every day of the week. This is contrasted with reading print books for 43 minutes a day. (Kaiser Family Foundation 2005). This trend leads to hyper-cognition which can lead to superficial thinking, the inability to concentrate, and the reduced capacity to think deeply (Carr 2010).

It is also creating a potential crisis in higher education learning environments based solely on deep cognitive premises of previous generations without technology. According to Gunn (2019), there needs to be adaptation to the hyper-cognitive learning styles of a new generation of students.

DEEP COGNITION AND HYPER-COGNITION

Research indicates that prevalent technology use rewires our brains around attention and cognition. Hayles (2007) calls this phenomenon *deep attention* and *hyper attention*. Newport (2016) refers to this observable fact as *deep work* and *shallow work*. In his best-selling book entitled *Deep Work*, Newport (2016) defines deep work as the ability to focus on one cognitively challenging task at a time without distractions. This focused concentration pushes cognitive capabilities to their limit, increases intensity on tasks, increases productivity, gives one the ability to learn hard things quickly, and charges intellectual development. Deep work produces high quality output which is a result of time spent coupled with intensity of focus. In a connected age we need this skill and are healthier and more productive for it. However, it has become increasingly difficult to develop. Deep work is rare (Newport 2016). Ironically, while prison is isolating and horrendous, for some it may actually be seen as a site for deep work to be nurtured.

For purposes of this book, we use the terms deep cognition and hyper-cognition as opposed to deep work and shallow work, though they are basically the same concepts. As stated previously, deep cognition includes a high ability to concentrate on one object at a time. Our schools and higher education institutions were created with this type of cognition paramount. Deep cognition is characterized by reflective and critical thinking with a bent toward nuance and the ability to hold opposing arguments (Newport 2016).

In contrast, hyper-cognition is increasingly prevalent and will continue to be as children raised on technology enter schools. Hyper-cognition is not new in human evolution; it developed first to accommodate basic survival instincts. Deep cognition is the luxury of secure societies and environments which are conducive to deep attention and is harder to access in locations where survival mode is chronic (Hayles 2007). Deep cognition and hyper-cognition are both essential for productive lives and often appear on continuums. Often dualistic thinking is employed when discussing technology and its effects on human cognition. The question should not be whether one is better or worse than another, but what type of cognition is needed in what context and for what task (Hayles 2007; Newport 2016).

THE PRISON EXPERIENCE AND DEEP COGNITION

The authors first became experientially aware of deep cognition when teaching computer and literacy classes in Accra, Ghana to students who had no access to media or technology. These students' ability to focus and concentrate on learning tasks was uncanny. The authors remember how quickly they attained unfamiliar computer skills (most had never sat at a computer before) as well as their ability to concentrate on reading and completing books and writing assignments without boredom or agitation as compared to American students. Students sat for undistracted hours intently focused and were able to learn new computer and literacy skills quickly and with excellence. This ability had nothing to do with the students themselves. But it did reflect the absence of media-saturated environments.

The authors have seen this same phenomenon in prison classrooms where students had no access to cell phones, computers, very little television, and occasional radio. Teaching a writing class over several years the authors have observed students finishing books, writing for hours, demonstrating sophisticated analysis, and bringing profound insights to discussions. Prison students perform better and produce more writing than university students in the same course outside the prison. On reading the same book as one being read in the authors' college classes, *On Writing by Stephen King* (2010), the prison students were observed to demonstrate greater ease with finishing the book, talking about it and analyzing and applying concepts to their own writing as well as seemingly getting more enjoyment of the task than the college students who read it in a college course. The prison group demonstrated astute and close reading not typically demonstrated by the college classes. It should be noted that the prison writers did self-select to be in the course so they may have come with more interest and determination than had they been assigned to the course. However, the college students at least in some instances had similar choices. The authors observed prison writers engage in their writing with no regard for time and focus for long periods of writing up to nearly an hour with little discomfort, agitation, or distraction. The groups were highly reflective with the students demonstrating ability for self-reflection and sociological imagination.

Other programs and college professors have witnessed the same experience. Since 2001, Bard College has offered liberal arts degrees in prison to hundreds of incarcerated men and women at Eastern Correctional Facility and Taconic Correctional Facility in New York. This is a rigorous and competitive program with graduates earning degrees in subjects ranging from Mandarin to advanced mathematics. Prison students learn quickly in settings with few distractions and intense time on task. The prison students can do long uninterrupted batches of intellectual work leading to college completion often at Ivy League standards, in one instance leading prisoners to defeat Harvard University students in a debate (Burns 2019). After release, some graduates go on to rewarding careers and elite graduate and professional programs. Karpowitz, one of the initial founders of the Bard Prison Initiative, does not specifically use the term deep cognition but does refer to the making of intellectuals and the development of the intellectual mind without access to the internet, cell phones, and electronic resources on a consistent basis. He does herald the deep cognitive work where this select group of prison college students learn challenging languages, read difficult texts, and engage in critical thinking on a regular basis, for hours at a time. According to Karpowitz, this intense focus, concentration, and intellectual presence in the classroom prison is as good, if not more engaging, than many college classrooms on the outside (Karpowitz 2017). There is little doubt that the Bard Initiative has fortuitously utilized the circumstances of imprisonment for the work of deep cognition. None of these findings are surprising, but they speak to the unexpected opportunity that prison can afford for intellectual development.

Mikita Brottman, author and professor described a book club in a maximum-security prison engaging prison students in challenging reading. This demands deep cognition. Brottman describes the book club with no technology—only books, time, and one another. She engages in her own deep thinking, self-reflection, and self-scrutiny about the group:

> At first, I was surprised to find the prisoners' responses to be so insightful, thought provoking, and articulate. Then I wondered why I'd been expecting any less from them because they've been in prison for most of their lives, or because they murdered another human being. Why do we find it so difficult to believe that men who've killed are as capable of literary appreciation as anyone else? Is it because we consider them fundamentally lacking in empathy? If a convicted murderer turns out to have a refined literary sensibility, might it suggest that his crime was caused not by an innate pathology but by the same kind of momentary bad decision anybody could make. If so, is it merely [an] accident of circumstance that separates "the murderer" from "you and me"? (2016, xxv)

Regarding technology, one of Brottman's students upon returning home said, "I read so many books in prison, now there's all this other stuff to catch up on" (2016, 226). For prisoners returning home after incarceration, there is anecdotal evidence to suggest that once returning citizens have access to cell phones, lap tops and the like; learning to use them is relatively easy as it relates to text messaging, accessing websites, using search engines, email, websites, Instagram, Twitter, blogs, Facebook, and the like. This shallow learning comes quickly once a returning citizen has access (Newport 2016).

More research on the relationships between deep cognition, limited technology, and prison experience is needed, but anecdotal evidence suggests that in these media deserts like prisons, mindfulness is increased with positive effects on intra and interpersonal communication (Cooper 2011; Schwartz 2016). This evidence coupled with neuro research on the brain indicates that the lack of access to technology seems to have a bright side. Particularly for prisoners who have spent decades behind bars, their brains have not gone through the rewiring to adapt to technology. Chapters 6 and 7 delve into this phenomenon as well by examining the role of silence and solitude and the making of the intellectual which coincides with technological deserts.

Arguably, the absence of technology in the development of deep cognition puts the returning prisoner at a decided advantage to the rest of us who are bombarded with technology. With the increasing speed with which we are controlled by social media and the internet, the ability as well as time and space for reflection is receding. The exception to this phenomenon may be US prisons as they stand today.

This is not to say that prisons should not have access to technology—they need to. However, in terms of the potential to produce deep cognitive work this lack can be an asset. The current absence of technology in prison environments paradoxically are potential sites for the development of deep cognition.

THE GIFT OF BALANCED COGNITION

According to Joshua Gunn, "Sustained thought and reflection have been hard-won luxuries for humans: to read a novel or meditate on a philosophical problem, we need environments that encourage reflection, and these are a relatively recent achievement" (2019). Individuals who can access both deep cognition and utilize hyper cognition will likely be most successful in the workplace, as adult learners and transformative thinkers (Gunn 2019; Newport 2016; Hayles 2007; Clark 2008).

Building bridges between the two cognitions, deep and hyper, so that individuals are proficient with both print- based and digital-based tools must be the goal for successful life and work (Hayles 2007, Newport 2016). Individuals who are able to engage in deep cognition while managing the hyper-cognitive world of fragmented tasks, multiple activities, and ongoing distractions may find success. The authors make the case that the returning prisoner is positioned well to find success. One such case is Marvin, highlighted in Chapter 8, a fifty-year-old man who had just returned from completing a twenty-five-year sentence. While incarcerated he wrote short stories, meditated, worked out, read, and used the time to develop deep cognitive skills including the ability for critical thinking and reflective practice. Upon returning home, he learned how to use email, social media (Facebook in particular), cell phone operation, and basic computer operations within weeks (in twenty-five years he had never been on a computer or cell phone). But while adapting to this shallow technology (easy to learn), he has maintained his meditative practices, reading, writing, and exercise, realizing that these deep work practices are essential to his continued growth and development even more so than the new technology. He is a centered individual, anchored in both mind and emotion, easing himself back into the work force and interpersonal relationships with a wisdom born through deep cognition.

RE-ENTRY—HYPER-COGNITION
AND DEEP COGNITION

95% of prisoners incarcerated in state prisons will be released back to their communities at some point (The National Resource Center 2019). Far more individuals are in state custody and are the majority of prisoners in the US (The National Resource Center 2019). From the 6.9 million monitored with the US carceral system (federal, state, local prisons, and 4.7 million on parole and probation) in 2015; 641,100 people were released to their communities. The trend is a decreasing number of individuals sent to prisons, at a reported

14% drop in 2020, largely due to releases connected with COVID-19 (Vera Institute 2021). Re-entry solutions mainly address education, employment, housing, health, mental health, women and families, voting and licensing decisions (Uggen, Larson and Shannon 2016; Love, Roberts and Klingele 2013).

Accordingly, if we want to think about effective re-entry initiatives, we must think about technology and preparation to re-enter a society that has changed immensely—characterized by hyper-cognition, the attention switching and constant stimulation. It can be argued that prisoners and former prisoners know a great deal about hyper-cognition because of the carceral environment and neighborhoods some came from where they had to be hyper vigilant to danger and be able to read their environments. There is a difference between hyper vigilance and hyper-cognition, however. Hyper vigilant behavior is a heightened alertness that aims to prevent danger and is often caused by past trauma. Hyper-cognition is not connected to trauma or danger but connected to the ongoing, sometimes over stimulation of digital technology and the way the brain functions (Gunn 2019).

If the hyper vigilance so necessary in prison can be harnessed and understood and translated to hyper-cognition, returning citizens may fare well with technology as long as they have access.

For many like Brian, the authors' former student, who returned from prison with little exposure to technology, he learned how to use his cell phone quickly. Upon enrolling in college, he wrote most of his assignments on his cell phone, not having a laptop of his own and no computer training. He had trouble navigating platforms and websites to apply and register for college as well as communicating with professors (Miller, Mondesir, Stater and Schwartz 2014). Without exposure to technology or the skills to navigate it, life after incarceration can be made exponentially more difficult, particularly as it surrounds employment, further education and training, and everyday communication.

Several individuals in the authors' prison creative writing classes are preparing to leave prison after having served as much as twenty-five years of incarceration. These men are aware that they need to learn how to use technology. They look out the prison windows and watch individuals walking past with cell phones pressed to their ears. Those with families to go home to say that they will learn how to use technology through young family members. Most learn to navigate these tools quickly as traversing the internet is not cognitively complex.

What can't be learned quickly is deep cognition. However, they have read extensively, wrote volumes, meditated regularly, and nurtured silence and solitude to their emotional, spiritual, and intellectual benefit. Deep cognitive skills are already developed in part because of the prison environment and the choices they made within it. Once back in society they will be bombarded with hyper-cognitive demands. Each must then strive to maintain a balance between the nurtured "gift" of deep cognition and the world of technology and hyper-cognition.

REFERENCES

Aday, R. (2003). *Aging prisoners: Crisis in American correction*s. Westport: Praeger Publishers.

Alexander, M. (November 8, 2018). The newest Jim crow: Recent criminal justice reforms contain the seeds of a frightening system of "e-carceration." *The New York Times Opinion Sunday Review*.

Bronson, J. (April 25, 2019). Prisoners in 2017. Bureau of Justice Statistics. https://www.bjs.gov/index.cfm?ty=pbdetail&iid=6546

Brottman, M. (2016). *The maximum-security book club: Reading literature in a men's prison*. New York: HarperCollins Publishers.

Burns, K. [Executive Producer], Botstein, S. [Producer], Novick, L. [Director] (2019). *College behind bars*. USA. Skiff Mountain Films.

Carr, N. G. (2010). *The shallows: What the internet is doing to our brains*. New York: W.W. Norton.

Carson, E. A., and Sabol, W. (2016). *Aging of the state prison population, 1993–2013*. Bureau of Justice Statistics.

Clark, A. (2008). *Supersizing the mind: Embodiment, action, and cognitive extension*. New York: Oxford University Press.

Cooper, T. (2011). *Fast Media Fast*. Boulder, CO: Gaeta Press.

Gramlich, J. (2018). America's incarceration rate is at a two-decade low. Factank: Pew Research Center https://www.pewresearch.org/fact-tank/2018/05/02/americas-incarceration-rate-is-at-a-two-decade-low/

Gunn, J. (2019). Hyper and Deep Cognition. Oral Presentation at LaGuardia Community College.

Hayles, K.N. (2007). Hyper and Deep Attention: The Generational Divide in Cognitive Modes. *Profession*. Modern Language Association. (Pp.187–199).

Kaiser Family Foundation. (March 9, 2005). *Generation M: Media in the Lives of 8–18 Year Olds*.

Karpowitz, D. (2017). *College in Prison: Reading in an Age of Mass Incarceration*. New Brunswick, NJ: Rutgers University Press.

Kilgore, J., Sanders, E., and Hayes, M. (2018). No more shackles: Why we must end the use of electronic monitors for People on Parole. The Center for Media Justice.

Love, M.C., Roberts, J. and Klingele, C. (2013). Collateral consequences of criminal convictions: Law, policy and practice. Books. 56. https://digitalcommons.wcl.american.edu

Martinez, J. (November 7, 2016). Jail tech: Phones, tablets, and software behind bars. PC Business.

Mediajustice #NoDigitalPrisons. https://mediajustice.org/challengingecarceration/

Miller, B., Mondesir, J., Stater, T., & Schwartz, J. (2014). Returning to school after incarceration: Policy, prisoners, and the classroom. In J. Schwartz, D. Rosser-Mims, B. Drayton, and T. Guy. (Eds.) *Swimming Upstream: Black Males in Adult Education. New Directions in Adult and Continuing Education.* San Francisco, CA: Jossey-Bass.

McLuhan, M. (1964). *Understanding media.* Routledge: London.

Morris, C. (2015, August 13). New online learning program prepares inmates for life after prison, *Diverse.* www.diverseeducation.com

The National Reentry Resource Center. (2019). http://csgjusticecenter.org/nrrc/facts-and-trends/

Newport, C. (2016). *Deep work.* New York: Grand Central Publishing.

Perrin, A. and Kumar, M. (2019). About three-in-ten U.S. adults say they are "almost constantly" online. Factank News in the Numbers. Pew Research Center. Washington, DC.

Rubenstein, J., Meyer, D. and Evans, J. (2001). Executive control of cognitive processes in task switching. *Journal of Experimental Psychology: Human Perception and Performance.* 27: 763–797).

Schwartz, J. (2016). Disconnect to Connect: Emotional Responses to Loss of Technology During Hurricane Sandy in *Emotions, Technology, and Behaviors* edited by Tettegah, S. and Espelage, D. Amsterdam: Elsevier.

Smith, A. (2017). Record shares of Americans now own smartphones, have home broadband. Factank News in the Numbers. Pew Research Center. Washington, DC.

Uggen, C., Larson, R. and Shannon, S. (2016). 6 million lost voters: State-level estimates of felony disenfranchisement (Washington, DC: The Sentencing Project, 2016), available at sentencingproject.org/publications/6-million-lost-voters-state-level-estimates-felony-disenfranchisement-2016/

Vera Institute. (2021). People in jail and prison in 2020. http://vera.org/people-in-jail-and-prison-in-2020

Chapter 12

Non-Verbal Communication

In the previous chapter, we defined hyper-vigilance as heightened alertness utilized to prevent danger. Often this vigilance is the result of past trauma and exposure to real or perceived ongoing danger. Because of the incarceration experience, prisoners are hyper-vigilant upon their return.

For example, some returning citizens select certain seats in classrooms, restaurants, or other public settings facing the entrance/exit doors, seldom sitting with their back to the door (Miller, Mondesir, Stater and Schwartz 2017). This is a hyper-vigilant, non-verbal behavior designed to assure easy egress in case of a volatile or dangerous encounter. Hyper-vigilant behavior can be bodily defense postures, fleeing an environment perceived as a threat, puffing the chest, aggressive gestures, or assuming overly stern facial expressions. In most instances, these behaviors are non-verbal. In acute instances of stress, the body produces survival chemicals like dopamine, adrenaline, and endorphins triggering instinctive bodily responses (Martinelli 2010).

Hyper-vigilant behavior has associations with post-traumatic stress disorder (henceforth, PTSD). The clinical criteria for PTSD are direct/indirect exposure or witnessing trauma; or learning that a relative or close friend was exposed to trauma manifesting in upsetting memories, nightmares, flashbacks, emotional distress, physical reactivity after reminders of trauma, or trauma triggers (American Psychiatric Association, 2013). Some prisoners have PTSD while others do not. The occurrence of PTSD is dependent on a variety of factors including but not limited to degree of and length of exposure to trauma, tolerance of trauma, coping and support systems, ongoing and prevalence of symptoms, and quality of treatment (American Psychiatric Association 2013).

For purposes of this chapter, hyper-vigilance is not examined as a severe response to trauma that has unhealthy manifestations, but rather in its less acute occurrence an important non-verbal response and awareness of potentially positive use. Once again, we turn what is perceived as a negative and look at the concept from a positive perspective. We begin by defining non-verbal communication and providing a brief overview of this communication skill.

OVERVIEW OF NON-VERBAL COMMUNICATION

The study of non-verbal communication commenced in 1872 with the publication of Charles Darwin's book *The Expression of the Emotions in Man and Animals* (Darwin 1872). Thereafter into the 1920s there was a halt in the research on non-verbal communication due to the behaviorist work of B. F. Skinner. The 1950s saw a resurgence in the study with the work of Ray Birdwhistell. Birdwhistell is considered the founder of kinesics (see Birdwhistell 1952), the study of human movement. Beginning in 1959 and through the 1960s, the renowned anthropologist, Edward Hall, published his classic book on proxemics, *The Hidden Dimension* the study of how geography and space affects our communication. Other researchers studied eye contact, pupil dilation, and personal space (Hall 1966) and during the 1970s, Hall and others continued their research (Hall 1966, 1973) as non-verbal communication became popularized with books like Fast's (1970) *Body Language.*

From its inception, non-verbal communication has been an interdisciplinary field attracting scholars from anthropology, ethology, psychiatry, communication studies, linguistics, and only recently criminal justice. The role of non-verbal communication is now recognized in racial stereotyping, stop and frisk policies, body camera usage, interactions between police and civilians which include posturing, facial expression, eye contact, gesture, tone of voice, and invasion of personal space.

Non-verbal communication does not often get the credit it deserves as a focus of study considering that 55% of human communication is through body language, 38% through paralanguage (voice, tone, intonation), and only 7% through spoken word with non-verbal communication particularly effective in emotional communication (Mehrabian 1981, 1972). However disputed these exact percentages might be and whatever limitations Albert Mehrabian's research had, most scholars of non-verbal communication agree that much of our communication comes through non-verbal channels within the social contexts of culture, environment, and individual cognitive schemata.

PROXEMICS, PERSONAL SPACE, TERRITORIALITY, AND THE PRISON EXPERIENCE

Proxemics is one sub-category of non-verbal communication that has profound implications on the prisoners' experience. It is the study of how space and environment impact human behavior, communication, and social interaction. In relation to corrections facilities it includes the architecture and location of the prisons, amount of space assigned to each prisoner, the amount and quality of personal space and privacy, exposure to natural light, access to fresh air, sanitary conditions, ability to access nature, wall colors, size of cells, sharing of jail cells, density of prison populations, ceiling heights, and freedom to traverse through spaces. It also includes the claiming of personal space, invasion of personal and private space, and territoriality—ownership or occupancy of certain areas or possessions as one's own.

Historically prisons were architecturally designed for control and large-scale confinement from origins in medieval dungeons to modern maximum-security penitentiaries (Johnston 2001). One prison architect said that the construction of prisons give strong non-verbal messages of control with outdated views of punishment. According to Wall (2016), architecture sends a silent message to everyone walking into a place. It tells you what to expect and how to behave. Prisons are the same.

With incarceration rates on decline, the First Step Act (prison reforms to bail and sentencing) in place, and jails like Rikers Island closing, talk of architectural design of prison spaces and social responsibility is not uncommon. Within the last decade, there has been a movement among young architects, planners, and designers to decode oppression in architecture and look at how architectural space can be used as a tool for social justice (Mortice 2017; O'Donnell 2018). These architects design prisons that reflect system reform, are more humane, and responsive to the goal of rehabilitation (Wall 2016).

This is done in part through thoughtful understanding of proxemics. This understanding begins first by placing prisons in the communities, or near the communities, that prisoners come from instead of far away in distant rural communities making traveling for family members visits long, hard, and nearly impossible. Nearness to prisoners' neighborhoods and loved ones is an issue of proxemics. In addition to prison location, the prison itself communicates and affects prisoners' rehabilitation. According to Kenneth Ricci, a New York architect devoted to criminal-justice facilities "Environment cues behavior. You maximize safety by designing for good sight lines, reasonable decibel levels, and daylight and exterior views, especially of nature, which measurably reduces adrenaline levels" (Adler 2019, 1).

Proxemics also includes personal space, overcrowding, territoriality, and solitary confinement. Human beings require both personal space and privacy. With prison overcrowding a global prison problem and 115 countries exceeding their official prison capacities, severe instances of overcrowding such as prisoners sleeping in shifts, on top of each other, or having to share beds are not uncommon. Overcrowding and lack of privacy can cause or exacerbate mental health problems, increase violence, self-harm, and suicide (Penal Reform International 2019).

Communication scholars identify four main spaces or distances between people (sometimes dependent on culture) that indicate the kind of communication that occurs. They are intimate space (0–18 inches between individuals), personal space (18 inches–4 feet, social space (4 feet–12 feet) and public space (12 feet +) (Hall 1966, 1973). These spaces are invisible barriers, bubbles, or boundaries that humans create around themselves. In prison, personal space is protected, sought out, and understood because it is essential not only to appropriate communication but because it is sometimes scarce, invaded, challenged, and necessary for survival and emotional well-being. Ironically, solitary confinement often provides the most personal space for individuals. While solitary confinement can create severe debilitating distress, it is occasionally welcomed by prisoners seeking more personal space and privacy.

Territoriality, another facet of proxemics, was first recognized in animals as they lay claim to areas of ownership and protect that space from others (Beebe, Beebe, & Redmond 2008; Hall 1966, 1973). From this behavioral perspective, territoriality is a product of human instinct akin to that of animals (Malmberg 1980). Since the 1980s, human territoriality has been studied from a sociopolitical lens, signaling the obtaining and maintaining territory as demonstrations of power and sometimes oppression (Sack 1986). We see territoriality at play in gendered communication, nation states and nationalism, and gentrification (Wood 2007). In the case of prisons, territoriality presents itself in gang affiliation, dormitory ownership of beds and immediate areas, seating arrangements in the cafeteria, control of the television room or other public prison spaces. The stall space (telephone booths, prison toilets), and possessions (prison clothing, books, toiletries, writing material, photographs, etc.) also represent areas of territoriality. Invasion of one's territory can be a serious offense among prisoners potentially leading to violence. Invasion of one's territory by correctional officers is unfortunately common, too often debilitating and dehumanizing, though on occasion necessary for the safety of prisoners. Prisoners spend a good deal of time and energy creating, maintaining, and protecting personal space and territory (Sibley and van Hoven 2009).

KINESICS—BODY MOTION, GESTURES, AND FACIAL EXPRESSION

As mentioned previously, anthropologist Ray Birdwhistell (1952) is credited for coining the term, kinesics, which comes from the Greek word, kinein "to move." Kinesics covers non-verbal messages such as facial expression, gesture, and posture. Body language or movement can project aggression, weakness, fear, strength, dominance, confidence, attraction, or set up boundaries as defense (Waiflein 2013).

Prisons are controlled movement environments with usually zero contact rules: no touching or talking in certain instances. Prisoners learn to gesture with their hands as in the power fist or hands to the heart to indicate respect. These are important forms of acknowledgment, affirmation, and recognition. This type of sign language is used, for example, in the chow hall (prison cafeteria) if prisoners are not allowed to speak. Individuals use finger and hand gestures to "text." Prison gangs often have special signals and signs for their group members reinforcing group inclusivity, bonding, and solidarity. These can be highly sophisticated gesture "languages."

In terms of walking and posture, some prisoners carry themselves with their chin up and chest out to present masculinity and dominance, but not to threaten. Immediately upon going to jail, image is everything. How a prisoner walks into a new situation or compound and how they carry themselves displays either strength or weakness. Other prisoners read the body language for signs of paranoia or vulnerability. Through the stance, posture, and gait, the non-verbal message that you are tough is sent because you never want to be viewed as weak.

The face and especially the eyes are considered the pathway to the soul. The prison experience requires that individuals maintain facial expressions that communicate strength and neutrality. Emotions of fear or anxiety are often masked. Eye contact, or oculesics, is also particularly important when entering a new setting. According to one formerly incarcerated citizen who reviewed this chapter before publication, you need to hold your head up, look at everyone in the eyes, give eye contact, and look without looking so that you understand your surroundings and who you are with. Prisoners learn to read their surroundings, putting people in categories as either a threat or not. This decoding is a survival tactic. They can then determine who to befriend and who to avoid.

PHYSICAL APPEARANCE AND IDENTITY WORK

Identity work is the effort put forth to modify or adapt one's identity to a specific setting, so that you will be engaged with, listened to, and accepted within that context (Goffman, 1958; Phelan and Hunt 1998; Erikson 1974). In effect, rather than being, acting, talking, and relating authentically, all people engage in identity work by adjusting behaviors and identity to be accepted.

For prison settings that acceptance can include protection, gang membership, status, rank, and companionship (Phelan and Hunt 1998). Identity work requires self-awareness and the ability to "read a room" which is the quick analysis of the interpersonal dynamics of any given social situation including but not limited to threat, safety, and power. Perceptive identity workers can navigate different settings so that they are not a threat to people and that they fit into the setting.

Much of this reading of a room comes from the ability to use and understand non-verbal personal appearance demonstrated by clothing, body adornment including jewelry, and prison tattoos. In prison tattoos can be powerful, non-verbal symbols of gang membership, status and rank within a gang, and stripes earned. They can also symbolize toughness, racism, or refusal to accept authority. Tattoos may also signal the length of stay in prison, crimes committed, or loved ones and family members on the outside. The *loca* is a special type of tattoo that signifies the prisoner's neighborhood and community. Other tattoos symbolize the individual's prison experience (Demello 1993). At least one study links increased recidivism and criminal thinking styles with tattoo adornment (Rozycki Lozano, Morgan, Murray and Varghese 2011).

Beyond tattoos, one's personal appearance and identity is communicated through cleanliness and olfactics, the dynamics of smell. Generally, the same clothing is worn by everyone in prison. Any distinctions that can differentiate or express identity in a non-threatening manner, therefore, are cherished. These are all non-verbal constructs that operate in all social settings—offices, homes, work sites, public places—but are particularly signifying in prisons because of the ongoing crowding of individuals in relatively small spaces and the human need to establish one's own identity.

CHRONEMICS

Chronemics is the study of how time is quantified, managed, and used in communication. It is the study of human time-experiencing and human communication. There are human temporal processes besides the scientific and technical. These are genetic time, biological time, perceptual time, psychological time, and sociocultural time. Our ability to time-bind as humans distinguishes us from animals (Bruneau, 2012).

In prison you are "given time." Counting days, weeks, months, or years is an active process. Time is on everyone's mind whether it is remembering (or regretting) the past, attempting to live in the present moment, or envisioning and planning.

Generally, in the institutional experience, time is quantified carefully for order and control. It is monochronemic in approach: there is a set time to wake up, to eat meals, to turn out the lights, for recreation, cell searches, and "on the count" (roll call). Much like the military, time is exacting and predictable but controlled by someone other than the prisoner. If guards want to have a roll call in the middle of the night to disturb prisoners' sleep, prisoners have no control of the timing of those instances. This method of controlling time and deprivation of hours for sleep has also been used as torture and punishment.

Beyond this predictability and regimentation of time during most prison days, for many prisoners there are long stretches of personal time that are relatively free. Prisoners can become time haunted, waiting to be released or as some say, "you do the time, don't let the time do you." This phrase means to fill the time with useful activity. However constructed, time in prison is another powerful non-verbal construct.

SOCIAL AND CULTURAL COMPETENCE AND THE PRISON EXPERIENCE

Returning citizens often utilize and translate the non-verbal negotiation skills learned through the prison experience to effective social and cultural competence. As stated previously, relating to and interacting with others, also thinking about relationships or about whom to avoid, constitutes a very important part of prison life. Much of this identity work is involved in decoding and encoding non-verbal messages (Sibley and van Hoven 2009). This kind of social agency or social capital has been demonstrated and observed by multiple research studies (Dirsuweit 1999; Baer 2005).

From the perspective of proxemics, prisoners frequently adjust to prison spaces, use spatial tactics, and employ spatial strategies. In response to the alienating environment that is prison, many prisoners are skilled at seeking out "dark corners," where it might be possible to pursue activities out of sight of the guards. Some are also adept at making their own spaces or territories whether in the cell, prison yard, or library. These territories are a means of distancing oneself from real or imagined threats, and a way of retaining a sense of home in an institutional setting (Sibley and van Hoven 2009).

Translated outside the prison, these skills include an alert sensitivity to non-verbal cues. With these skills come the ability to understand how dominance, control, and power are often communicated non-verbally in the workplace, apartments, and homes, for example.

The prison experience can make an individual resourceful. Returning citizens understand that space matters, space speaks, and space affects both attitude and behavior. A good example is when one author used this skill, refined in prison, to revamp the workspace and offices for a program he directed, effectively changing its atmosphere and dynamics for the positive. The space before was drab and the furniture was arranged in separate cubicles so that communication was obstructed. The author opened the space, decorated, brought color to the walls, and arranged furniture in circular and open places to encourage interaction.

In terms of kinesics, body language decoding is an important adaptive social behavior and social competence. Skilled and healthy decoders can perceive, interpret and respond to emotions and affective cues (Sokolov et al. 2011). Astute decoding of body language, eye contact, facial expressions, and gestures have generally been attributed to females (Briton and Hall 1995; Arseny et al. 2011), but there is reason to suspect that the prison experience heightens awareness of kinesics cues in both males and females.

While some returning citizens may be adept at reading kinesic cues, some recently released individuals may have trouble with correctly decoding particularly aggressive body language. This has been suggested in the research of Kert and de Gelder, who stated,

> Our study shows that violent offenders, aggressive men who had committed a violent offence with a male victim, and who have a strong tendency to get involved in fights, have problems with mixed emotional signals with a particular bias towards threatening body language, resulting in lower task performance and incorrect interpretations of happy signals (face or body) when a threatening context (body or scene) is provided (2013, 409).

This is not surprising when one considers the cognitive schemata that most violent offenders bring to prison and the prison setting itself. Despite these findings, it is the perspective of both Kert and Gelder and the authors of this book that learned responses to threatening triggers can be modified, especially in the young and non-psychopathic. In recent years, cognitive-behavioral interventions have shown great promise (Kert and de Gelder 2013; Schwartz and Schwartz 2012).

With this qualification in mind, prisoners' keen decoding skills that were a matter of survival in prison can be translated to job interviews, the workplace, partner relationships, family dynamics, and other social settings. What was once a skill of survival is now a potential asset in interpersonal environments where being alert to kinesic cues can make one a sensitive employee, employer, partner, or group member.

As mentioned earlier, prisoners often have long stretches of time with nothing to do. When prisoners "use the time," some learn to structure time with activity. There is time for identity work which is not only a survival skill within hostile settings, but includes self-reflection, developing a core sense of self, self-evolution, as well as the making of friends within prison, including giving to and caring about others. The prison experience can be used to develop an identity of resilience, flexibility, and structure with an appreciation of the simple things of life and small luxuries. Some embrace this gift.

Some non-verbal communication is universal like smiling, frowning, and looks of terror, globally recognized facial expressions that depict emotions of happiness, sadness and fear. However, other non-verbal codes are culturally determined and vary from culture to culture. These include hand gestures, kissing in public, head coverings, and personal space. Skilled non-verbal decoders usually have exposure to different kinds of peoples and cultures, are comfortable with individuals of different backgrounds, and can be border crossers (Wood 2007).

Prison sometimes places individuals together who would not ordinarily be. Such is the case of Mario [pseudonym]. In a not uncommon moment of transparency and reflection in the prison writing group, Mario talked about growing up in an all-white Italian neighborhood in Brooklyn, New York. This neighborhood was segregated both ethnically and racially. His prison experience placed him in integrated environments with individuals across cultural and racial lines. Racially and ethnically, he was a minority within his cell block. As this 40-year old man told it, this was a positive experience for him. In his case, this border crossing transformed the way he understood race, language, and ethnic differences in America. The integration of his space in prison clearly impacted Mario's perspectives of "the other" in positive ways (Mario, personal communication, November 2019).

CODA

Further research is needed that explores the social and cultural competency some prisoners develop because of the non-verbally dense prison environment. However, what we know from current research is that living the experience of incarceration requires non-verbal proficiency and decoding and encoding to survive well, skills capable of translation for outside social and cultural competence. Prison demands that individuals "read" people. Effective reading of people is crucial for interpersonal communication, relationship skills, and negotiation.

In an era of prison reform returning citizens, as a result of this unique lived experience, should be included in reform conversations including the design of new prisons with prison architects. Returning citizens are the experts and the clients of spatial intelligence as it concerns prisons; they come with a vantage point that should be tapped. Finally, we make the case that along with developed social and cultural competence comes the development of empathy and a sensitivity to the pain of others. These unique gifts, often non-verbally understood and employed in giving back to others and in prison reform, will be the subjects of the remaining chapters.

REFERENCES

Adler, J. (March 4, 2019). Architecture and Prison Reform. Architectural Record. http://www.architecturalrecord.com/articles/13919-architecture-and-prison-reform

American Psychiatric Association. (2013). *Diagnostic and Statistical Manual of Mental Disorders* (*DSM-5*). http://gynecology.sbmu.ac.ir/uploads/4_5911178616359616931.pdf

Arseny A., Sokolov, Krüger, S., Enck, P., Krägeloh-Mann, I. and Pavlova, M. (2011). Gender affects body language reading. Frontiers in Psychology. 2:16.

Baer, L. (2005). Visual imprints on the prison landscape: A study on the decorations in prison cells. *Tijdschrift voor Economische en Sociale Geografie*. 96:209–17

Beebe, S.A., Beebe, S.J. and Redmond, M. (2008). *Interpersonal communication*. 5th Edition, Boston: MA: Pearson Education.

Birdwhistell, R. (1952). *Introduction to kinesics: An annotation system for analysis of body motion and gesture.* Washington, DC: Department of State, Foreign Service Institute.

Briton, N.J. and Hall, J. A. (1995). Beliefs about female and male nonverbal communication. *Sex Roles* 32, 79–90.

Bruneau, T. (2012). Chronemics: Time-binding and the construction of personal time. *ETC: A Review of General Semantics.*

Darwin, C. (1872). *The expression of the emotions in man and animals*. London: John Murray.

Demello, M. (1993). The convict body: Tattooing among male American prisoners. *Anthropology Today*. 9:6. Pp 10–13.

Dirsuweit, T. (1999). Carceral spaces in South Africa: A case study of institutional power, sexuality and transgression in a women's prison. *Geoforum*. 30: 71–83.

Erikson, E. (1974). *Dimensions of identity. Jefferson Lectures in the Humanities*. New York: W.W. Norton & Company.

Fast, J. (1970). *Body language*. Lanham, MD: Rowman & Littlefield.

Goffman, E. (1958). *The presentation of self in everyday life*. Harmondsworth: Penguin.

Hall, E. (1973). *The silent language*. New York: Anchor Books.

Hall, E. (1966). *The hidden dimension*. New York: Anchor Books.

Johnston, N. (2001). *Forms of constraint: A history of prison architecture*. Chicago: University of Illinois Press.

Kert, M. and de Gelder, B. (2013). When a smile becomes a fist: The perception of facial and bodily expressions of emotion in violent offenders. *Exp Brain Res*. 228(4): 399–410.

Malmberg, T. (1980). *Human Territoriality: Survey of behavioral territories in man with preliminary analysis and discussion of meaning*. New York: NY.

Martinelli, R. (December 2010). Murder or stress-induced hypervigilance? Officer Johannes Mehrabian, A. and Wiener, M. (1967). Decoding of inconsistent communications. *Journal of Personality and social Psychology,* 6, 109–114.

Mehrabian, A. (1981). Silent messages: Communication of emotions and attitudes. (2nd Ed.) Belmont, CA: Wadsworth.

Mehrabian, A. (1972). *Nonverbal communication.* Aldine-Atherton, Illinois: Chicago.

Miller, B., Mondesir, J., Stater, T. and Schwartz, J. (2017). Returning to school after incarceration. In J. R. Chaney and J. Schwartz (Eds.) *Race, education, and reintegrating formerly incarcerated citizens: Counterstories and Counterspaces.* (Pp.121–130) Lexington Books.

Mortice, Z. (Oct. 24, 2017). Decoding oppression in architecture: Design as a tool for social justice. Redshift. https: www.autodesk.com/redshift/design-for-social-justice/

O'Donnell, K. (October 2, 2018). Who does the design include, benefit, or harm? American Institute for Architecture. https://www.aia.org. articles.216051-who-does-design-include-benefit-or-harm

Penal Reform International. (2019). Overcrowding. https://www.penalreform.org/issues/prison-conditions/key-facts/overcrowding/

Phelan, M.P. and Hunt, S. A., (1998). Prison gang members' tattoos as identity work: The visual communication of moral careers. *Symbolic Interaction.* 21:3. pp 277–298.

Rozycki Lozano, A. T., Morgan, R.D., Murray, D.D., & Varghese, F. (2011). Prison tattoos as a reflection of the criminal lifestyle. *International Journal of Offender Therapy and Comparative Criminology,* 55(4), 509–529.

Sack, R. (1986). Human territoriality: Its theory and history. Vol. 7 CUP Archive.

Schwartz. J. and Schwartz, P. (Producers) & Osborne, R. (Documentarian). (2012). *A New Normal: Young Men of Color, Trauma, & Engagement in Learning* [Documentary]. New York City: City University of New York. https://www. facebook.com/anewnormalyoungmenofcolor.

Sibley, D. and van Hoven, B. (2009). The contamination of personal space: boundary construction in a prison environment. Area (2009) 41.2, 198–206 doi: 10.1111/j.1475–4762.2008.00855.x

Sokolov, A., Kruger, S., Enck, P., Krageloh-Mann, I., and Pavlova, M. (2011). Gender affects body language reading. *Frontiers in Psychology.* 2:16.

Waiflein, M. (2013). The progression of the field of kinesics. Illinois State University. Senior Theses, Anthropology.

Wall, I. (September 28, 2016) Architecture and prisons: Why design matters. Interview *The Guardian*: US Edition.

Wood, J. (2007). *Gendered lives: 7th Edition.* Belmont: CA: Holly J. Allen. doi: 10.1007/s00221-013-3557-6

PART IV

Learning that Transforms the World

Chapter 13

Giving Back

According to prison chaplain, counselor, confessor, and international writer Richard Rohr, "It has been acceptable for some time in America to remain *wound identified*" that is, using one's victimhood as one's identity, one's ticket to sympathy, and one's excuse for not serving (2011, 3,10). Alternatively, he speaks about transforming one's wounds to serve others; to give back to the world from a place of woundedness. Although the experience differs in type and intensity, all incarceration experiences produce wounding. How this emotional, psychological, or physical wounding is transformed into community solidarity and social activism is the crux of this chapter.

WOUNDED HEALER

The concept of the wounded healer may have originated from Greek mythology but was contemporaneously reexamined by Carl Jung (2002) in his psychiatric research. Of course, the prime example of the wounded healer is Christ. From a spiritual perspective Henri Nouwen, internationally recognized priest and author, expounds on service and ministering to others through one's own woundedness and what Nouwen identifies as the fundamental woundedness of all human nature. His body of work focuses on how one's brokenness can become a source of strength and healing for others (1972). Suffering, then, is the foci of service. Whether it is identifying the suffering in ourselves through direct experience or the suffering of our own times within our hearts, helping others is born in the recognition of our own pain. And for Nouwen, this is in the image of Christ. "We heal from our own wounds" (1972).

Nowhere is this more applicable than to prisoners. For many formerly imprisoned persons, the wounds of incarceration are frequently transformed to heal others. This wound transformation is different from being wound identified (Williams 2015). It is healthier and outward aimed, rather than

155

insular and inward. Reflecting on one's experience of incarceration along with others who share the experience, creates desire to give back to those left behind (Schwartz 2018). This often happens in community solidarity and with the purpose of systemic and institutional change.

COMMUNITY SOLIDARITY AND SOCIAL JUSTICE ACTIVISM

Black athletes have a long and brave history of giving back and of social resistance. Successful athletes, once they have gained financial rewards and public notoriety, often pay a high price for utilizing their positions to speak out against injustice. Colin Kaepernick is the American football quarterback who was among the first to "take a knee" to protest police brutality during the playing of the national anthem protesting police brutality. He joins a legacy of athletes in the likes of Jesse Owens, Muhammed Ali, Tommie Smith and John Carlos who used their notoriety to protest injustice often at great cost to their careers. Since the 2020 tragedy in Minneapolis where a Black man, George Floyd was choked to death by a police officer; we see athletes again calling for change in police tactics and law enforcement departments. But athletes are not the sole arbitrators of solidarity and social activism. Thousands of men and women who survived and thrived after periods of incarceration have stood against oppression.

Chapter 6 maintains that some prisoners become organic intellectuals in the tradition of social activist scholarship and that education is a powerful tool for transformation both individually and collectively in the service of social justice. This connects to the legacy of Black scholars that framed much public and resistance writing. These include Frederick Douglass, Marcus Garvey, Booker T. Washington, W.E.B. DuBois, James Baldwin, Cornell West, Michael Eric Dyson, Henry Louis Gates Jr., James H. Cone, and Peter J. Gomes, bell hooks, Derrick Bell, Joyce A. Ladner, and Kimberle Crenshaw, among others. These public intellectuals use and continue to give back through their scholarship in the service of social justice. Not a few are or were political prisoners including Angela Davis, Huey Newton, Nelson Mandela, Assata Shakur, Leonard Peltier, Susan Rosenberg, and Elizam Escobar.

THE PRISON ACTIVIST

We know that at least 95% of prisoners in the United States will be released from prison at some time (Hughes and Wilson 2020). This means there is a large community of formerly incarcerated persons. For many of them, this mutuality of experience naturally breeds solidarity, the recognition of being "all in this together." This solidarity is a commitment to strengthen community and to act for equity and social justice. It puts the group as a priority not just the welfare of the individual. In some ways, prisoners' solidarity and community share similarities with those found among war veterans. Like the returning soldier, the person returning from prison has a shared life experience so impactful that those affected are never the same, never forget, and bond deeply. Giving back is in the DNA of most returning citizens; it is woven into the fabric of their lives. As previously mentioned, giving back may take diverse forms from social justice protest, political and policy activism to scholarship to social, financial, and emotional support. Whatever the vehicle, the voices of those directly impacted by the system, are integral in the reentry process and solutions related to incarceration. People closest to the problem are especially suited to provide strategic leadership and are powerfully involved in developing their own solutions.

Unfortunately, community solidarity and the agency of prisoners is infrequently included in scholarly literature and policy discussions. Conversely, prisoners are too often portrayed as dependent upon government or community organizations, wound identified, and framed through a deficit lens. And although returning citizens do have need for housing, jobs, education, and justifiably lean on supportive services for help, there are a myriad of examples of incarcerated and formerly incarcerated men and women organizing and advocating for themselves (Williams 2015).

Drawing from the framework of the wounded healer and community solidarity, the remainder of this chapter highlights movements, individual leaders, prison reform, and prison advocacy organizations founded and led by imprisoned persons and returning citizens. The choices for inclusion are far from exhaustive nor are they wholly representative of the myriad ways people have transformed their incarceration experiences. The first example is from history and within prison walls.

THE CASE OF ATTICA

A classic example of prisoner solidarity is the Attica prison uprising in 1971 and the resulting prison reform. On September 9, 1971, approximately 1,300 New York State Attica Correctional Facility prisoners protested abusive and neglectful treatment and conditions and ultimately took over the Attica maximum security prison for four days and nights. The tragic aftermath is now history. Thirty-nine prisoners and guards died with over a hundred individuals severely wounded. The overwhelming violence and murders were committed by law enforcement, not the prisoners (Thomson 2016). The entire story is horrific and needs to be told repeatedly. Suffice it to say that the sacrifice that many Attica prisoners made led to some reform at Attica and contributed in developing the Community Model in other prisons (Clear, Cole, and Reisig 2016). At Attica, prisoners eventually received improved food and medical care, extended visiting hours, expanded employment, and educational opportunities. Beyond Attica, many grassroots organizations like the Osborne Association and the Fortune Society were energized and the criminal justice system became less repressive (Thompson 2016). Clearly, there was a backlash to the uprising that tempered and restrained massive and structural reform, but policymakers as well as returning citizens took to prisoner rights activism for decades to follow. In the words of Pulitzer Prize winning historian and writer, Heather Ann Thompson from her comprehensive book, *Blood in the Water*:

> The Attica uprising of 1971 happened because ordinary men, poor men, disfranchised men, and men of color had simply had enough of being treated as less than human. That desire, and their fight, is by far Attica's most important legacy . . . America's incarcerated people have never stopped struggling against this country's worst and most punitive practices (2016, 570–571).

Lewis M. Steel tempers Thompson's assessment. Steel was one of two civil rights lawyers who represented the Auburn 6, six prisoner reform protesters involved in a peaceful hostage takeover drawing attention to the overcrowded and deplorable conditions at Auburn Correctional Facility. This protest was a precursor to Attica. Steel negotiated on the part of Attica prisoners and in Attica's aftermath, spent his career seeking racial progress and prison reform. Steel believed the legacy of Attica, despite some short-term progress, made prisons like Attica more repressive for decades to come.

According to Steel, Americans on the outside must work for prison reform. Former prisoners, families affected, and allies must make significant reform a high priority. There are a multitude of reform issues: the curtailment of solitary confinement, bail reform, oversight of prosecutors, restoration of educational and rehabilitative programs, family and advocate access to prisons, decarceration, electronic monitoring, prison closings and relocation, safety of prisoners, pay for work, and now appropriate precautions against pandemics (2016). The next sections exemplify precisely this, returned citizens who actively engage in reform efforts.

FORMERLY INCARCERATED AND CONVICTED
PEOPLES AND FAMILIES MOVEMENT

Foucault defined the Russian practice of multiple locations, levels of prison social control, and state regulated repression as the *carceral archipelago* (1975). This term was based on Solzhenitsyn's *The Gulag Archipelago* (2007), Stalin's early-20th century sphere of informers, spies, interrogators, secret police, prisons, jails, and camps—a system of social control, and oppression. Today's American mass incarceration system with the tendrils of ongoing control and widespread regulation extending to sanction and reentry systems (probation, parole, e-carceration, electronic monitoring, etc.) is America's carceral archipelago (Williams 2015).

Movements like Formerly Incarcerated and Convicted Peoples Movement (henceforth, FICPFM) address this carceral archipelago from a multitude of vantage points to end mass incarceration. FICPFM is a national network of over fifty advocacy organizations led by people with criminal records from over thirty-five states. This network elevates the contribution and expertise of those most affected by the carceral archipelago. It includes organizations like: All of Us Or None, A New Way of Life, College and Community Fellowship, Communities United for Restorative Youth Justice, Haywood Burns Institute, JustLeadershipUSA, Legal Services for Prisoners with Children, The Ordinary People Society and Voice of the Experienced, among others.

FICPFM is the brainchild of Forward Justice, a Southern law, policy, and strategy center addressing racial, social, and economic disparities and partners with human rights organizations at the forefront of social movements. It emphasizes expanding opportunities for people affected by injustice (https://forwardjustice.org/ficpfm-movement) FICPFM's platform includes demands for an end to mass incarceration and the incarceration of children, sexual harassment of prisoners, racial profiling, immigration detention and deportation, and prison as a source of slave labor. Freedom for political prisoners, voting rights, equality, respect, dignity for persons in prison and their children, and quality medical treatment are additional demands.

Two members of the FICPFM coalition are JustLeadershipUSA (JLUSA); and the school for Justice at Colombia School of Social Work, the brainchild of Kathy Boudin and Cheryl Wilkins; both agencies were founded by individuals with histories of incarceration. A recent study documents the work of formerly incarcerated persons engaged in policy, programs, advocacy, social service, and social activism related to dismantling the carceral state. Sturm and Tae (2017) drew on forty-eight in-depth interviews with these leaders conducted over a period of fourteen months. The authors call the individuals *leaders with conviction* after the Leading with Conviction program of

JustLeadership The study found that these individuals possess capabilities born of their experiences enabling them to uniquely advance prison and criminal legal system reforms. This kind of leadership assumed importance during the Trump presidency. Notwithstanding the purported benefits of the First Step Act of 2018, the Trump era tested the strength of criminal justice reform movements and coalition's collective efforts to dismantle mass incarceration and the American carceral archipelago (2017). Born of the incarceration experience, these leaders contribute unique social capital:

> Remaining deeply tied to individuals and communities affected by incarceration as they become upwardly mobile while infusing these relationships with resources and relationships developed through their education, employment, and activism. . . leaders with conviction may provide the only meaningful connection that justice involved individuals and communities have to high-quality social capital. (Sturm and Tae 2017, 2)

Incarceration counterstories bring new knowledge and credibility to America's understanding of the criminal justice system. Leaders who can tell this counterstory and combine it with education have access and social capital that is powerful.

> [Formerly Incarcerated Leaders]Bring their narrative and multiple forms of knowledge into venues where they form relationships with influential people who have had little or no direct contact with people who have been in prison and have had no exposure to people who have turned their lives around and become leaders. [Formerly incarcerated leaders through] their education and boundaries spanning employment are in contact with many high impact situations and people beyond the reach of many people who have not been to prison. (Sturm and Tae 2017, 2)

FIGHTING TO OVERCOME RECORDS
AND CREATE EQUALITY—FORCE

According to one member of Fighting to Overcome Records and Create Equality (henceforth, FORCE), a Chicago faith-based organization led by formerly incarcerated men and women; his job "is to pay forward." By promoting and advocating for voter registration, working with the homeless, directing legislative campaigns, and advocating for policy change, he is returning the support and empathy he received. This paying forward is an old concept, and this reciprocity is one driving force for including persons formerly in prison as organizational board and executive staff members. FORCE is just one example of both volunteer and salaried community and faith-based organizations led by returned citizens. Smart Justice in Kentucky, the Center for NuLeadership on Human Justice and Healing, and Center for Justice at Columbia University, both in New York, are other notable models.

In the case of FORCE, it is faith-based, and a bulk of research finds religious initiatives effective in rehabilitation and reduced recidivism (Jensen and Gibbons 2002; O'Connor and Perreyclear 2002; O'Connor, Ryan, and Parkikh 1998). However, detractors believe rehabilitative efforts, particularly religious, to be a disguise for neoliberalism and socializing for the labor market and conformity to the status quo (Haney 2010; Peck and Theodore 2008). According to Flores and Cossyleon, both perspectives can be true. As in the case of FORCE, faith and redemption take on unique agency and power when civic engagement advancing the rights of people with criminal records is taken on and led by returning citizens themselves. They practice disruptive religion and organize to move legislative bills through the Illinois general assembly. They use house meetings, creating platforms for renewal, lobbying at the state capitol, and securing support from elected officials for policies like the Sealing Bill (Illinois HB 3061) that allows the courts to consider the sealing of criminal records for eight categories of felony convictions. This bill was successfully passed through FORCE's efforts (Flores and Cossyleon 2017).

FORCE members use civil religion to lobby legislative campaigns to fight for the rights of the formerly incarcerated, advocating for themselves. In constructing a prosocial, collective subjectivity that validates themselves as reformed, there is agency, independence from the state, decision-making, voice and giving back through broader transformation of society as well as individual transformation (Flores and Cossyleon 2017).

In the words of one leader, "Man, I always challenge these people who are at the table discussing issues pertaining to people with records, and ain't nobody at the table with a record!" (Williams 2015). Through FORCE and other organizations like it, returning citizens are at the table.

GIVING BACK—SCOTLAND, PENAL REFORM

This book has primarily focused on the American penal system. If truth be told, though, America has much to learn from other countries. Since 2008, Scotland has experimented with life coaching. This is part of larger Scottish penal reform centering on short prison sentences and what Scotland calls "RooP"—routes out of prison. RooP utilizes life coaches, most of whom are formerly incarcerated men, to support the successful transition and resettlement of individuals back to society (Schinkel and Whyte 2012).

Each life coach is at least two years away from an offending past and working with the project utilizes and builds on their assets. This one-to-one, person centered support from workers with valuable and varied life experience, is central to the project. One life coach spoke of the opportunity to give something back that working with RooP has afforded him (RooP—Routes out of Prison website).

Life coaches approach work *with* not *for* or *to* prisoners. This working *with* is key to success in peer mentoring of repeat offenders. While developing employability is included in coaching, transformative learning of life skills such as relationship maintenance and identity development is stressed. Individual work on self-identifying as students, leaders, and friends as opposed to identifying with the incarceration experience; how one self-identifies is a central outcome of this giving back through mentoring. Sometimes the peer mentor and mentee establish lifelong friendships as well. The next section focuses on a unique American program out of an unlikely location—a District Attorney's office.

ComALERT

Giving back was the very foundation of co-author Chaney's revitalized life when he served as Executive Director of ComALERT (Community and Law Enforcement Resources Together) from 2009 to 2014. This highly successful reentry program, the first of its kind, was operated by a prosecutor's office. Created by the Kings County District Attorney's Office in Brooklyn, New York, ComALERT provided wraparound service assistance, including employment and substance abuse treatment, to the large number of men and women returning to live in Brooklyn under parole supervision.

Established in 1999 by the progressive and innovative Charles J. Hynes, who also developed the nationally acclaimed Drug Treatment Alternative-to-Prison program for drug offenders; ComALERT's success influenced the development of New York State's County Reentry Task Force currently operating in twenty New York counties. In a thirty-month evaluation report, authored by Dr. Bruce Western of Harvard University; this research revealed that when compared to a control group of people who did not participate in ComALERT, ComALERT participants were twice as likely not to be rearrested within one year of prison release. Two years after release, ComALERT graduates had a 29% rearrest rate while the control group's rearrest rate was 59% (Western and Jacobs 2007).

In 2007, in a bold and unprecedented move for the agency, District Attorney Hynes hired Chaney, an individual whose criminal history included periods of incarceration, as a member of the Brooklyn District Attorney's Office administrative management team. Appointed as ComALERT's Executive

Director in 2009, Chaney formed key community and agency alliances that over time expanded the program to offer over eighteen resources and services. Many of these service offerings including onsite mentoring and GED classes, were inspired from needs he either personally experienced or directly observed during his five years of incarceration.

ComALERT's leadership model is not unusual, and Chaney's story is but one more example of giving back to others who endured the same experience, and how many do so with a fervor, passion, insight, and experiential leadership. Returning citizens frequently serve on commissions and boards, providing public speaking and media presentations, teaching, and are heavily involved in advocacy, policy change, and social reintegration. Sometimes, leadership roles include those in community-based organizations that support job readiness training, skills development in writing, community development, and legal assistance. A wide range of organizations, networks, and systems, employment, activism and volunteerism, private, public, and non-profit sectors, government agencies, law firms, consulting, and academia are led by, or receive technical assistance from, carceral involved individuals (Sturm and Tae 2017).

WOMEN AGAINST MASS INCARCERATION (WAMI)

Tiheba Bain is the Director of Women Against Mass Incarceration (henceforth WAMI) in Bridgeport, Connecticut, an organizational member of the National Council for Incarcerated and Formerly Incarcerated Women and Girls, a justice activism movement. Tiheba is also a mother, recent college graduate, published author, and a returned citizen (Bain and Halberstam 2017).

There has been a dramatic increase in the number of incarcerated women in the last decades; from 1980 and 2017, this increase was more than 750%. (The Sentencing Project 2019). Despite this increase, their plight remains relatively unseen. Tiheba's organization aims to make these women visible as well as reduce their rate of incarceration.

WAMI is a grassroots post-conviction organization, supporting advocacy, consulting, and political activism around women's rights as human rights. Most of all coaching, mentoring, facilitating of workshops and seminars for personal growth and rebuilding families and communities are led and organized by formerly incarcerated women. Tiheba works tirelessly partnering with churches, community-based organizations, government representatives, and agency departments to empower women, thereby enriching the community. She is a strong public speaker and often lobbies at state and local events for policy and budgeting changes.

WAMI also supports The Vine—transitional housing for formerly incarcerated women and their children, a home founded on Christian principles. This structured temporary housing program assists with sustainable reintegration while transitioning residents to permanent housing. It provides a safe and stable living environment while building stepping-stones of empowerment, self-worth, and confidence by promoting positive lifestyle changes. It is a place of refuge according to Bain (J. Bain, personal correspondence, June 17, 2020).

The national organization, of which WAMI is a part, works for the clemency of women serving extraordinarily long sentences, women who are ill with terminal or long-term diseases, or criminalized survivors of violence as well as elderly women through both commutations and executive pardons. The National Council also works to monitor, and in some cases dismantle, aspects of the Adoption and Safe Families Act (ASFA) that has been used to discriminate against and break up Black and Brown families. The group targets and weakens legislation like this that hold discriminatory practices in place. This group of women also support grassroots organizing through grant-making partnerships called the FreeHer Fund that restore or expand the rights of currently and/or formerly incarcerated women and girls who lead projects directly impacting the criminal justice legal system. It is apropos that the National Council for Incarcerated and Formerly Incarcerated Women and Girls slogan is "Nothing About Us Without Us!" (https://www.nationalcouncil.us/).

Women like Tiheba, those closest to the experience of incarceration and the communities most surveilled and criminalized under current and past policies, are key to determining solutions. She and Carol Soto, a founding member of the National Council, make themselves accountable to their communities and transforming their own experiences of incarceration for positive change.

RESTORATION WRITERS' GROUP

Carol Soto is central to the Restoration Writers' Group, a literary collaborative in Brooklyn, New York, created by co-author Schwartz. This group provides social and emotional support to persons returning home especially during the first year after their release. It also creates a community space where writers can develop their skills in a safe and encouraging environment through guided feedback, constructive criticism, and structured reading and writing activities. Carol does all of this. With an understanding and compassion born of her own lived experience she writes, encourages, advocates, and supports with her entire being.

The group began in October of 2018 and Mike Colbert, having just been released that month, was at the first meeting. Colbert was in some ways the catalyst for this returning citizens' group. After a couple of months, the group held steady at 3–6 members on any given week. During the COVID-19 pandemic and quarantine, the group went online and held its meetings via Zoom and FaceTime.

Recently the group has morphed into a support group and is less about writing and development. The group advocates for its members to secure housing, food, and employment while maintaining emotional support. Colbert speaks to the dual role of writing and giving back in an excerpt from one of his pieces:

> Yes, sometimes the writer takes himself out of the prison becoming a citizen of conscious thought or solutions. He is no longer . . . a problem but a solution re-educating self into self-awareness toward research, history, political science which captivates an imagination beyond his own experience of life's mistakes [then he can] spiritually give back and realize that perhaps his life was destined and drawn to where they are comforting the heart and the mind [of others] (Michael Colbert (unpublished journal).

CODA

Individuals mentioned in this chapter have been condemned to unimaginably painful spaces. And yet, they collectively access the gift of giving back born of the universal experience of woundedness. The issue here is not whether this wounding was self-inflicted, other inflicted, justly or unjustly inflicted, individually or systematically induced, but how the experience is transformed and the recognition that each one of us are, in some fashion, wounded. The individuals and groups exemplified in this chapter are wounded healers, and we could all do well to learn from them. In the words of Nouwen "When we become aware that we do not have to escape our pains, but that we can mobilize them into a common search for life, those very pains are transformed from expressions of despair into signs of hope" (1972, 93).

REFERENCES

Bain, T. and Halberstam, J. (2017). Mentoring: Compassion without condescension. In Editors Chaney, J.R. and Schwartz, J. *Race, education, and reintegrating formerly incarcerated citizens: Counterstories and counterspaces.* Lanham, MD: Lexington Books.

Clear, T. R., Cole, G. F. and Reisig, M. D. (2016). *American corrections*. (11th Ed.) Belmont, CA: Wadsworth.

Flores, E. and Cossyleon, J. (2017). I went through it so you don't have to: Faith-based community organizing for the formerly incarcerated. *Journal for the Scientific Study of Religion*. 55(4): 662–676.

Foucault, M. (1975). *Discipline and punish: Te birth of Prison*. Translated by Sheridan, Alan. London: Penguin. p. 333. ISBN 0713910402. OCLC 809640229.

Haney, L. (2010). Working through Mass Incarceration: Gender and the Politics of Prison Labor from East to West. *Signs*, 36(1), 73–97. doi:10.1086/652917

Hughes, T. and Wilson, D. Reentry Trends (May 26, 2020) In The U.S. Reentry Trends in the United States Inmates returning to the community after serving time in prison. Bureau of Justice Statistics. https://www.bjs.gov/content/pub/pdf/reentry.pdf

Jensen, K. and Gibbons, S. (2002). Shame and Religion as Factors in the Rehabilitation of Serious Offenders December 2002. *Journal of Offender Rehabilitation,* 35(3–4):209–224. DOI: 10.1300/J076v35n03_11

Jung, C. G. (2002). *Psychology of the unconscious*. Mineola, NY: Dover Publications.

Nouwen, H. (1972). *The wounded healer*. New York: Doubleday.

O'Connor, T. P. and Perreyclear, M. (2002). Prison religion in action and its influence on offender rehabilitation. *Journal of Offender Rehabilitation*, 35(3–4), 11–33. https://doi.org/10.1300/J076v35n03_02

O'Connor, T., Ryan, P. and Parikh, C. (1998). A model program for churches and ex-offender reintegration. *Journal of Offender Rehabilitation*, v28 n1–2 p107–26.

Peck, J. and Theodore, N. (2008). Carceral Chicago: Making the ex-offender employability crisis. *International Journal of Urban and Regional Research*. https://doi.org/10.1111/j.1468-2427.2008.00785.

Rohr, R. (2011). *Falling upward: A spirituality for the two halves of life*. San Francisco: Jossey-Bass.

RooP, Routes out of prison. (2020) https://www.understandingglasgow.com/asset_based_approaches/routes_out_of_prison

Schinkel, M. and Whyte, B. (2012). Routes out of prison using life coaches to assist resettlement. *The Howard Journal of Criminal Justice*. Vol. 51, No. 4 pp. 359–371.

Schwartz, J. (Executive Producer), Jacobson, B. & Parker, T. (Directors). (2018). *Counterstory after incarceration*. https://filmfreeway.com/CounterstoryAfterIncarceration

Solzhenitsyn, A. I. (2007). *The Gulag Archipelago, 1918–1956: An experiment in literary investigation*. New York: Harper Perennial Modern Classics.

Steel, L. (September 26, 2016). Understanding the Legacy of the Attica Prison Uprising. *The Nation*. https://www.thenation.com/article/archive/understanding-the-legacy-of-the-attica-prison-uprising/

Sturm, S. and Tae, H. (2017). Leading with conviction: The transformative role of formerly incarcerated leaders in reducing mass incarceration. Columbia Public Law Research Paper No. 14–547 (2017). https://scholarship.law.columbia.edu/faculty_scholarship/2033

The Sentencing Project. (June 2019). Incarcerated women and girls report. https://www.sentencingproject.org/wp-content/uploads/2016/02/Incarcerated-Women-and-Girls.pdf

Thompson, H. (2016). *Blood in the water: The Attica prison uprising of 1971 and its legacy*. New York: Penguin Random House.

Western, B. and Jacobs E. (2007). Report on the Evaluation of the ComALERT Prisoner Reentry Program.

Williams, Q. (2015). Dissertation ProQuest. *Returning citizens? The path from prison to politics among the formerly incarcerated*. Loyola: University of Chicago.

Chapter 14

Criminal Justice Reform: Everyone's Responsibility

In 2018, 2.2 million individuals had been imprisoned in correctional facilities in the United States, with another 10 million having experienced incarceration. Roughly $200 billion is spent on the criminal justice system per year in the US. There is a significant loss of income to the communities, predominantly male figures, due to imprisonment. The emotional and social cost to families is also high as a society we are collectively morally and economically diminished (Bureau of Justice Statistics 2018).

As recently as 2010, after four decades of steady growth, prison populations have slightly declined because of bipartisan opposition to mass incarceration in Congress and concerted prison reform efforts by a host of organizations, individuals, politicians, and returning citizens (Pfaff 2017). Prison reform is one of very few issues that Congress across political parties can agree on. The attitude toward incarceration has shifted from one of punishment to rehabilitation. Taking advantage of current attitudes toward reform and rehabilitation seems crucial and urgent as time has shown prison reform to be volatile.

HISTORICAL CONTEXT

In the US and Europe, prisons did not always exist as we know them today. Instead, corporal punishment, capital punishment (or the death penalty), and various forms of public humiliation were used as a means of discipline for behaviors deemed punishable. Beginning with Philadelphia's Walnut Street Jail in the late 1700s, day jails and prisons were introduced. These were considered more humane as they replaced corporal or capital punishment. As discussed in previous chapters, the start of the penitentiary movement in 1820 with Auburn Prison was part of prison reform. This movement was not without controversy; In its modern incarnation of solitary confinement, cells, and lengthy stays, it was considered reform when first conceptualized. Later, additional prison reforms were created that separated prisoners by gender, age, and security classification, with an ongoing tension between punishment and rehabilitation.

Scholars consider the 1960s and early 1970s the height of prisoners' rights movement, particularly following the Attica uprising of September 1971, as previously discussed in this book. Many of the prisoners' demands were implemented across New York prisons and had implications across the country. These demands included more nutritious food, frequent showers, visitation rights, less mail censorship, and clothing allocations. Unfortunately, the later 1970s saw a backlash to Attica and the Civil Rights Movement in the form of racist and anti-rehabilitative approaches (Thompson 2017). There were reforms calling for rehabilitation rather than punishment but through the eras, the same social control, domination, punishment, and oppression permeated the prison system. Prison reform is not new but approaches thought to be rehabilitative sometimes themselves become another form of punishment, e.g., solitary confinement, e-carceration, and draconian responses to parole violations. This is not to say that these attempts to reform are not good, but because the history of corrections in America is endemic to social control and oppression, they can have unforeseen byproducts.

SECOND CHANCE ACT OF 2007

The Second Chance Act, a congressional act, signed by George W. Bush on April 9, 2008, was designed to reauthorize grant programs for reentry of returning citizens into the community as part of the Omnibus Crime Control and Safe Streets Act of 1968. It was mainly designed to assist prisoners returning to the communities. It established federal grant reform awards to over 800 government agencies and non-profits for reentry programming with the goals of reducing recidivism and increasing public safety. These grants focused on mental health, substance abuse, housing and homelessness, education and employment, and children and families. The Act allowed eligible prisoners to be considered for halfway house (temporary transitional housing supportive of reentry) placement during their final year of incarceration. The act was passed with bipartisan support and with support of law enforcement, corrections, returning citizens, courts, behavioral health, and educators. For the fiscal year 2018, $85 million was awarded to grantees across the country with the goal of addressing prison reform (Second Chance Act Fact Sheet 2018).

FAIR SENTENCING ACT OF 2010

The Fair Sentencing Act was a congressional act signed by President Barack Obama on August 2, 2010, which reversed the severe maximum sentences for drug-related crimes as a result of the crack cocaine epidemic that had heightened disparity in cocaine sentencing. The main thrust of this reform Act reduces the sentencing disparities for possession of crack cocaine and the possession of powder cocaine. Basically, this is a distinction that has racial implications because higher sentences for crack cocaine affected people of color and poor communities while the disparate lower sentences were given to wealthier white possessors of powder cocaine.

The second portion of this Act eliminated the five-year mandatory mini-mum sentence for simple possession of crack cocaine (The Fair Sentencing Act 2010). The Act includes other provisions but the two noted are of most significance.

THE FIRST STEP ACT

Signed on December 21, 2018, by the 155th Congress of the US and President Donald Trump, the First Step Act retroactively applies the Fair Sentencing Act of 2010. Additionally, the First Step Act enables incarcerated man and women convicted of certain "non-violent and non-heinous" offenses to earn prison "time credits" that are applied toward early release. To earn these time credits prisoners must attend approved evidence-based recidivism reduction pro-gramming or productive activities. These include: Aggression Replacement Training, Substance Abuse Strategies, Moral Reconation Therapy, Reasoning and Rehabilitation, Relapse Prevention Therapy, and Thinking for a Change, a/k/a T4C (Federal Sentencing Alliance 2019).

In addition to applying time credits toward early release, the Act prohibits restraints on pregnant prisoners and expands compassionate release to ter-minally ill patients. In some cases it places prisoners closer to their families, reduces and restricts enhanced sentencing for prior drug felonies, secures the Second Chance Act, creates grant programs to evaluate and improve educational methods at prisons, establishes home confinement for low-risk prisoners, provides de-escalating training for correctional officers and evidence-based treatment for opioid and heroin abuse while altering of juve-nile solitary confinement guidelines, etc. (Federal Sentencing Alliance 2019).

The First Step Act also expands the possibility for prison labor and devel-opment of the federal prison industry programs, including the marketing of products produced by prisoners. Some prison reformers are concerned that the legislation leaves much to be desired but is a start. There is also concern that it may benefit the private prison industry more than prisoners (Horn 2019).

STATE PRISON REFORMS

Mass incarceration overall is a state and local problem, not a federal one. In some ways state-level reform efforts matter more than federal because most crimes are prosecuted locally (Kaleem 2018)., and only 8% of all prisoners are in federal custody. Areas of reform that state and local officials and activists are advocating include reducing prison populations, as well as decriminalizing or legalizing marijuana use. Within these broad categories reformers, advocates, and politicians across many states are instituting bail and sentencing reform, reining in prosecutorial discretion, raising the age for prosecuting minors, abolishing involuntary servitude, expanding the vote for prisoners and returning citizens, and eliminating the collateral consequences of conviction.

The New York State 2017 Criminal Justice Reform Act includes bail reform laws, changing the bail system for pre-trial detainees, and closing the notorious Rikers Island. Also included are proportional penalties for low level crimes, the closing of 24 adult and juvenile detention centers, pre-trial services, and the right to a speedy trial. The New York Protect Our Courts Act is designed to ensure that everyone can access the courts without fear of being arrested by Immigration and Customs Enforcement (New York State Legislature 2019).

Across states, the decrease in prison populations results from the reduction of imprisonment for minor crimes. This includes eliminating "stop and frisk," the controversial police practice where an individual is stopped for questioning, then patted down to check for weapons, often resulting in an arrest. Stop and frisk has proven to be racially biased due to racial profiling—people of color are more likely to experience this practice. Improved police training and new policing strategies, bail reform, probation and parole changes, and prosecutorial reform have also aided in the decarceration effort (Pfaff 2017).

Under federal law, marijuana is still an illegal drug. However, small amounts of marijuana possession have been decriminalized in several states including Colorado, Alaska, California, Connecticut, Delaware, Hawaii, Illinois, Maine, Maryland, and Massachusetts. By the end of 2020, nearly 40 states may have some form of legal marijuana use (Zhang 2020). These kinds of societal changes propel criminal justice reform. Between legalization and decriminalization, arrests for marijuana use and possession have significantly declined (Kaleem 2018). There also appears to be a new wave of local district attorneys less interested prosecuting and incarcerating low level, non-violent property crimes and crimes of desperation caused by poverty, addiction, or mental illness (Kaleem 2018). Much of the most recent reform revolves around non-violent marijuana crimes and includes retroactive expungement for those who have committed them (Tony 2019).

Many states, particularly Michigan, California, Florida, and New York, have worked on issues related to elder parole, fair and timely parole, monitoring the special prosecutor in cases of police misconduct, restoring voting rights to people in prison and on parole, caps on solitary confinement, ending police secrecy, ending the lifetime ban on jury duty, increasing protection for juveniles interrogated by police, providing medication-assisted treatment, and the repeal of loitering laws for the purpose of prostitution. The ending of rogue DNA databanks, expanding laws allowing survivors of trafficking to clear criminal records, and police statistics and transparency initiatives are also in process (Goldberg and Brand 2020).

Despite the aforementioned reform acts some scholars, like John Pfaff, are concerned that they do not go far enough and that the current reforms only go after the "low hanging fruit"—drug and non-violent crimes, reduced sentencing, and private prisons. Pfaff argues that the bigger challenges are limiting prosecutorial power, initiating more realistic responses to crimes of violence, and acknowledging the racial geography of crime and punishment (Pfaff 2017). Pfaff cautions that unless these larger issues are addressed, reform will not go far enough.

PRISON ABOLITION

Prison abolitionists argue that prisons cannot be reformed; they need to be eliminated (Prison Moratorium Project (2020). Although the premise of this book is that the gift of transformative learning can often emerge from the dark experience of incarceration, the authors believe that prison abolition should be societies' long-term vision and goal. That does not mean that there should be no consequences for wrongdoing or that the safety of all is not paramount, but we need to move toward new visions of what imprisonment means, and toward the kind of society that does not need prisons, because prisons as institutions have never been spaces of rehabilitation.

In the 1960s and 70s in the US, prison abolition was a real conversation with serious consideration by administrators, academicians, and activists. During that time, people were really thinking beyond reform to abolition. This was when US state and federal prisons held approximately 200,000 prisoners, a time before mass incarceration, and the growth of the prison industrial complex. This was before the emergence of legislation and policies including the Sentencing Reform Act of 1984, "tough on crime," the politics of law and order, the Anti-Drug Abuse Act of 1986, and the "three strikes" law (Raphael and Stoll 2014). Prison abolition seemed possible.

Prison abolition is different than prison reform. Prison reform seeks to work within the system to improve conditions and policies that affect prisons. Prison abolition's long-term goal is to dismantle the prison system in favor of working toward economic equality. Toward this end, prison abolitionists call for all people to enjoy equal access to affordable housing, universal healthcare, quality mental health and voluntary drug treatment, community-based recreation and enrichment, equal educational opportunities, and fair wages. Prison abolition calls for an end to racist drug policies, housing, education, and crime policies. The premise is that underlying societal issues and context are ultimately responsible for why prisons are deemed necessary.

In the 60s and 70s Angela Davis became an early and vibrant prison abolitionist, and remains consistent in her anti-racist stance (Kendi 2016). Davis believes our criminal justice system is malignantly evil and imagines that this broken system requires an undoing of society. Abolition is not an isolated reform but an alternative vision of the world. According to Davis, abolition is a creative endeavor requiring forethought and strategy. It is about destroying the present system for something new. Davis thinks prisons are obsolete (2003).

Is prison abolition possible? We must certainly try to imagine a world with no prisons are not only possible, but preferable. If prisons cannot be substantially reformed because of their endemic nature, then prison abolition may be; essential. Historically, prison reform has not been successful. Reforms often fall short of real change. More drastic measures, including the possibility of full abolition, may therefore be required (Sullivan 1990).

EVERYONE'S RESPONSIBILITY

Arguably, California has led the way in American Prison reform (Arango 2019) because of a multitude of ordinary concerned citizens, prison abolition and reform organizations, returning citizens, and prisoners (Gilmore 2019). Perhaps the most extraordinary contribution to the California Prison Reform Movement began on July 8, 2013, when nearly 30,000 people incarcerated throughout California refused meals. The prisoners' demands included five core items: 1) eliminate group punishment for individual rules violations; 2) abolish debriefing policies and modify active/inactive gang status criteria; 3) end long-term solitary confinement; 4) provide adequate food; and 5) expand and provide constructive programs and privileges for indefinite Security Housing Unit (henceforth, SHU) prisoners (Gilmore 2019). SHU prisoners are kept in extreme isolation, in tight, often windowless spaces for long periods of time.

What is even more remarkable about this nation's largest ever prison hunger strike, which was finally suspended on September 5, 2013, was that it was organized by prisoners in the SHU at Pelican Bay State Prison who protested indefinite solitary confinement for having gang ties. These were individuals in a supermax prison, some who had been held for as long as 23 years in isolation in windowless 11 x 7 cells. They originally organized the hunger strike by shouting down the prison corridor to one another. Toward the end of the strike, they were force fed by correctional officers, but not until their protests drove California lawmakers to hold public hearings on the conditions inside maximum security prisons. Almost 7 years later, they won a decisive victory for prison reform, however incomplete (Law 2018; Arango 2019; Gilmore 2019).

If prisoners in Pelican Bay's SHU could organize a 60-day hunger strike despite their confinement, anyone can contribute something and be part of the solution from their own cells or corners of influence and agency. According to Ruth Wilson Gilmore, an abolitionist and prison scholar who, along with Angela Davis, used her public scholarship for the public good, California's progress came from organizing from the ground up. People working on a variety of problems, in many different settings both inside and outside of prison facilitated this progress. Californians worked with university and agricultural groups, unions like the United Farm Workers, laborers, grassroots non-profits, and prison educators. In some cases, ordinary citizens who had never been involved in prison reform began creating petitions, writing letters, attending protest rallies, and voting.

The California Prison Moratorium Project, according to Gilmore, aimed to "build an international movement to end the Prison Industrial Complex by challenging the belief that caging and controlling people makes us safe" (critical resistance.org/about/; National Lawyers Guild). The Project linked with environmental justice advocates, and the Central California Environmental Justice Network to lobby for carceral change. In looking for solutions, advocates discussed the possibilities of prisons run by non-profits and how housing, mental health, and educational institutions could be part of the solution.

Gilmore goes on to explain that abolition campaigns in California even reached into elementary classrooms, in efforts modeled after the Black Panthers and La Raza in the 1960s, when prison reformers and abolitionists organized teachers, developed K–12 curriculum to embrace the struggle. Education for transformational learning, learning that changes society can happen (Gilmore 2019). Beginning with children, these people are working on a variety of angles on imprisonment, in many different settings. This is practical abolitionist work, affecting values and structuralism to create a more just world (Gilmore 2019).

Anyone can join in this fight. There are multiple reform organizations that people can join and support. The Center for Prison Reform, a Washington, DC–based nationwide coalition and lobby group supports and collaborates with over forty organizations and 373 nationwide affiliates working toward national reform (Center for Prison Reform 2020).

There are conservative as well as liberal groups, like Families Against Mandatory Minimums (henceforth, FAMM), funded in part by both the Koch brothers and Mark Zuckerberg, a billionaire business and political family and billionaire founder of Facebook, respectively. As discussed in the previous chapter, many organizations are led by individuals who have "done time." Such is the case of FAMM (Shinal 2017).

In education, individuals have worked tirelessly to restore the Pell Grant for prisoners' college education which President Bill Clinton eliminated in 1994 as part of the tough on crime initiative. The result of this action had profound consequences for prisoners' lives, rehabilitation, and recidivism (Ubah 2004). As mentioned in Chapter 7, the authors are strongly encouraged by successful legislative efforts that promise to restore Pell eligibility for many incarcerated men and women, as well as for those convicted of drug offenses, because of the education component of a $23 billion COVID-19 relief package enacted in December 2020 (Murakami 2020).

Scholarly activists research and write about abolition and reform in academic journals like *Dialogues in Social Justice: An Adult Education Journal* out of the University of North Carolina. These kinds of contributions are crucial in providing evidence-based data to guide reform efforts. Other scholars create partnerships between universities and prisons. Examples of these include the Bard College Initiative, Pitt Prison Education Project, and the Michigan Prison Creative Arts Project. Successful smaller education outreach initiatives have also emerged, including the promising collaboration between the New York State Department of Correction and Community Supervision's Queensboro Correctional Facility and City University of New York's LaGuardia College in New York City. Reentry as well as in-prison teaching opportunities exist for educators. There are events to attend like the HALT solitary rallies in New York City and Bail Reform Projects and INCITE! whose mission is to respond to gender-based violence within the criminal justice system. The approaches used toward protesting, policy research and advocacy, prison teaching, public scholarship, and handling local initiatives involving how we manage education, race equality, healthcare, and housing have a direct bearing on whether prison abolition is possible.

As so aptly articulated by Aisha Karefa-Smart, niece of prolific African American writer and activist James Baldwin, social activism is in the daily choices we make; we can all be activists (CUNY's LaGuardia College Conference 2017). An example of daily activism may be as simple as shopping at small locally owned businesses owned by long-time members of a marginalized community. This is a form of proactively countering the ill effects of gentrification of communities to which many prisoners are now returning.

For individuals wanting to work not for reform but abolition, there is the Critical Resistance Movement a nationwide organization with headquarters in Oakland, California, with additional chapters in New York City, Los Angeles, and Portland, Oregon—a loose network of organizations and activists which one can join. The Empty Cages Collective in England, Wales, and Scotland is working toward building resistance to the prison industrial complex and abolition in Europe and internally (www.prisonaboliton.org/take-action/get-involved/).

The arguments and perspectives on reform and abolition are nuanced and complicated, and there is not one monolithic view of how change should develop. The authors are not necessarily advocating for prison abolition, there should be ramifications for violent crime and some individuals need imprisonment. However, what that imprisonment looks like is a subject of reform.

However, most people can agree that institutional change must occur if America is to remain a civilized society. For everyone, there is something to do from our own corners of the world which match our interests, expertise, time, and social justice calling. We can join or donate to the aforementioned organizations; protest; visit prisoners; volunteer in correctional facilities; work on reentry projects; and create higher education opportunities for prisoners and returning citizens. We can also lobby to better regulate our prosecutors; expand reform goals beyond low-level drug crimes to tackle sentencing for individuals convicted of violent crimes; or simply change our speech around criminal justice, such as using *people convicted of violent crimes*, as opposed to *violent offenders*. Change begins with the individual's willingness to spread the word, learn more, then address the organized neglect and constructive abandonment in our prisons, including preventable illnesses and deaths. As a society each of us need to show up and be present. The ultimate abolition of prisons is not about absence but presence (Gilmore 2019).

Beyond individual transformative thinking, we also need collective transformation—a transformation of consciousness to refigure our world, a change of collective consciousness to understand where power lies, unmasking the fiction of race, the humanity of all, telling formerly untold stories, and embracing history from multiple perspectives. In America we are still completing the work of destruction caused by slavery (Kendi 2016; Blackman 2008). Prison reform and abolition is about completing this labor of emancipation, and we need everyone to participate. This collective labor seems like heavy lifting and perhaps it is. However, in the words of many other labor movements "An injury to one is an injury of all" (Haywood 1929). We are all responsible.

REFERENCES

Arango, T. (January 21, 2019). *The New York Times.* In California, Criminal Justice reform offers a lesson for the nation.

Blackman, D. (2008). *Slavery by Another Name: The Re-Enslavement of Black Americans from the Civil War to World War II.* New York: Anchor Books.

Bureau of Justice Statistics. (2018). United States Justice Department. https://www. bjs.gov/

Center for Prison Reform. (2020). Washington, DC. https://centerforprisonreform. org/prison-reform-organizations/

Davis, A. (2003). *Are prisons obsolete?* New York: Seven Stories Press.

Department of Corrections, State of Rhode Island. (2020). Second Chance Act. Retrieved 7/11/2020. http://www.doc.ri.gov/documents/reentry/FAQ%20-%20 2nd%20Chance%20Act.pdf

Fair Sentencing Act, (2010). Pub.L. 111–220. US Law. Washington, DC.

Federal Sentencing Alliance (2019). The first step act of 2018 and prison reform: Recidivism reduction programs & productive activities time credits analysis. Middleton: Delaware.

Gilmore, R. W. (December 9, 2012). Don't Reform Prisons, Abolish Them. YouTube youtube.com/watch?v=akirVY5Mqsg

Gilmore, R. W. (April 17, 2019) Ruth Wilson Gilmore Talk. Youtube.com/ watch?v=YeOY9Z3rZ94

Goldberg, N. and Brand, D. (2020). What to look for in criminal justice reform in New York in 2020. *Brooklyn Daily Eagle.*

Haywood, W.D. (1929). *The autobiography of big Bill Haywood.* New York: International Publishers Co. pp. 186.

Horn, S. (2019). First step act passes—includes federal sentencing, prison reforms. *Prison Legal News.* Lake Worth Beach, FL.

Is Prison Abolition Possible? News Beat Apple Podcasts. (December 20, 2018). usnewsbeat.com/2018/12/20is-prison-abolition-possible/

Kaleem, J. (December 30, 2018). The feds just passed criminal justice reform. Here's why state-level efforts matter more. *Los Angeles Times.*

Kendi, I. (2016). *Stamped from the beginning: The definitive history of racist ideas in America.* New York: Bold Type Books.

Law, V. (July 3, 2018). As long as solitary exists, they will find a way to use it. *The Nation.*

Mooney, E. and Hopwood, S. (June 10, 2019). Reinstate Pell Grants for Prisoners. *National Review.*

Murakami, K. (December 22, 2020). Congressional Deal Would Give Higher Ed $23B, Inside Higher Education Congressional Deal Would Give Higher Ed $23B [insidehighered.us2.list-manage.com]

New York State Legislature. Protect our courts act. https://www.nysenate.gov/legislation/bills/2019/s425

Pfaff, J. (2017). *Locked in: The true causes of mass incarceration and how to achieve real reform.* New York: Basic Books

Prison Moratorium Project. (2020). No More Prison. (www.nomoreprisons.org)

Raphael, S. and Stoll, M. (2014). A new approach to reducing incarceration while maintaining low rates of crime. The Hamilton Project: Brookings Institute. Washington, DC.

Second Chance Act Fact Sheet. Retrieved 7/11/2020. Bureau of Justice Assistance, US Department of Justice, National Reentry Resource Center April 2018. https://csgjusticecenter.org/wp-content/uploads/2020/02/July-2018_SCA_factsheet.pdf

Shinal, J. (November 13, 2017). These conservative ex-prisoners are now fighting for prison reform, with backing from Mark Zuckerberg. CNBC. https://www.cnbc.com/2017/11/11/chan-zuckerberg-supporting-conservative-prison-reform-groups.html

Sullivan, L. (1990). *The Prison Reform Movement: Forlorn Hope.* Twayne Publishers: Boston

Thompson, H. A. (2017). *Blood in the Water.* New York: Vintage Books.

Tony, M. (2019). Criminal justice impacts of marijuana legalization, decriminalization examined. Union Town, PA: *Herald Standard.*

Ubah, C. (2004). Abolition of Pell Grants for higher education of prisoners. *Journal of Offender Rehabilitation*, 39:2, 73–85.

Zhang, M. (2020). How state marijuana legalization became a boon for corruption. *Politico.* https://www.politico.com/news/2020/12/27/marijuana-legalization-corruption-450529

Conclusion

With a few exceptions, this book is written from the perspective of the American prison experience. During the last days of writing, however, the authors visited four men's and women's prisons in Gulu and Jinja, Uganda in East Africa. It was there in Northern Uganda where the authors were reminded that transformative learning and the prison experience of gifts from the dark is not a phenomenon of the United States alone but one of global proportion. Two events stood out during the visits, one at the Gulu Main Women's Prison and the other in the Jinja Men's Prison.

The women looked radiant as they modeled gorgeous dresses they had designed and tailored in a prison sewing class. The process included complicated measurements and proficient use of old Singer sewing machines in the prison classroom. While conversing, one woman translated English to Acholi and Swahili for the others, and each spoke of the transformative learning that the prison, particularly the prison sewing class afforded them. They revealed how they never thought they could sew anything but now possessed a marketable skill. They also spoke of the new sense of self they possessed—transformation.

Not only did they have new tailoring skills that could translate to a small business on the outside to support themselves and their families; they have new approaches to life, to themselves, and a new way of thinking. Within the squalor that is the Gulu Women's Prison Yard where helplessness, desperation, and negativity abound, these women received a gift from the dark—new self-respect and transformation. The authors were privileged to have been an audience to this phenomenon.

The other event was in the Jinja Men's Maximum-Security Prison. Walking in the authors observed a group of elderly men between 70 and 98 years old, in yellow prison uniforms. They were huddled and crouching in a row on the concrete floor accepting pieces of fruit from a prison official in a tan military uniform with a burgundy beret. This was a gracious act, as fruit was a rare commodity and not part of what the government diet provided. We later learned that this official was the commander, in charge of the entire facility, and his actions exemplified the mission and vision of the prisons in Uganda—of rehabilitation, reintegration, and humane treatment of all. Uganda adheres to the *Nelson Mandela Rules, the United Nations Standard Minimum Rules for the Treatment of Prisoners* which was adopted in 1955 but revised and improved in 2015. Uganda is considered third after South Africa in implementing this human rights approach to prison management (personal conversation with Assistant Superintendent of Prisons, Kuboi Ben Moses, Jinja Main Prison, February 26, 2020).

The commander took the authors on a tour which included a carpentry workshop where men used chopped trees to construct beautifully constructed mahogany bed frames, desks, and tables. We also observed an animal husbandry project that taught prisoners how to keep birds and chickens; masonry including brick making and laying; and classes in basket weaving, all valuable skill in the region. Jinja Main Prison also offered religious training; maintained soccer and basketball fields, and had adult education classes ranging from adult literacy through pre-university and university courses. Despite the prison structure that was built in 1930 to house 400 inmates and is now severely overcrowded with 1523 prisoners, the prison seemed progressive and safe when compared to many American prisons. The authors' impressions of the prisons were also surprising because of the historical context of Idi Amin, Uganda's brutal dictator and Joseph Kony, a domestic terrorist and leader of the child soldiers, in a country once riddled with terror and trauma.

However, the ways in which some of the Gulu prisoners spoke of their experiences sounded familiar to the testimonies heard in the United States and the stories of the lived experiences of Gramsci, Himes, Frankl, Mandela, Abbott, and Assata which began this book. It is, therefore, safe to say that the darkness of the prison experience is unique in its potential for transformative learning anywhere in the globe. There is something about the experience that has potential to transform.

In reflecting upon Uganda and ending this book, we recall the words of Reginald Dwayne Betts an American poet, writer, and teacher who spent eight years in prison and who shared the podium with the authors at one time. Mr. Betts comments were mentioned in the introduction to this book, but they bear repeating at the close as well:

> the gaps we have when we were incarcerated should not be erased. I'm not saying incarceration in any way should be glorified, but it is a reality. Some of it can be an asset and we shouldn't erase it. Shame makes you silent. To ignore this gap means we don't value at all that time in our lives; this time contributes to who we are. We must open up the space. (Dwayne Betts, May 3, 2019 Conference at BMCC Re-Entry/Entry Conference)

This book is an effort to "open up the space," to avoid erasure and to silence shame. The global and historical experience of living in prisons continues to call all of us to live more humanely and to learn from those who bring gifts from the dark for us to open. Gifts are meant to be shared.

Index

On Writing by Stephen King (King), 134
organic intellectual: activism of, 73;
    adult education of, 67; body of, 89;
    counterstories of, 69; emotional
    learning of, 107–8; Gramsci on,
    68–69; growth mindset for, 84–85;
    making of, 71; power of, 70;
    prisoners as, 69–71; prison writing
    by, 72–73; in solitude, 71–72;
    traditional contrasted with, 68–71
O'Toole, S., 92

Paracelsus, 90
Parker, Theodore, 20
parole, 62, 101, 137, 170, 173
pathology: BCP contrasted with, 121–
    22; of family, xiii, 117–18
Patterson, M., 80
Paul, Apostle, 63
pedagogy, 15–16
pedagogy of discomfort, 105–6
Pelican Bay State Prison, 175
Pell grants: Clinton limiting, 78, 176;
    incarcerated individuals banned
    from, 77–79; restoration of, 79
Pena, Dario, 82
penance, 62
Pennsylvania Model, of
    rehabilitation, 56
personal space, 142–43, 144
Pfaff, John, 173
philanthropy, 79
Phillips, J., 63
physical appearance, 145–46
Pilates, Joseph, 90
The Pilgrim's Progress (Bunyan), 3
Plato, 89–90
Post-Traumatic Stress Disorder
    (PTSD): in CRT, 104–5; in formerly
    incarcerated individuals, 104; from
    prison experience, 22, 104–5; in
    reentry, 141
The Practice of Silence and Solitude
    (McKay, B., and McKay, K.), 62
prayer, 63

pregnancy, in incarcerated
    mothers, 45–46
prerelease mentoring, 35
prison. *See specific topics*
prison abolition, 173–74, 177
prison activist. *See* activism
prison-based programs, 31
prison experience: Attica, Rosenberg
    and, 99–101; deep cognition in, 133–
    36; EI and, 99–101; emotional labor
    vs. emotional learning in, 106–9;
    as gift, ix, 4, 84, 85; pedagogy of
    discomfort in, 105–6; proxemics,
    personal space, territoriality
    and, 142–44; PTSD from, 22,
    104–5, 109–10; social and cultural
    competence in, 147–49; technology
    in, 129–38
prison industrial complex, 20. *See also*
    mass incarceration
prisonization: Clemmer coining, 27;
    deprivation model, 29; disorienting
    dilemma of, 31; importation model,
    29–30; individual choice impacted
    by, 28; inmate code influencing,
    30–31; rehabilitation impacted by, 27
Prison Notebooks (Gramsci), 5,
    69–70, 72, 73
prison officers, 36
prison reform: at Auburn Prison,
    169–70; of Criminal Justice Reform
    Act, 172; demand for, ix; Protect Our
    Courts Act, 172; Scottish, 161–62,
    177. *See also* criminal justice reform
Prison Studies (Malcolm X), 67
prison theatre, 82–83
Prison to College project, 35
prison writing: activism impacted
    by, 73; cell as ideal for, 4; in deep
    cognition, 134–35; as education,
    50; of Frankl, 7–8; Franklin
    on, 3; of Gramsci, 5; of Himes,
    6–7; of incarcerated women, 48;
    Malcolm X impacted by, 72; of
    organic intellectual, 72–73; peoples

historians for, 4; at Queensboro
Correctional Facility, 21, 72–73;
of Restoration Writers' Group,
vii, 74, 124, 158, 164–65; Shakur
impacting, 49; as transformational
learning, 3, 108–9
Protect Our Courts Act, 172
proxemics, 142; architecture impacting,
143–44; personal space in, 144;
solitude in, 143
PTSD. *See* Post-Traumatic
Stress Disorder
Pulitzer Prize, x, 10
punitive technology, 130–31

The Quality of Hurt (Himes), 6
Queensboro Correctional
Facility, 21, 72–73
Quiet (Cain), 58, 59

race: gender and, 42–43; incarcerated
women impacted by, 11–12;
institutionalizing, 18; judicial
system influenced by, 41–42;
as social construct, 126; War on
Drugs against, 43. *See also* Critical
Race Theory
*Race, Education, and Reintegrating
Formerly Incarcerated Citizens*
(Chaney, Schwartz), 34
racial discrimination: of
colleges, 83–84; Covid-19
influenced by, 19–20
racial trauma: DSM-5 excluding, 104;
microaggressions impacting, 105
racism: apartheid and, 9; in education,
19; gentrification as, 19; higher
education impacted by, 19,
81; Himes impacted by, 6–7;
individual choice impacted by,
41; institutionalization of, 49;
microaggressions influenced by,
33–34; of New Jim Crow, 36,
131; of prison officers, 36; in
stereotypes, 118

reading, 68
REAL. *See* Restoring Education and
Learning Act
reentry: BCP aiding, 122; cognition
impacting, 136–37; internet
aiding, 130; PTSD during, 141;
questions regarding, 10; technology
impacting, 136–38
reflection, 62
reform. *See* prison reform
rehabilitation, 56; through exercise,
92; prisonization impacting,
27; transformative learning
impacting, 28–29
religion: in Black family, 123–24;
incarcerated individuals
impacted by, 63–64
resiliency, 125–26; of incarcerated
women, 46–47; transformative
learning and, 48
Restoration Writers' Group, giving back
of, vii, 74, 124, 158, 164–65
restorative justice, 124
Restoring Education and Learning Act
(REAL), 79
Return to Life (Pilates), 90
Rikers Island, 44
Robben Island, 9
Rockefeller, Nelson, 70
Rohr, Richard, 17, 155
Rosenberg, Susan, xii, 99, 100–
102, 108, 110
Ryan, William, 119

Sanders, E., 131
scholarship, xii, 5, 48–50, 71
Schwartz, Joni, xi–xii, 33, 34
Scottish penal reform, 161–62, 177
SCP. *See* Second Chance Pell
Experimental Sites
Second Chance Act (2008), 170
Second Chance Pell Experimental Sites
Initiative (SCP), 77, 79
self-examination: through Shakespeare,
83; through study, 61–62

About the Authors

Joni Schwartz is Professor of Humanities at the City University of New York's LaGuardia Community College and adjunct professor at John Jay College of Criminal Justice Graduate Studies Program. Dr. Schwartz is the founder of three adult education centers in Brooklyn, NY, serving returning citizens and has led prison writing groups at New York State's Queensboro Correctional Facility. She is a critical researcher, social activist scholar, mother, and grandmother. She is the co-author of *Learning to Disclose: A Journey of Transracial Adoption*, co-lead editor for the peer review journal *Dialogues in Social Justice*, and co-editor of *Race, Education, and Reintegrating Formerly Incarcerated Citizens: Counterstories & Counterspaces*. Dr. Schwartz has also authored twenty-four scholarly publications and is the producer of two documentary films.

John R. Chaney is an Assistant Professor and director of Criminal Justice programs for City University of New York's LaGuardia Community College. Professor Chaney has served as the Executive Director for the Brooklyn District Attorney's Office's nationally acclaimed ComALERT reentry program, and as coordinator for the NY State Division of Criminal Justice Services' Kings County Reentry Task Force. He is also a co-editor and contributing author of *Race, Education, and Reintegrating Formerly Incarcerated Citizens: Counterstories & Counterspaces*. A scholar/activist, Professor Chaney has provided technical assistance for the Criminal Justice section for the American Bar Association; the ACCES-VR division for the New York State Department of Education; and Nevada Workforce Connections. He is the recipient of several awards for his distinguished work, including formal recognition from the New York City and State legislatures.